Problems of Knowledge

Problems of Knowledge

A Critical Introduction to Epistemology

Michael Williams

OXFORD

UNIVERSITY PRESS

Great Clarendon Street, Oxford OX2 6DP

Oxford University Press is a department of the University of Oxford.
It furthers the University's objective of excellence in research, scholarship,
and education by publishing worldwide in

Oxford New York

Athens Auckland Bangkok Bogotá Buenos Aires Cape Town
Chennai Dar es Salaam Delhi Florence Hong Kong Istanbul Karachi
Kolkata Kuala Lumpur Madrid Melbourne Mexico City Mumbai Nairobi
Paris São Paulo Shanghai Singapore Taipei Tokyo Toronto Warsaw

with associated companies in Berlin Ibadan

Oxford is a registered trade mark of Oxford University Press
in the UK and in certain other countries

Published in the United States
by Oxford University Press Inc., New York

© Michael Williams 2001

British Library Cataloguing in Publication Data

Data available

Library of Congress Cataloging in Publication Data

Data available

ISBN 0–19–289256–8

1 3 5 7 9 10 8 6 4 2

Typeset in Minion by RefineCatch Limited, Bungay, Suffolk
Printed in Great Britain by
T.J. International Ltd, Padstow, Cornwall

For Paul

Preface

The title of this book is an allusion to A. J. Ayer's *The Problem of Knowledge*, first published in 1956. I studied with Ayer back in the 1960s, so the allusion is in part a gesture of respect towards a teacher of whom I retain fond memories. But that is not its sole point. I also regard Ayer's book as a model of a certain kind of philosophical writing.

Ayer's book is meant to appeal to a wide range of readers. It offers a general account of the aims and methods of philosophical theorizing about human knowledge, designed to be accessible to the beginning undergraduate or curious non-specialist. At the same time, it is not a textbook. On the contrary, Ayer always discusses problems in a way that allows him to develop his own distinctive line, with the result that his arguments are interesting to specialists as well as beginners. This is what I have tried to do too. For those acquainted with my work, this book combines the Sellarsian themes of *Groundless Belief* with the diagnostic ideas and contextualist approach to knowledge developed in *Unnatural Doubts*.

Does it still make sense to attempt what Ayer attempted? Some philosophers will argue that, since Ayer's day, philosophy has become too technically developed for serious philosophical ideas to be made accessible to the average reader. While I do not deny the value of technical work, I am not so pessimistic. I think that philosophical ideas are important, so that they ought to circulate outside narrowly professional circles; and I think that they can be made to do so, if not in full rigorous detail, then at least not in hopelessly garbled form. Anyway, for good or ill, I have tried to follow Ayer's lead. Whether I have succeeded is for others to judge.

Baltimore MD
November 2000

Contents

Contents

Acknowledgements

I am sure that I owe intellectual debts to more people than I can remember. But the following have influenced me greatly, either through their writings, personal discussion, or both: Laurence BonJour, Robert Brandom, Stewart Cohen, Fred Dretske, Robert Fogelin, Paul Horwich, Hilary Kornblith, John McDowell, David Lewis, Hilary Putnam, Richard Rorty, Ernest Sosa, Barry Stroud, and Timothy Williamson. I owe special thanks to Ernest Sosa, John Skorupski, and Meredith Williams, who read complete drafts of the manuscript. Their comments forced me to make substantial changes and (I hope) improvements. The influence of the late Wilfrid Sellars, together with that of Quine, Davidson, and Wittgenstein, is obvious throughout. Sellars's great essay, 'Empiricism and the Philosophy of Mind', decisively influenced my early thoughts about epistemology and continues to shape my thinking to this day.

One seems forced to choose between the picture of an elephant which rests on a tortoise (What supports the tortoise?) and the picture of a great Hegelian serpent of knowledge with its tail in its mouth (Where does it begin?). Neither will do.

(Wilfrid Sellars)

Introduction

The Very Idea of a Theory of Knowledge

What is epistemology?

What is epistemology? The short answer is: the branch of philosophy that concerns itself with human knowledge, which is why it is also called 'the theory of knowledge'. But this tells us next to nothing. Why do we feel the need for a theory of knowledge? What would such a theory be *about*, and how would we argue for (or against) it? Moreover, what is implied by saying that epistemology is a branch of *philosophy*? What is special about philosophical investigations of knowledge? How do they differ from discussion of 'knowledge' or 'cognition' on the part of sociologists or psychologists?

Many philosophers today deny that philosophical questions about knowledge have any special character. They argue that epistemology needs to be 'naturalized': that is, made continuous with one or more of the sciences, cognitive psychology perhaps. Other philosophers assert that epistemology is dead. These views can be hard to tell apart: the distinction between radical transformation and outright abolition is not clear-cut. However, I think that naturalism is mistaken and that the obituaries for epistemology are premature.

Five problems

To understand what is distinctive about a given type of theorizing, a good opening move is to ask what problem (or problems) it is meant to address. With respect to epistemology, I suggest that we distinguish five (really problem-areas or families). They are:

1. *The analytic problem.* What is knowledge? (Or if we prefer, what do or should we *mean* by 'knowledge'?) For example, how is (or should) knowledge be distinguished from mere belief or opinion? What we want here, ideally, is a precise explication or *analysis* of the *concept* of knowledge.

2. *The problem of demarcation.* This divides into two sub-problems. (a) The *external* problem asks: given some account of what knowledge is, can we determine in a principled way what sorts of things we might reasonably expect to know about? Or as

is sometimes said, can we determine the scope and limits of human knowledge? Do some subjects lie within the province of knowledge while others are fated to remain in the province of opinion (or faith)? Do some apparently significant forms of discourse lie outside the realm of the 'factual' or 'meaningful' altogether? The aim here is to draw a boundary separating the province of knowledge from other cognitive domains (or perhaps the cognitive from the non-cognitive). (b) The *internal* problem asks whether there are important boundaries *within* the province of knowledge. For example, many philosophers have held that there is a fundamental distinction between knowledge that is *a posteriori* or 'empirical' and knowledge that is *a priori* or non-empirical. Empirical knowledge is held to depend (in one way or another) on experience or observation, whereas *a priori* knowledge is supposed to be independent of experience, pure mathematics providing the clearest example. However, other philosophers have denied that any such distinction can be drawn.

3. *The problem of method.* This has to do with how is knowledge to be obtained or sought. I suggest that we distinguish three sub-problems. (a) The problem of *unity* poses the question: Is there just one way of acquiring knowledge, or are there several, depending on the sort of knowledge in question? For example, some philosophers have held that there are fundamental differences between the natural and the social or 'human' sciences. (b) The *ameliorative* problem asks: can we improve our ways of seeking knowledge? In the seventeenth century this problem was of central concern to philosophers intent on defending new scientific advances against what they regarded as the sterile dogmatism of scholasticism (the semi-official version of Aristotle's philosophical and scientific opinions that was taught in the universities or 'schools'). (c) Last but not least, there is the problem of *reason* or *rationality*. The concern here is whether there are methods of inquiry, or of fixing belief, that are distinctively rational and, if so, what are they?

4. *The problem of scepticism.* Is it possible to obtain knowledge *at all?* This problem is pressing because there are powerful arguments, some very ancient, for the conclusion that it is not. For example, although knowledge cannot rest on brute assumptions, all arguments must come to an end somewhere. It appears to follow that, ultimately, everyone's views rest on assumptions that he cannot justify and so do not amount to genuine knowledge. The problem here, then, is to come to terms with arguments for philosophical scepticism, the thesis that knowledge is impossible. Since there is a powerful case for connecting knowledge with justification, the problem of scepticism is intimately linked with the *problem of justification.*

5. *The problem of value.* The problems just sketched are significant only if knowledge is worth having. But is it, and if so why? Supposing we want it, what do we want it for? Do we want it in an unqualified way, or only for some purposes or in some situations? Is knowledge the only goal of inquiry, or are there others of equal (or greater) importance?

Obviously, these problems are not independent. How we deal with one will impose serious constraints on how we deal with others. But how a given philosopher judges their relative importance will shape his sense of what an epistemological theory needs to accomplish and how it might be argued for. This is typical in philosophy, where really deep disagreements concern not just the correctness of answers to a given set of questions but extend to the questions themselves.

The centrality of scepticism

Many philosophers have accorded the problem of scepticism a privileged status in the theory of knowledge. Indeed, they have pretty much identified the philosophical problem of knowledge with this problem. Ayer's *The Problem of Knowledge* is a case in point.[1]

There is a lot to be said for this view. It is generally agreed that the modern era in philosophy begins with Descartes (1596–1650), and that Descartes's decisive move is to induce philosophy to take an emphatically epistemological turn.[2]

Descartes writes during a period of great intellectual ferment when (among other things) the medieval view of the world, a somewhat unstable synthesis of Aristotelian philosophy and Christian theology, is coming under increasing pressure from newly emerging scientific ideas. Dissatisfied with the school-learning of his day and eager to promote the new science, Descartes argues for a radical break with the past. He aims to construct a view of the world and our knowledge of it from the ground up. In carrying out this reconstruction, he claims to accept as basic principles only things that, logically speaking, cannot be doubted. In effect, he uses sceptical argument as a filter for eliminating all dubious opinions: we are to accept only propositions that resist the most determined sceptical assault. Confident that he has found such propositions, Descartes is not in the end a sceptic. Nevertheless, his 'method of doubt' moves sceptical problems to centre-stage.

In addition to these historical considerations, there is a powerful theoretical case to be made for the view that sceptical problems are the driving force behind philosophical theories of knowledge. One of the most illuminating ways to understand the difference between traditional theories of knowledge is to see them as taking off from competing ideas about where sceptical arguments go wrong. (I shall explain all this in detail in Chapters 5 and 6.)

Putting concern with scepticism at the centre of epistemology makes very clear what is distinctive about philosophical theorizing about knowledge. Such theorizing responds to deep worries about whether knowledge is so much as possible. This cannot be a straightforwardly scientific issue since scepticism calls in question all putative knowledge, scientific knowledge included.

I agree that, in philosophy's modern era, scepticism has been epistemology's *dominant* problem. Accordingly, the problem of scepticism will receive special attention in this book. Nevertheless, two points should be borne in mind.

The first is that the threat of scepticism has never been the only motive for philosophical reflection on human knowledge. A useful distinction here is that between a philosopher's *goal* and his *task*: that is, between what he hopes to accomplish and how he thinks he must proceed.[3] Scepticism has been the dominant epistemological problem in the modern era, not because 'refuting the sceptic' is always the *goal* of epistemological theorizing, but because coming to terms with sceptical argumentation is almost invariably one of its central tasks. For example, if we suspect that some types of claim are more vulnerable to sceptical undermining than others, exploring the limits of scepticism will offer a way of drawing significant demarcations. Or again, if we can put a finger on how sceptical arguments go wrong, we can expect to learn useful lessons about knowledge and justification. We do not have to be in the market for sceptical conclusions to take an interest in sceptical arguments.

The second point is that, although modern epistemology has shown a definite tendency to follow the Cartesian paradigm, putting scepticism first, my characterization of epistemology in terms of a list of problems leaves open the possibility of taking other approaches. This aspect of my account of epistemology will be important when we discuss whether the subject has come to the end of the road.

Epistemology and the 'Western tradition'

Of my five problems, the problem of value is the least discussed by contemporary philosophers.[4] But all the other problems depend on it. If knowledge didn't *matter*, we shouldn't waste time wondering how to define it, obtain it, or draw lines around it. Nor would we care about refuting the sceptic. If we saw no value in knowledge, scepticism might still be a *puzzle* but it wouldn't be a *problem*. However, I take it that knowledge does matter (to most of us, at least some of the time); or if not knowledge according to some very strict criterion, then other epistemological concepts, such as justification or rationality. Why?

One answer is that concern with knowledge (or its close relatives) is so deeply embedded in our Western intellectual tradition as not to be optional. This tradition, which in its philosophical and scientific aspects traces its origins to classical Greece, is on the whole and in the largest sense a *rationalist* and *critical* tradition. Science and philosophy begin when ideas about the origin and nature of the universe are decoupled from myth and religion and treated as theories to be argued about: that is, compared with (and perhaps supplanted by) competing theories. As Karl Popper has noted, this broadly rationalist approach to understanding the world can be thought of as a kind of 'second-order' tradition: what it hands on is not particular beliefs—regarded as sacred, ancestral, and so more or less unquestionable—but a practice of critically examining current ideas so as to retain only those that pass muster.[5] Our having inherited this tradition explains our tendency to contrast knowledge with prejudice or the (merely) traditional. The distinction is invidious, which is another way of saying that knowledge matters. And this is not just a local prejudice. Once we become aware that even our most cherished views can be challenged, there is no going back to a pre-critical, traditionalist outlook. This is why concern with knowledge is no longer optional.

The rationalist outlook can be applied to itself. When it is, we get epistemology: a third-order, meta-critical tradition of reflection on our epistemological goals and procedures. We get a tradition of inquiry centred on the sort of questions we began with.

Given this account of epistemology, it is easy to see why scepticism is especially difficult to ignore. Scepticism is the skeleton in Western rationalism's closet: an argumentatively sophisticated attack on rational argumentation itself. It represents the extreme case of a tradition of critical inquiry reflexively applied. From the very beginnings of Western philosophy, there has been a counter-tradition arguing that the limits of reason are much more confining than epistemological optimists like to think, that the very idea of reason is a snare and a delusion and that, even if we could get it, scientific or philosophical knowledge would not be what it is cracked up to be. If scepticism cannot be refuted, the rational outlook undermines itself.

I think that this is all correct. But as we shall see, there is a way in which the problem of value is moot. To be thinkers at all, we have to be in the knowledge business.

Epistemology and metaphysics

The fact that epistemological interests arise readily from a rationalist, inquiry-and-argument-centred approach to making sense of the world has a lot to do with philosophy generally, not just epistemology.

'Philosophy' is commonly used generically to apply to any body of doctrine dealing with 'ultimate' questions about the world and our place in it, so that just about any cultural tradition can be thought of as embodying a philosophy. However, in referring to 'Western' philosophy we are talking about something much more specific: not a particular body of doctrine but a distinctive tradition of theoretical inquiry that has lately hardened into an academic discipline. This tradition is distinguished, I suggest, by its taking epistemological problems to be among its essential concerns. I am not saying that philosophy, in this narrower sense, is the exclusive possession of the Western tradition. But it certainly has a special salience in that tradition. In the modern period, no doubt, this has a lot to do with the fact that physical science in its developed form is a Western creation.

Some philosophers will think that it is overdoing things to tie philosophy so closely to preoccupation with epistemological questions. Epistemological inquiry may be important to philosophy (or to a lot of philosophers), but there is more to philosophy than epistemology. For example, there is metaphysics.

Some say that the term 'metaphysics' was coined to apply to some books of Aristotle, which according to a traditional ordering came after (Greek, *meta*) the *Physics*. Others, however, suggest that 'metaphysics' originally meant 'beyond physics'. Aristotle himself did not use the term, speaking instead of 'first philosophy', which he famously defined as the study of 'being as being'. This phrase is less mysterious than it sounds: he meant the study of fundamental principles that underlie or are presupposed by the various special sciences. For Aristotle, the investigation of such matters involves theology, which certainly takes us beyond physics. But it is possible to understand metaphysics in a more general and more secular way.

Metaphysics investigates concepts that, because of their pervasive applicability, are not the property of any particular science. Compare the concept of 'cause' (still the focus of lively debate) with that of 'electron' or 'inclusive fitness'. The latter two concepts are the property of particular sciences: respectively, physics and evolutionary biology. But since all sciences seek causes, the idea of causation is not. But what exactly are we (or should we be) saying when we identify something as the cause of something else? Or, shifting out of the semantic mode, what exactly is a causal relationship (between objects or events in the world)? Is there just one kind of causation, or are there several?

Along these lines, we can draw a rough-and-ready distinction between metaphysical questions (about what, say, causal relations are) and epistemological questions (about how causal relations can be known to obtain). But we should not take the boundary too seriously. Metaphysical issues are never discussed in an epistemological vacuum. Views about what causal relations are will always be constrained by considerations as to how such relations can be known to obtain. Moreover, views about what we are looking for in our quest for causes are bound to affect our views about how to look: in other words, such views are closely bound up with the problem of method, one of our fundamental epistemological problems. The point that metaphysics deals with that 'nature' of such and such, rather than with our knowledge of it, should not tempt us into thinking that a sharp line can be drawn between metaphysical and epistemological concerns.

Another aspect of metaphysics, as 'first philosophy', is its concern with *ontological* issues: issues about what ultimately exists or is ultimately real. An example of an ontological problem has to do with the interpretation of mathematics. Do we have to recognize numbers as really existing, though of course not in the spatio-temporal manner of more familiar physical objects? 'Platonism' in the philosophy of mathematics answers 'Yes'. Platonism gets much of its intuitive force from the apparent objectivity of mathematical results and the sense of *discovery* that accompanies mathematical innovations. But to other philosophers and mathematicians Platonism seems extravagant, for reasons that are at least partly epistemological. Anti-Platonists doubt that humans have a special faculty for exploring an immaterial realm, beyond time and space. For them, mathematics is a human construction. Its objects 'exist' only to the extent that we can devise recipes for specifying them: for example, a number answering to a certain description exists if there is a way of calculating it. Again, we find no reason to suppose that metaphysical issues can be cleanly detached from epistemological concerns.

I began by asking what makes epistemology a philosophical enterprise. We now see that there is a way in which this apparently straightforward question gets things backwards. Concern with fundamental epistemological issues is, at least in part, what makes problems philosophical.

Contemplation and power

I have suggested that as heirs to a broadly rationalistic intellectual tradition we inevitably see value in knowledge. Even philosophical critics of rationalism pay reason the back-handed compliment of arguing against its pretensions. Still, someone might say, this only means that we do value knowledge, not that we should. True enough: this is why the epistemological tradition recognizes the value of knowledge as a *problem*. Responding to this problem, philosophers have put forward various views about why knowledge is worth having. Particularly worth noting is the difference between the dominant tendency in ancient philosophy (the Greeks) and modern philosophy (seventeenth century onwards).

Plato and Aristotle both hold that a life devoted to the pursuit (or perhaps enjoyment) of knowledge is the best life there is. Behind this idea is the thought that, in exercising our intellectual faculties, we are acting in the way that is most distinctively human: human beings, as the familiar definition has it, are *rational* animals—that is, distinguished from other animals precisely by their (potential) rationality. From this standpoint, there can hardly be a problem about the value of knowledge. To ask 'What is the value of knowledge?' is like asking 'What is the point of being human?' Knowledge does not have to be *good for* anything: for beings like ourselves, it is an end in itself.

Modern philosophers tend to take a more utilitarian position. The modern thought is that knowledge is valuable because it gives us power, particularly over the natural world. To take this view is to value knowledge for its consequences rather than as an end in itself. This view is advocated by Descartes and, even more forcefully, by Francis Bacon, for whom the goal of inquiry is 'the relief of man's estate'. It is familiar to all students of the humanities ('So what's the use of all this philosophy?'). Its appeal is rooted in the rise of modern science and science's eventual association with unprecedented advances in technology.

This is a familiar story: for the ancients, knowledge is contemplative and intrinsically valuable, whereas for the moderns it is experimental and valuable instrumentally. But while there is certainly something to this contrast, it is not quite right. For many ancient philosophers, as much as for most moderns, knowledge is instrumentally valuable, only not in quite the same way.

Ancient philosophy, it has been plausibly argued, is practical through and through. For the ancients, philosophy is at bottom a certain way of life: the philosophical way. This is why the ancients are happy to describe as 'philosophers' statesmen who, though they wrote nothing, lived in a certain way. On this account, ancient philosophy is not what philosophy is today: a primarily (or even exclusively) theoretical undertaking. The ancient understanding of philosophy still echoes strongly in the popular conception of the subject and often causes embarrassment to professional philosophers when they find themselves in conversation with the laity, who are disappointed to find that professional philosophers are not always outstandingly wise or even full of advice.

The practical orientation of ancient philosophy need not downgrade philosophy's theoretical component. On the contrary, a distinguishing feature of the philosophical life is the importance it accords to knowledge. To know how best to live, we need to know the nature of things: ourselves and the world we live in. Lacking knowledge of either the world or ourselves, we shall be bound to live in unsatisfactory, even self-defeating ways. To be sure, if our inquiries lead us to conclude that the capacity for knowledge, through the exercise of reason, is the defining feature of humanity, we may well end up treating knowledge as a basic goal of beings like ourselves, hence intrinsically valuable. Nevertheless, even this recognition of the intrinsic importance of knowledge takes its place in an overarching practical project of living according to nature.[6]

The ancient ideal of a life guided by knowledge is an ideal of self-control. To live according to one's own knowledge is the very opposite of living in accordance with customs, habits, or inarticulate 'know-how'. This is the point of Socrates' saying 'The unexamined life is not worth living'. But to guide the life of an individual, knowledge must be something possessed by that individual. This controlling function gives knowledge an individualist cast: we cannot think of knowledge as socially distributed. Today, of course, this is the natural way to think of scientific knowledge, which is too extensive, too complicated, and too specialized to be mastered by any one person. In contrast to self-control, technological effectiveness demands the social dispersal of knowledge.

The ancient understanding of the value of knowledge leads to a conception of knowledge that is not just individualistic but also aristocratic. Self-examination presupposes leisure: time to reflect. It also presupposes logical and theoretical abilities of a high order. Knowledge, as the ancients conceive it, is not for everyone. Of course, even today not all knowledge is for everyone either. But this is the result of specialization and the premium placed on expertise. It reflects the division of cognitive labour. Unlike the ancient philosopher, the expert does not present himself as a higher human type.

If it is correct to see ancient philosophy, or much of it, as essentially practical, we cannot differentiate ancient and modern conceptions of the value of knowledge simply in terms of the contrast between intrinsic and instrumental worth. I do not say that the ancients do not value knowledge for itself. But people today do that too. Much research is undertaken without expectation of practical payoff; and even John Dewey, the prophet of American pragmatism, recognized the 'aesthetic' delight in contriving elegant theoretical explanations for complicated phenomena. Still, there is an important distinction between ancient philosophy and modern in the way in which knowledge is seen as *instrumentally* valuable. For both ancients and moderns, knowledge is power. But whereas for the moderns this means power over the world, for the ancients it means power over oneself.

Why this difference? The answer is surely that, in the ancient world, knowledge was not for the most part power in the modern sense. The most technically advanced of the physical sciences—astronomy—deepened our understanding of the movements of the heavenly bodies but hardly put us in a position to do much about them. True, for societies steeped in divination, improving horoscopes was a practical incentive to astronomical research; and calendar reform was an intermittent spur to astronomical theorizing. But on the whole, in the ancient world, mastery over nature was not a plausible goal of inquiry.

Not all the Greek philosophers value knowledge in the ways just described. The notable exceptions are the sceptics. The ancient sceptics suspend judgement on the question of whether we are capable of knowing the real nature of things and even on the question of whether there is any real nature to be known. They feel free to question the possibility of knowledge because they also doubt its value. In their eyes, the key to happiness is to give up worrying about determining the truth and to learn instead to be content with local opinion. Accordingly, they do not see scepticism as a problem. Quite the reverse: to the problem of how to live, scepticism is the solution.

In modern philosophy, by contrast, scepticism is almost universally seen as a problem, if not *the* problem. At the same time, scepticism is not generally thought of as something to be practised: 'the sceptic' is just a literary conceit, a personification of certain challenging arguments, rather than a real-life opponent. This is as it should be. Few, if any, of us are thoroughgoing sceptics, and this is not just a matter of fashion or habit. In a world in which knowledge *is* power, whether we like it or not, thoroughgoing scepticism is not an option.

We might think that, if scepticism is such a purely theoretical affair, it is just a puzzle after all, fine for those who like that sort of thing, but hardly of compelling interest to anyone else. This is not so. Although, when its implications are fully understood, philosophical scepticism is difficult—maybe impossible—to swallow, sceptical ideas are enormously influential in contemporary culture, which is characterized by pervasive and deeply felt misgivings about rationality, justification, and truth. Sceptical ideas, I believe, underpin such widely accepted doctrines as 'social constructivism', according to which what people believe is wholly a function of social, institutional, and political influences, so that 'reason' is only the mask of power; relativism, which says that things are only 'true for' a particular person or 'culture'; and 'standpoint epistemologies', according to which social differentiation by gender, race, class, or tribe gives rise to distinct 'ways of knowing', there being no possibility of justification according to common standards.

How can I combine this point about the influence of scepticism with the claim that none of us is a thoroughgoing sceptic? The answer is that reflection on scepticism tends to induce a kind of intellectual split personality. When we reflect theoretically, scepticism can easily seem unavoidable. But in more everyday contexts, no one behaves or thinks like a sceptic. Hume was perhaps the first philosopher to call attention to this. Sceptical doubts, which triumph in the study, vanish like smoke when we return to the affairs of common life.[7] This is a deep insight. But Hume doesn't get things quite right. While scepticism fades in the light of day, it continues to exert a subterranean influence beyond the narrow confines of purely theoretical inquiry. One index of our culture's being pervaded by sceptical doubt is a tendency towards stridency and suspiciousness. We continue to judge and to argue, while suspecting that such practices are really a sham. The less confident we feel, the more insistent we become. Or we see our opponents, not as fellow inquirers, but as driven by disreputable motives, which it is our duty to expose. Argument gives way to unmasking (though, if scepticism is correct, why suppose that there is anything to explanations like this?).

Scepticism is of much more than 'purely academic' interest. Indeed, this is true of epistemological questions generally. In the next section, I explain why.

Descriptive and normative

I mentioned that many philosophers today think that epistemology should be naturalized: turned into or replaced by some form of natural-scientific inquiry. However, insofar as epistemological theories respond to sceptical concerns, epistemology cannot be a straightforwardly scientific subject. The sceptic raises questions about the very possibility of knowledge, scientific knowledge included (or even especially).

This is hardly news to epistemological naturalists. They may well agree that sceptically centred epistemology cannot be naturalized, but they will turn the argument on its head and claim that this is all the more reason to move beyond modern philosophy's obsession with scepticism. For all the discussion scepticism has attracted, they may say, there is still no agreed response. Perhaps it is time to try something else.

We will not be in a position to evaluate such suggestions until we know more about scepticism (and naturalism). However, a point emerging from our discussion of the value of knowledge provides the beginnings of a more general account of what makes epistemological questions distinctively philosophical. This is that epistemological distinctions are invidious. 'Knowledge' is an honorific title we confer on our paradigm cognitive achievements, which is why there is an important question about the nature of knowledge. As an important honorific term, 'knowledge' is bound to be contested.

More generally, 'know' is a 'success-term' like 'win' or 'pass' (a test). Knowing is not just a factual state or condition but a particular *normative status*. Such statuses are related to appropriate factual states: winning depends on crossing the line before any other competitor. But they also depend on meeting certain norms or standards which define, not what you *do* do, but what you *must* or *ought* to do. To characterize someone's claim as expressing or not expressing knowledge is to pass judgement on it. Epistemic judgements are thus a particular kind of *value-judgement*. It is far from obvious that investigations with such a strongly normative component can be fully 'naturalized'.

Returning to our list of basic epistemological problems, it is clear that they all possess this normative or evaluative dimension. They are not just about how what we *do* believe but what (in some sense) we *must, ought,* or are *entitled* to believe; not just with how we in fact conduct our inquiries but how we *should* or *may* conduct them. In this respect, epistemology is like ethics or political philosophy, neither of which is concerned simply with how people do act or organize their social relations, but with how they should do so. Of course, with respect to moral or political questions, there are all sorts of factual questions about what people actually do, what they think they ought to do, how various political arrangements actually function, and so on. But if the question is 'What ought we to do?', 'What are the correct moral standards to apply here?', or 'How should we strike a political balance between freedom and equality?', more than purely factual considerations will be involved.

This normative dimension distinguishes philosophical theories of knowledge from straightforwardly factual inquiries and explains why demarcational (and related methodological) issues are so significant. Because epistemological distinctions are invidious, ideas about epistemological demarcation always involve putting some claims or methods above others: mathematics above empirical science, empirical science above metaphysics or religion, logic above rhetoric, and so on. Demarcational projects use epistemological criteria to sort areas of discourse into factual and non-factual, truth-seeking and merely expressive, and, at the extreme, meaningful and meaningless. Such projects amount to proposals for a map of culture: a guide to what forms of discourse are 'serious' and what are not. Disputes about demarcation—including disputes about whether demarcational projects should be countenanced at all—are disputes about the shape of our culture and so, in the end, of our lives.

Notes

1. Ayer (1956).
2. Descartes, *Discourse on Method* and *Meditations on First Philosophy*, in Cottingham *et al.* (1984).
3. I owe this useful terminology to Robert Fogelin.
4. An exception to the rule is to be found in those naturalistically inclined philosophers who argue that our knowledge-gathering activities are best understood in an evolutionary perspective. From an evolutionary standpoint, there is an interesting question as to why knowledge, or a capacity for learning, should be preferred to wired-in true beliefs. See Dretske, 'The Need to Know', in Clay and Lehrer (1989). This volume contains a number of worthwhile papers on recent work in epistemology.
5. 'Towards a Rational Theory of Tradition', in Popper (1963).
6. These remarks on the practical character of ancient philosophy are derived from Hadot (1995). According to Hadot, ancient philosophy insists on a distinction between philosophy and discourse about philosophy. The philosophical life is thus not simply a life lived in accordance with philosophical precepts or doctrines. Rather, the practice of philosophical reflection, understood as a kind of mental discipline or 'spiritual exercise', is an essential *component* of the philosophical life. In later antiquity, it became standard practice to divide philosophy into three divisions: logic (which incorporates what we think of as epistemology), physics (what we would think of as natural science), and ethics. All three divisions have practical significance, and not just in the sense that physics and ethics are tailored to fit together in sustaining a certain picture of the good life. Rather, strange as it sounds, all three divisions of philosophy play an essential role in the practice of mental discipline. The function of logic is to discipline the intellect and of ethics to discipline the will. And physics? To discipline desire: reflection on the physical nature of things peels away adventitious human valuations, helping us to become indifferent to things that are in themselves indifferent. We are thus able to live more equably in an uncertain world, or rather a world in which only one thing is certain: that everything human will pass away sooner or later, most notably ourselves. It is in this spirit that Plato, in his *Phaedo*, has Socrates characterize philosophy as preparation for death, drawing the response that ordinary people would agree, since they think that philosophers are half-dead already.
7. Hume (1978), Book 1, Conclusion.

1

The Standard Analysis

The analytic problem

I begin with the analytic problem. I do so simply as a matter of expository convenience: as a way of introducing some ideas that will prove important later. This may seem a surprising thing to say. It is natural to suppose that the analytic problem enjoys a certain priority over the other problems, for surely our attitude to them must depend on what we take knowledge to be. However, we should not read too much into this obvious point.

In the first place, some of our other problems may invoke only 'lowest common denominator' ideas about knowledge: ideas that just about any account of the concept of knowledge would have to recognize. Many philosophers think of the problem of scepticism this way. If they are right, the problem of scepticism will swing free of detailed solutions to the analytic problem.

Furthermore, relations of influence between solutions to the analytic problem and our views about other epistemological issues do not go only one way. For example, our views about what knowledge is may be shaped by reflections on where we think knowledge is available and where it isn't: that is, our response to the analytic problem may be affected by prior thoughts about demarcation. Or we may be more certain that we have a workable distinction between knowing and merely surmising than we are that any particular analysis of that distinction is correct. Thus we may want to rethink a particular account of knowledge if we find that it encourages scepticism. We need not approach our other questions in the light of a dogmatic commitment to a particular response to the analytic problem.

The analytic problem challenges us to say just what knowledge is, but in a special way. When we ask 'What is knowledge?' philosophically, we mean 'Don't just tell us some ancillary facts about knowledge: tell us what it is essentially'. Such philosophical questions are often said to differ from scientific questions by being purely conceptual: that is, about meaning rather than fact. In my view, the distinction between factual and conceptual questions is fraught with problems. But in a general way, it is not hard to see what philosophers who explain the character of philosophical inquiry in terms of this distinction have in mind. When we ask 'What is knowledge?' in a philosophical tone of voice, we are not trying to get a grip on the natural world which, in some sense, exists independently of us. Rather, we are looking for a reflective understanding of evaluative practices that are our own creation. Epistemic standards, we might say, are like the rules of a game. Epistemological inquiry is thus 'purely conceptual' because concerned with our own conventions.

Does this mean that conceptual issues are just 'verbal', hence (by definition) trivial? There are really two objections here. The first is that determining the meaning of a commonly understood term can hardly be much of a problem. The second is that it can hardly be of much importance.

Taking the first objection, it is unquestionably true that we *already* understand the concept of knowledge, in the sense that we have a practical mastery of the verb 'to know'. We readily make epistemological distinctions involving the concept of knowledge ('You don't know, you're only guessing') and, because language is a social institution, we do so in ways that command a reasonable degree of consensus. However, in seeking a philosophical account of the concept of knowledge, we are trying to go beyond this kind of practical mastery to an explicit articulation of whatever it is that makes knowledge distinctive. It is not obvious how to do this, or even that it can be done at all.[1]

This brings us to the second objection. Here a concession is in order: analysing the concept of knowledge will never be just a matter of discovery, for even if we agreed about what 'knowledge' *does* mean, we might disagree over what it *ought* to mean. 'Know' is an honorific term—to credit someone with knowledge is to accord her opinion a strongly positive epistemic status—and so there are almost bound to be disputes about what the standards for deserving such a status ought to be. But even so, definition isn't arbitrary. Proposals as to how knowledge is or ought to be understood must be examined in the light of both our reasons for having the concept in the first place and the consequences that would result from drawing its boundaries one way rather than another. Think of our concept of human life: the emergence of modern life-support technology makes it harder to decide what counts as being alive, and it is doubtful whether our everyday, rough-and-ready understanding of the distinction between life and death settles the matter. But how we draw the line has serious implications for our treatment of the seriously ill.

In trying to understand how we do or should think about knowledge, we are in quest of what is sometimes called 'reflective equilibrium'. We are looking to make explicit our conception of knowledge in a way that harmonizes with our sense of what our best examples of knowledge are, where knowledge can reasonably be sought and where it cannot, and so on. In this quest, nothing is sacrosanct: our account of knowledge can be modified in the light of particular judgements; but equally, particular judgements can change in the light of an explicit account of knowledge. This reinforces the point that the analytic problem enjoys no absolute priority over other epistemological questions.

The standard analysis

Epistemology is mainly concerned with *propositional* knowledge—knowing *that* such and such—the sort of knowledge whose content is given by complete sentences. Making propositional knowledge the primary object of attention is a significant choice of theoretical orientation.

Propositional knowledge is not the only kind of knowledge. There is acquaintance or familiarity with people and places: I know the new Dean slightly or Manchester well. Also, there is practical mastery or 'know-how': I know how to ride a bike or how to get around London. But neither acquaintance nor know-how is wholly independent of propositional knowledge. One cannot know a city without knowing lots of facts about it; and acquiring practical skills typically involves learning rules of thumb. It is therefore tempting to think of propositional knowledge as theoretically fundamental. But whether this is really the right view is far from obvious.

For now, however, I want to put questions about the primacy of propositional knowledge to one side. The fact is that, even if we focus on propositional knowledge, the prospects for an illuminating general analysis do not look good, since propositional knowledge seems endlessly varied. I know that it will rain tomorrow, that the bird on the fence is a woodpecker, that the accused was in Edinburgh on the night in question, that $e = mc^2$, that the wallpaper looks to have a greenish tint, that Napoleon was victorious at Austerlitz, that $2 + 2 = 4$, that skids are more likely on wet roads, that my name is 'Michael Williams', that I should eat less fat, that genocide is an unspeakable crime: the list could go on and on. Faced with such variety, we might reasonably wonder whether it makes sense to ask what conditions a person must meet to qualify for having knowledge of this kind, or whether it makes sense to treat propositional knowledge as a 'kind' at all. Certainly, any general analysis of propositional knowledge will be very abstract.

Philosophers concerned with the analytic problem want a set of conditions for knowing that are *severally necessary* and *jointly sufficient*. To say that they are severally necessary is to say that, in order to count as knowing, a person must meet them all: if he fails to meet *any one* of them, he will not count as knowing. To say that they are jointly sufficient is to say that, if he does meet them all, he will count as knowing.

A condition (or set of conditions) can be sufficient without being necessary and necessary without being sufficient. Consider an examination, which you can pass by getting a certain score on any one of its three parts. Getting such a score on Part 1 will be sufficient for you to pass, but it won't be necessary since you can also pass by getting that score on some other part. But now change the rules and imagine that, in order to pass, you have to achieve a certain minimum score on every part. In this case, getting a suitable score on Part 1 will be necessary for passing but will not be sufficient, since you need also to do comparably well on Parts 2 and 3.

Supposing that we come up with some set of putatively necessary and sufficient conditions for knowledge, how do we test it for correctness? The usual procedure involves thought experiments. Given a list of conditions, we see if we can describe a case such that either (a) we are unwilling to describe it as a case of knowing, even though it meets all the conditions, or (b) we are strongly inclined to count it as a case of knowing, even though it fails to meet one or more of them. The first type of case will suggest that our conditions are not sufficient, though they may still be necessary; the second that they are not all necessary, though they may be sufficient. Either way we have a *counterexample* to the proposed analysis.

These reactions to cases are often referred to as 'intuitions'. Referring to them this way is harmless provided that it does not tempt us into treating them as set in stone. They are not. Initial reactions may change in the light of a more detailed description of the case or with the introduction of further cases for comparison; or they may be idiosyncratic, so that other inquirers do not share them. They may even be incoherent. If our 'ordinary' concept of know- ledge is in part the product of past epistemological theorizing, our intuitions may reflect fragments of distinct epistemological traditions, and so resist syn- thesis. Also, we should never forget that our idea of knowledge embodies a normative ideal, open to criticism. Maybe we have intuitions that we would be better off without.

Kinds of knowledge

The starting point in analysing the concept of knowledge—determining what knowledge is—is to ask what knowledge is *not*. Among philosophers, from Plato to the present, there has been more or less complete consensus that knowledge excludes three things: ignorance, error, and (mere) opinion, though how and why it excludes them remains controversial.

Many philosophers (including, arguably, Plato himself) have held some version of what I shall call 'the standard analysis'.[2] According to this analysis, in its basic form, S knows that p (where 'S' stands for an arbitrary person and 'p' for an arbitrary proposition) if and only if:

1.   S believes that p. (The belief condition.)
2.   p is true. (The truth condition.)
3(J).   S's belief that p is appropriately justified. (The justification condition.)

The analysis bears its rationale on its face. The belief condition excludes ignorance, the truth condition excludes error, and the justification condition excludes mere opinion.

The standard analysis is generally thought to state the 'truth conditions' for 'S knows that p'. However, we should not let this way of putting things mislead us into thinking that, in claiming or attributing knowledge, we are issuing a straightforward empirical description of ourselves or another person. We are doing much more than that. In advancing a knowledge-claim,[3] I express my commitment to the truth of some proposition: this is the point of the belief condition. But I also represent myself as epistemically entitled to this commitment, thus authorizing or entitling others to join me in it. This 'performative' aspect of knowledge-talk has been noted by a numerous philosophers. For example, Ayer writes that, in saying 'I know', I 'claim the right to be sure'. Austin says that, in representing myself as knowing, I guarantee the truth of what I have said. Similarly, in attributing knowledge to another person, I concede both the truth of what he believes and his right to believe it. And in advancing this double endorsement, I take on the same commitments and lay claim to the same entitlements. Thus Robert Brandom describes knowledge as a peculiar kind of 'complex, hybrid normative [Brandom says 'deontic'] status'. It is *complex* because it involves elements of commitment *and* entitlement. It is *hybrid* because, in attributing knowledge to another person, we imply things about *our* commitments and entitlements, not just his.[4]

Clearly, the standard analysis gives only the most schematic analysis of knowledge. It is neutral with respect to exactly what kind of justification knowledge demands and on the question of whether propositional knowledge constitutes a coherent kind of knowledge. It applies as well to *a priori* knowledge, the purely rational knowledge generally thought to be exemplified by pure mathematics, as to *a posteriori* knowledge, the sort that depends on observation and experience. All the standard analysis says is that knowledge depends essentially on justification, leaving it to further investigation to determine what sort of justification is required. Indeed, odd as it sounds, the standard analysis suggests that the theory of knowledge's main concern is not really knowledge but justification, for that is where the detailed problems lie.

Belief and truth

The standard analysis treats knowledge as a special kind of belief: belief that is both true and justified. But we must be clear that, unlike belief, knowledge isn't, or isn't just, a psychological state. To be a knower is to occupy a special normative status: to hold a belief that merits a special kind of positive evaluation. We certainly should not think of knowledge as on a par with subjectively identifiable mental states, such as pain.

To treat knowledge as a special kind of belief is not wholly uncontroversial. In his philosophical utopia, the *Republic*, Plato argues that knowledge and belief are wholly different, indeed incompatible, states of mind. Knowledge differs from belief by being infallible, by which he appears to mean that knowledge consists in the absolutely certain or mistake-proof apprehension of necessary truths. This conception of knowledge leads him to conclude that knowledge and belief must take different objects: the subject-matters where we can have knowledge (e.g. mathematics) must be different from those that are matters of opinion (e.g. the material world).

The belief condition excludes ignorance: you can't have knowledge about matters on which you have no views. In the standard analysis, belief is just relatively unrestricted acceptance: that is, believing is more than accepting for the sake of argument. Since even Plato will agree with this, when he marks out different domains for knowledge and belief, he must have in mind a much richer conception of belief, one that has implications for how 'beliefs' arise or can be justified. So the conflict is more real than apparent. Everyone agrees that knowledge is more than mere opinion.

Plato's accounts of knowledge and belief are evidently highly theorized. But it has been argued that ordinary usage also suggests an opposition between knowledge and belief. Upon hearing some very bad news, I might say 'I know it happened, but I just can't bring myself to believe it'. However, we should be wary of taking remarks like this too literally. I do not mean that I *don't* accept the facts, only that I find accepting them particularly distressing, so that I wish I didn't have to; or that, when not forced to face up to things, I tend to revert to old ways of thinking and acting: the distressing information hasn't yet fully sunk in (in which case my knowledge will be as unsettled as my belief).

This much is true: it is generally misleading to *say* 'I believe' when I could just as well say 'I know'. If you ask me which way to go at a fork in the road, it would be misleading for me to say 'I *believe* we should go left' when I have carefully checked the route and know which way to turn. However, there are various reasons why it might be inappropriate to *say* something. In the present instance, the reason is that it is generally misleading to make a weaker claim when a stronger one would be in order. But this does not make the weaker claim *false*. Thus the moral is not that knowing excludes believing but that knowing involves more than *merely* believing, as the standard analysis says.

Moving on, because knowledge contrasts not just with ignorance but also with error, only *true* beliefs count as knowledge: I cannot *know* that the battle of Hastings was fought in 1056, since it wasn't. 'Know' is a success term, which means that we only attribute knowledge to another person when we are ourselves prepared to endorse that person's assertion or belief. Admittedly, on receiving my disappointing examination results I might say, 'But I just *knew* the date was 1056'. However, all this means is that I felt sure: it was just as if I knew, though unfortunately I didn't.

There is, in philosophy, a long and continuing tradition connecting knowledge not just with truth but with certainty. Of course, certainty in the sense of a *feeling* of assurance is not sufficient for knowledge. It is not even necessary. (Think of the nervous examinee who knows the answers but never feels fully confident.) When philosophers like Plato contrast knowledge with belief, on the grounds that the infallible cannot be identified with the fallible, their demand is for objective certainty: knowledge that is proof against error.

Plato is right to link belief with fallibility. The concept of belief owes much of its point to the way it allows us, in evaluating another person's epistemic state, to distinguish between what that person *takes* to be the case and what *really is* the case. It is essential to the concept of belief that there should be *differences* of opinion, so that we attribute false as well as true beliefs. By contrast, the very idea of false knowledge is an oxymoron. (If we meant anything by 'false knowledge' it would be something we thought was knowledge that turned out not to be.) Because knowledge is a form of true belief, it is inconsistent to say that someone knows something that is false. However, this way of excluding error has nothing to do with being mistake-proof. All the 'factive' character of knowledge implies is that if you turn out to have been wrong, then you didn't really know: you just thought you did.

Plato demands much more. He restricts knowledge to knowledge of necessary truths, propositions that *cannot be false.* Perhaps they cannot even be fully understood without being seen to be true. Since facts concerning the physical world are contingent—they happen to hold, but might not have—the physical world is not an appropriate object of knowledge. More than this, Plato seems to want a *faculty* of knowledge, conceived as a error-proof mode of awareness. He wants knowledge to be self-guaranteeing. One consequence of understanding knowledge this way is that, when someone really knows something, he cannot fail to know that he knows it. This is not something that the standard analysis, in itself, requires.

How might a conception of knowledge as demanding as Plato's originate? One possibility is a tendency to think of knowledge as a subjectively identifiable mental state, on a par with pain, or for that matter belief. But whatever the source of this way of thinking, the standard analysis does not encourage it. If anything, the opposite is the case. By virtue of the truth condition on knowledge, in ascribing knowledge to someone we are doing more than characterize his subjective state: we are implying something about the world around him.

Why more?

The belief and truth conditions on knowledge are relatively straightforward in the sense that philosophers generally agree in *imposing* them, whatever their differences over how to *interpret* them. The justification condition is different. Two questions arise: why impose *any* third condition? And why must it involve justification?

To forgo a third condition is to equate knowledge with true belief. One could argue that there is a sense of 'knowledge' that makes this equation. I know the answers to the test questions if I get them right: knowledge, in this minimal sense, is simply correct information. On the other hand, we have normally acquired the relevant information from suitably authoritative sources, such as approved textbooks, and thus have reason to think it reliable. So it is not clear that correct information is ever really *mere* opinion. But even if it were, there is a more demanding but perfectly familiar sense of 'knowledge' for which merely getting things right is not enough. We can get things *right* for the *wrong* reasons, or for *no* reasons at all; and if we do, we have true belief but not knowledge. Playing roulette, I reason that after so many losses my number will definitely come up next time (the 'gambler's fallacy'); and I am right, it does. Did I know that it would? To be sure, I may say: 'I just *knew* it would win.' But I didn't really know. I was *convinced* and I turned out to be right. That is all.

Why do beliefs held for bad reasons or no reasons at all not count as knowledge, even though they happen to be true? That is the answer: they only *happen* to be true. A belief isn't knowledge if it is only accidentally true. This need to distinguish knowing from lucky guessing convinces most philosophers both that a third condition must be imposed and that it must have something to do with justification, for when I hold my beliefs for good reasons, their truth is not accidental. But is this familiar line of thought conclusive?

Perhaps not: the belief condition alone may be more of a constraint than first appears. Belief is a dispositional state, implying a certain degree of stability. To say I believe that the battle of Hastings was fought in 1066 is to imply that, other things being equal, this is the answer I am disposed to give whenever I am asked. If I guess the date—say by randomly picking it out on a multiple-choice history test—it is not clear that I have any real belief about when the battle took place. Perhaps I have no stable disposition to pick any date in particular and would pick another if retested. Along these lines, we could argue that lucky guessing does not provide a case of genuine belief. *A fortiori*, it does not provide a case of true belief without knowledge and so does not show the need for a third condition.

I think this objection fails. It does not really show that true belief, without justification, is sufficient for knowledge. But it derives its plausibility from a real insight: that where there is genuine belief, justification is always in the offing. Given that our beliefs are acquired, that they help us cope with our environment, and that we survive at all, it is unlikely that our ways of forming beliefs are wildly unreliable. More than this, there are deep connections between belief, truth, and meaning. Creatures who got everything wrong, or who were incapable of providing reasons for their 'beliefs', would not be believers at all. (These claims are controversial but, in the next chapter, we shall begin to see what can be said for them.)

Still, we might ask, why does justification *matter*? One answer to this question invokes the normative character of epistemic classification. A knower possesses a special kind of *entitlement*—epistemic entitlement—to hold to the proposition in question. Epistemic entitlement confers further entitlements: to use the claim as a basis for inferences or to authorize other people so to use it. So while, in a way, one may be entitled to make guesses and act on them—it isn't illegal—one is not normally entitled to advise others on the basis of mere guesswork.

A second answer is that, while true beliefs are what we need for getting on in the world, the only way to get them is by following the most reliable methods we know: paying attention to evidence, eliminating likely sources of error, and so on. We get true beliefs by paying attention to justification.

Of course, it is possible to take a more-than-pragmatic interest in knowledge: our goal may be understanding, not just utility. But the goal of understanding makes us want more than a ragbag of correct information: it makes us want our beliefs to hang together. This means having our more theoretical beliefs explain, and thus be confirmed by, a range of observations. An interest in understanding implies an interest in justification.

A final reason for valuing justification, and thus for excluding accidentally true beliefs from the status of knowledge, is suggested in Plato's *Meno*. There, Socrates remarks that, unlike the statues of the sculptor Daedalus, which were given to walking about, knowledge should be tied down. The point is that true beliefs are useful only if they are also *stable*. We don't want correct views to be vulnerable to the slightest objection or to our own passing whims. Justification is valuable as a source of stability in our beliefs.

Plato presses this point very hard, demanding infallible, thus absolutely stable, cognition. But we want to recognize beliefs that, while well-justified, are open to revision. Also, much knowledge doesn't need to be stable, because its usefulness is ephemeral. From the standpoint of rationality, the desirability of stabilizing one's beliefs needs to be balanced by a principle of 'clutter avoidance': not filling one's mind with useless information, no matter how well grounded.[5] Not that these considerations would impress Plato. Plato regards the ordinary sensible world—the subject of such ephemeral knowledge—as itself too unstable and indeterminate to be truly knowable. There is a gulf between Plato's epistemic ideals and our own, a point we will return to in Chapter 3.

Responsibility and grounding

We need to take account of two ways of understanding the phrase 'justified belief'. What exactly is supposed to be 'justified': a *person's believing* some particular proposition, or the *proposition* that he believes? There are two standpoints from which epistemic assessments of a person's beliefs can be made, corresponding to these two possibilities. Sometimes we focus on the person's entitlement to hold a certain view. But sometimes we are interested in whether the grounds on the basis of which he holds it are objectively adequate, whether they establish its truth, irrespective of whether he would be culpable for any defects.[6]

Looking at things from the first standpoint, we focus on whether a belief has been responsibly formed or is responsibly held. From this angle, justified belief is what we get by living up to appropriate standards of epistemic behaviour. For example, we can ask whether, in forming a certain belief, I have negligently ignored important counter-evidence. Call this 'epistemic responsibility' or 'personal justification'.

The second approach to epistemic assessment is more impersonal, object-ive, and outcome-oriented. From this angle, a belief of mine can be said to be objectively well justified when my epistemic procedure, in the circumstances in which it was executed, was *in fact* reliable: for example, when my grounds for holding a given proposition true really do establish its truth. We might be tempted to call this kind of justification 'evidential justification'; and indeed, adequate grounding does often involve possessing evidence, in the sense of knowing facts from which a conclusion may be inferred. But for reasons we shall get to, I want to leave open the possibility that it sometimes consists in the unselfconscious exercise of cognitive abilities. So instead of 'evidential justification', I shall use the more neutral term 'adequate grounding' ('grounding' for short).

I am not entirely sure that we should speak of two kinds or even two aspects of justification: usage strikes me as an uncertain guide in this matter. Suppose that I form an opinion on the basis of the best evidence I can gather but that, unknown to me and through no fault of mine, this evidence is defective or misleading. Is my belief justified? We *might* say: 'In a way, yes, but in another way, no.' If this sounds natural, then it is appropriate to speak of two kinds or two aspects of justification. But we might prefer to say: 'My belief was cer-tainly justified at the time, though the evidence I was relying on turned out not to be as strong as it appeared.' This reaction seems at least as natural as the first and perhaps more so. This gives us some reason to think that the primary sense of justification is personal. However, not much turns on the termino-logical issue. The important point is that there are two standpoints from which epistemic assessments can be made.

I think that there is a reason why this distinction is not clearly marked in ordinary usage. The point of setting standards for epistemic responsibility is to reduce the risk of error. Accordingly, epistemically responsible behaviour is itself a kind of grounding: by behaving in an epistemically responsible way, I increase the likelihood that the beliefs I form are true.

The point of the distinction between responsibility and objectively adequate grounding emerges most clearly from a third-person standpoint.

With respect to my own current beliefs, all I can do is to be as procedurally scrupulous as possible. But with respect to someone else's beliefs, I may have access to information that he lacks, and so may be able to see that his beliefs are not well grounded, even though his epistemic conduct is beyond reproach. And although I cannot *now* take myself to be entitled to a given belief and, at the same time, recognize that my evidence for it is defective, I can perfectly well adopt a third-person perspective on my former self. I can recognize *now* that I was non-culpably in error *then*, or that I had good evidence but failed to make proper use of it.

Now that we have the distinction between epistemic responsibility and adequate grounding in hand, what sort of justification is 'appropriate' for knowledge? It seems clear that the answer is 'both'.

Epistemic responsibility alone is not sufficient for knowledge. We may recognize a person is not to be faulted for undertaking a particular commitment, but we may know more about his epistemic situation than he does. For example, I believe that the match will kick off at 3.30 because I looked up the time in the newspaper. But you have just been on the phone to the editor, who has told you that there has been a misprint and the match is actually slated to start at 2.30. So you recognize that, although I am personally justified in my belief—I have not been irresponsible—the evidence I have for it is misleading. So even if there is an unexpected delay and the match does kick off at 3.30, we would not say that I knew it would do so.

Simply having adequate grounds for some true belief is not sufficient for knowledge either. I may reach a belief using a procedure that is in fact reliable, but which I ought to distrust. Perhaps I have strong (though misleading) evidence that it is unreliable. In such a case, beliefs reached via this procedure would be irresponsibly held and would not count as knowledge.

With these considerations in mind, we can refine the standard analysis to read:

1.   S believes that p.
2.   p is true.
3(p)   S is personally justified in believing that p.
3(g)   S believes that p on the basis of adequate grounds.

This is the standard analysis in its *extended* form.

Evidence and responsibility

The fact that the distinction between epistemic responsibility and adequate grounding only comes into its own from a third-person standpoint supports the idea that epistemic responsibility is the primary sense of justification. Judgements of responsibility and judgements about the objective adequacy of grounds fall apart when we make assessments of the beliefs of others (or our former selves) in the light of extra information. In a case like this, we may judge that the other person was entirely responsible in holding a particular view, although, given our extra information, we would not be. When we criticize a person's grounds, we express something about what we regard ourselves as entitled to believe, even though we may judge someone else's entitlements less severely.

Here is a further reason for thinking that epistemic responsibility is fundamental: epistemic responsibility is an essential component of rationality; and if we had no stake in rationality, we would have no interest in justification.

Someone might dispute this on the grounds that our fundamental interest is in having true beliefs, which we need in order to be successful in any of our undertakings. The thought is that this makes grounding the more important, since grounding makes our beliefs likely to be true. But why are we so interested in truth? Because it is irrational—epistemically irresponsible—not to be.

However, we might argue that, while these considerations suggest that epistemic responsibility is fundamental methodologically, grounding is more fundamental from a theoretical or explanatory point of view. And indeed, according to what has perhaps been the dominant view, personal justification is wholly dependent on a special kind of grounding: evidential justification, strictly so called. On this approach, one is epistemically responsible in believing a given proposition only if one's belief is based on adequate evidence. This conception of the relation between the two aspects of justification subjects personal justification, or epistemic responsibility, to what I shall call the 'Prior Grounding Requirement'. Because this requirement makes evidential justification so fundamental, it drains the notion of personal justification of much of its interest. This is perhaps the main reason why, traditionally, philosophers have not made much of the responsibility/grounding distinction.

There has been a dissident minority. William James, for example, rejected the 'Prior Grounding' conception of justification as overly 'intellectualist'. One of the fundamental insights of Pragmatism, James thought, was that not all responsible believing is believing-on-evidence.[7] By itself, however, this need not indicate serious disagreement. Philosophers who accept the Prior Grounding requirement need not hold that groundless believing is irresponsible *tout court*. They can recognize all kinds of reasons why we are justified, or at least not culpable, in holding beliefs we cannot back up. Sometimes practical considerations force us to make up our minds before the evidence is in. Or perhaps, as Hume thought, certain beliefs are 'natural'. As a matter of human psychology, we are going to hold them, whether or not we can support them by evidence; and we cannot be faulted for what we cannot help. But none of these justifications or exculpations is *epistemic*. We may therefore still be epistemically irresponsible, even if non-culpably so.

A more interesting thought is that 'intellectualism' is questionable *from an epistemic standpoint*. For example, by 'evidence' we mean known facts that give grounds for inferring further facts. This is what we have in mind when we speak of the experimental evidence in favour of a scientific hypothesis or of the evidence that led the jury to convict. Here justification takes the form of an explicit argument. But it is not obvious that all justification is like this. Many of our beliefs result from the unreflective use of our perceptual capacities and, in such cases, talk of evidence sounds strained. Mouse droppings are evidence that mice have got into the house: seeing the mice themselves run across the floor isn't.

In general, many beliefs are credible because they derive from a reliable source. Such sources could include the testimony of a dependable witness, a book written by an accredited authority, or direct personal observation under favourable conditions. So while justification may involve citing evidence for one's beliefs, it can also involve giving one's credentials or tracing one's belief to some reliable process of belief-formation. This is why I prefer 'grounding' to 'evidential justification'. However, if we are willing to count as 'evidential justification' anything that can legitimately be cited to demonstrate entitlement to an assertion, explaining personal in terms of evidential justification will not automatically induce a bias towards 'intellectualism'.

The Prior Grounding Requirement is intellectualist in a further way: it insists that one's beliefs be *based* on adequate grounds. But there is another possibility. This is that personal justification is more like innocence in a court of law: presumptive but in need of defence in the face of contrary evidence. On this view, personal justification has what Robert Brandom calls a 'default and challenge' structure: entitlement to one's beliefs is the default position; but entitlement is always vulnerable to undermining by evidence that one's epistemic performance is not up to par. Faced with such a challenge, one can retain entitlement only by producing evidence in favour of one's beliefs or of the reliability of one's methods. This conception of justification replaces the Prior Grounding Requirement with a *Defence Commitment*. Knowledgeable beliefs must be defensible, but not necessarily derived from evidence. This idea will prove significant when we turn our attention to scepticism.

Belief and the will

I have been talking about irresponsible believing: acquiring or retaining commitments that one ought not to hold. Some philosophers object to using this 'deontological' (i.e. rights and duties) vocabulary in matters concerning belief. Their thought is that talk about what one ought and ought not to do makes sense only with respect to actions that are *voluntary*. Or as is sometimes said, 'ought' implies 'can'. But belief is not generally subject to voluntary control. We do not choose our beliefs; we cannot believe or not believe at will. This is clearly true of perceptually based beliefs: I see what I see; choice doesn't come into it. But the same can be true of beliefs based on reasoning. An argument can compel assent. When we find an argument completely convincing, we have no choice about accepting its conclusion.

Obviously, there is something to the point about belief's not being generally a matter of choice. But we should not make too much of it. Though we do not always have direct control over what we believe, we have indirect control by virtue of our control over how we conduct inquiry. Perception may be a largely involuntary process, but if I want to see clearly what is going on, it is up to me to secure a good vantage-point. I control what I learn by making sure I get a good look, by looking carefully, by repeating my observations, and so on. A similar point can be made about beliefs based on reasoning. The link between reasoning and belief may not be voluntary; but it is still up to me whether I try to reason carefully, on the basis of all the relevant evidence I can find, whether I look at counter-evidence as well as evidence favourable to my initial ideas, and so on. We control our beliefs—both perceptually and intellectually—by virtue of how we inquire. This is why we are responsible for them. Notice that we would not even want our beliefs to be directly subject to the will. Rational control over belief is a matter of inquiring in such a way that observation and reasoning will lead us in the direction of true beliefs. The point of making observations is to ensure that our beliefs are partly under the control of external circumstances.

A final point: some talk of the involuntariness of belief makes acquiring and retaining a belief sound too much like the flipping of a switch. But the commitment involved in believing is a matter of what one does with a belief once acquired: that is, with making subsequent use of it in inference and action. We may involuntarily come to believe that p. But whether we act on this information, or use it as a basis for drawing further conclusions—that is to say, whether we retain a real commitment—is by no means automatic. If we get new information, which suggests that our previous information is either inaccurate or unreliably obtained, we will cease to treat p as information we can use. If we do not, we will be open to criticism on grounds of epistemic irresponsibility. This is all the voluntariness that epistemic evaluation needs.

Notes

1. This point will be familiar to readers of Plato's early dialogues. In these works, Socrates typically asks an interlocutor for a definition of a word that person might be expected to understand: for example, a general is asked to define 'courage' or a conspicuously religious person to define 'piety'. At first, the interlocutors simply give examples. When they try to formulate general definitions, the definitions, combined with other views that they find difficult to deny, lead to contradiction.

2. Because it is usually thought to go back a long way: arguably to Plato's *Theaetetus*. But see Kaplan (1985).

3. In speaking of knowledge-claims, I do not mean only claims beginning with 'I know

that . . .' or some equivalent phrase. Quite the contrary. Knowledge-claims are not usually, expressed by using the phrase 'I know that . . .'. If you ask me when the match kicks off, and I reply '3.30', you will be entitled to reproach me if it turns out that I was just picking a time out of the air. Absent contextual cues to the contrary, all assertions are implicit knowledge-claims. 'Knowledge-claim' is the default significance of assertions advanced in the normal course of communication. When I do say 'I know that . . .', I imply that I know that I know. The relation between knowing and knowing that one knows is not obvious. I discuss it in Chapter 4 below.

4. Ayer, (1956), ch. 1. J. L. Austin, 'Other Minds', in Austin (1961). Brandom (1994), ch. 4.
5. On clutter avoidance (and much else of epistemological interest), see Harman (1986).
6. Kornblith (1983), Engel (1992), and Fogelin (1994).
7. James, 'The Will to Believe', in Thayer (1982).

2
Knowledge Without Evidence

Gettier's problem

In the previous chapter, we were concerned with the necessity for imposing a justification condition on knowledge. A different question, posed in a brilliantly brief paper by Edmund Gettier, is whether adding this condition is sufficient.[1]

Gettier tells the following story:

Suppose that Smith and Jones have applied for a certain job. And suppose that Smith has strong evidence for the following conjunctive proposition:

(d) Jones is the man who will get the job, and Jones has ten coins in his pocket.

Smith's evidence for (d) might be that the president of the company assured him that Jones would in the end be selected, and that he, Smith, had counted the coins in Jones's pocket ten minutes ago. Proposition (d) entails:

(e) The man who will get the job has ten coins in his pocket.

Let us suppose that Smith sees the entailment from (d) to (e), and accepts (e) on the grounds of (d), for which he has strong evidence. In this case, Smith is clearly justified in believing that (e) is true.

But imagine, further, that unknown to Smith, he himself, not Jones, will get the job. And also unknown to Smith, he himself has ten coins in his pocket. Proposition (e) is then true, though proposition (d), from which Smith inferred (e), is false. In our examples, then, all the following are true: (i) (e) is true, (ii) Smith believes that (e) is true, and (iii) Smith is justified in believing that (e) is true. At the same time, Smith does not know that (e) is true . . .

Though all the conditions contained in the standard analysis are clearly met, no one would say that Smith knows that (e) is true. Accordingly, the standard analysis fails to give sufficient conditions for knowledge.

A striking feature of Gettier's example is that our reluctance to grant Smith knowledge has nothing to do with his having only low-grade evidence for his conclusion. Thus the suggestion that knowledge demands a high degree of justification will not solve the problem. By normal standards, Smith's evidence is more than adequate to support a claim to knowledge.

The main reason for imposing a justification condition in the first place is that accidentally true beliefs do not amount to knowledge. What Gettier notices is that a well-justified belief can be as fortuitously true as the baldest guess. Although Smith has good grounds, makes responsible use of them, and forms a belief that turns out to be true, the facts in virtue of which it is true have nothing to do with his reasons, so that his belief's being true is still just a matter of luck.

What philosophers think of as 'Gettier's problem' is to state necessary and sufficient conditions for knowledge in the face of Gettier-style counter-examples to the standard analysis. The problem has generated an enormous (some might say inordinate) amount of discussion. But in my view, though there are useful lessons to be learned from thinking about this problem, whether it needs to be—or even can be—definitively 'solved' is another question.

Two broad strategies for solving the problem are available. Conservative strategies try to supplement the justification condition, specifying more narrowly the kind of justification needed for knowledge. Radical strategies drop the justification clause entirely, proposing a *non-justificational* analysis of knowledge. If radicalism is defensible, justification is not necessary for knowledge after all, so this is the approach we shall consider first.

Knowledge without justification

The key idea of non-justificational analyses of knowledge is that knowledge demands a tight connection between a person's belief and the facts that make it true. Knowledge is belief that *co-varies with the facts.*

An early example is Goldman's *causal* theory of knowledge, according to which my belief that p counts as knowledge if and only if it is caused by the fact that p.[2] Goldman treats his causal condition as necessary and sufficient for knowledge. His view is not that the justification condition needs to be supplemented by a causal condition, but that knowledge has no essential connection with justification.

The application of Goldman's idea to Gettier's argument is straightforward. Smith's belief is true because of facts about Smith: principally, that he, like Jones, happens to have ten coins in his pocket. However, he is led to form his belief by facts about Jones. Since the facts that cause Smith to form his belief are distinct from those that make it true, his belief fails to meet the causal condition on knowledge.

At first glance, the causal theory fits some kinds of knowledge rather well: for example, knowledge gained by direct observation. I know that my dog is in the garden because I can see him there. His presence causes (by way of visual perception) my belief. Other kinds of knowledge, however, pose problems. I know that $2 + 2 = 4$, but it is not clear what would even be meant by supposing that there are *causal* relations to mathematical facts. We also seem to have some knowledge of the future, though my current beliefs can hardly be caused by facts that do not yet exist. It seems too restrictive to tie knowledge always and everywhere to causation.

Another suggestion is that knowledge demands a 'lawlike connection' between a person's belief and the state of affairs that make it true. Events can co-vary in a lawlike way even when neither causes the other: for example, when they have a common cause. But although lawlike relatedness is broader than strict causation, it still seems too restrictive. Do we really stand in lawlike connections to mathematical facts? Presumably not.[3]

A more general conception of co-variance is offered by Robert Nozick, who suggests that knowledge is belief that 'tracks the truth'.[4] Instead of condition 3(J), Nozick proposes

> 3(T)   If it were not the case that p, S would not believe that p.

To get a feel for how this works, imagine that I believe, truly, that someone is guilty of a crime but do so because I am ready to believe anything bad about him. Since my belief would have been the same irrespective of the facts, it does not count as knowledge. This seems right.

There is another way in which my beliefs can be only coincidentally true: namely that, if circumstances had been slightly different, I would *not* have held them, even though they would *still* have been true. This can easily come about when a belief is based on misleading evidence. Suppose that I believe, correctly, that last week the local railway station put on a special event involving steam engines; and suppose that, if the event had been cancelled, an acquaintance of mine who was planning to attend would have expressed his disappointment to me, so that I would not have believed that the event took place. In this instance 3(T) is satisfied. But suppose further that I believe such an event took place only because I heard the engines puffing away. Or so I thought: what I actually heard was a neighbour playing his records of train noises. If he hadn't happened to play them while I was at home, I would never have given any thought to events at the station. Surely my belief fails to count as knowledge. To deal with cases like this, Nozick adds

> 4(T)   If, in somewhat changed circumstances, it were still the case that p, I should still believe that p.

He calls 3(T) a 'variation' and 4(T) an 'adherence' condition.

The critical feature of 3(T) and 4(T) is that they are *subjunctive* conditionals: they say something about what S's beliefs *would have been* if (contrary to fact) p had not been true or circumstances had been slightly different. This may seem far-fetched. Why should we care about what someone's beliefs would have been, as opposed to what they actually are? To see why, compare the concept of knowledge with that of reliability, which also has an important subjunctive component. A reliable car will run properly in a variety of weather conditions. My car is not reliable simply because it started this pleasant morning, but because it would have started even if the weather had turned nasty. We can think of knowledge as a kind of reliability in our beliefs: truth reliability.

Nozick's suggestion seems to capture what the other views were after. A defining feature of lawlike statements—causal statements too—is that they allow us to infer various subjunctive conditionals, including contrary-to-fact conditionals. Because the temperature dropped, the thermometer went down. But if the temperature had remained constant, the thermometer reading would have remained constant too. Compare this case with the following generalization: all the coins in my pocket are dimes. We would not infer that, if this penny had been in my pocket, it would have been a dime. This generalization is not lawlike (unless I have a magic, wealth-increasing pocket).

This should ring a bell. The main reason for adding a third condition to the standard analysis is that beliefs do not count as knowledge if they are only accidentally true. Perhaps the kind of co-variance with the facts that distinguishes knowledge from accidentally true belief is best expressed by means of subjunctive conditionals, no matter what accounts for co-variance in particular cases.

Pure externalism

It seems plausible to suppose that, if someone knows something or other, he ought to realize or at least readily be able to determine that he does. Influenced by this thought, many philosophers have subscribed to the so-called 'K-K thesis': that if S knows that p, S knows that he knows that p. If we take this position, we will see knowledge as indefinitely iterative: knowing implies knowing that you know, which implies knowing that you know that you know, which implies . . . , and so on *ad infinitum*.

Non-justificationist accounts of knowledge deny that knowledge is iterative in this way. A crucial feature of any such analysis that is that, while it will set conditions that a person's beliefs must *in fact* meet, if they are to count as knowledge, it will not demand that the subject be aware that those conditions are fulfilled. For this reason, such theories of knowledge have come to be called 'externalist'. They make a person's knowledge depend on 'external' factors: that is, factors of which he may not be cognizant. From an externalist point of view, *knowing about* one's reliability is not required for 'first order' knowledge. I know something if my belief is in fact truth-reliable. If I have given no thought to my reliability, I do not know that my belief amounts to knowledge. But this just shows why the K-K thesis is false.

Justificationist accounts of knowledge are often thought of as 'internalist'. Knowledge requires having good grounds and making proper use of them. This is not something of which one can be unaware.

Against internalism, externalists are fond of pointing out that we often credit children, or even animals, with knowing all sorts of things. But, presumably, we do not suppose them to be in possession of elaborate justifications, which they can reflect on to assure themselves that they really do have knowledge. To know that I know something, I must have the concept of knowledge; and mastery of epistemological concepts looks like a more sophisticated accomplishment than simple factual knowledge.

It may be that externalist attributions of knowledge, say to children and animals, are less than literal. But it is not immediately obvious that this is so (which isn't to say that it isn't in the end correct). Even with adults, we are ready to count as instances of knowledge beliefs for which they have little or no justification, or for which anything they could produce by way of justification would be badly misguided.

Consider our most fundamental beliefs and inferential processes: for example, that we inhabit an external world not of our own making, or that putting your hand in the fire gives you a reason not to repeat the experiment. Sceptics doubt that we have any good reasons for such convictions, but do we need any? Or are certain beliefs and inferential propensities simply part of our basic cognitive equipment, as Hume suggested? Of course, we can try to think up justifications as 'rational reconstructions' of unreflectively held views, but to what end? Such rationalizations will amount only to 'arguments on paper'. They will have no connection with anyone's actual reasons for believing anything.[5]

These are fair points. However, it is important to see that the non-justificational accounts of knowledge under discussion do not merely allow knowledge to involve some external factors. Rather, these theories are *purely* or *radically* externalist, claiming that external factors *alone* give sufficient conditions for knowledge. In a similar vein, some epistemologies are purely internalist: they deny that external factors are ever relevant to a belief's epistemic status. There is no immediately obvious reason why an acceptable theory of knowledge should take either of these pure forms. The internalist/externalist distinction and the justificationist/non-justificationist distinction need not draw the same line.

Reliability as norm

Non-justificational epistemologies lay down certain rather general constraints on knowledge. Filling in the details, showing what truth-reliable information gathering and processing capacities humans and other animals actually have, is the business of cognitive psychology. Radically externalist theories of knowledge thus appear to fit in well with the idea that epistemology should be 'naturalized'. Indeed, this is an important source of their appeal.

The thought that epistemology either can or should be fully 'naturalized' conflates two senses of 'natural'. One contrast is between the natural and the supernatural; another is between the natural and the conventional or normative. Philosophical naturalists are anti-supernaturalists: their thought is that, because the natural world is the only world there is, there is no inquiry other than natural-scientific inquiry. However, epistemology does not resist 'naturalization' because it deals with the supernatural but because it is irreducibly normative. Of course, the question of what our epistemic norms actually are is an empirical question. But once some account of those norms is on the table, the question of whether to abide by or to modify them is on the table too. In epistemology, the line between descriptive analysis and normative proposal is *never* sharp. This point applies as much to non-justificational analyses as to more traditional approaches. They are not just explications of our actual concept of knowledge but implicit normative proposals.

The radical externalist's key notion is 'reliability'. This is not quite so straightforward an 'empirical description' as naturalistic epistemologists like to think. Reliability is a normative standard governing adequate performance. Because of this, any talk of reliability involves an implicit reference to a (possibly variable) range of conditions. What that range is (or ought to be) is something we decide, not something we simply discover.[6]

To see this, consider the view adopted by Goldman after he abandoned his simple causal theory of knowledge: the view that perceptual knowledge depends on reliable discriminative capacities.[7] As Goldman points out, whether my discriminative capacities are reliable depends in part on the alternatives that the world presents me with. Relatively coarse-grained abilities can be extremely reliable in an environment that doesn't demand refined discrimination. I can normally tell just by looking whether there is a barn by the side of the road. But suppose, Goldman suggests, that a certain local authority decides to prettify the countryside by erecting barn-façades, indistinguishable to the casual observer from the real thing. Driving through this region of Potemkin barns, I catch sight of what happens to be a real barn. Do I know that there is a barn by the road? We are reluctant to say so. Our ability to 'just see' such things is no longer reliable. But does the fact that our barn-spotting capabilities are reliable only within limits mean that we can't spot barns when we *aren't* in Barn Façade County? Presumably not.

The example is fanciful but the moral is not. If we are to explain ordinary knowledge in terms of truth-reliable methods, we must insist that 'reliability' be reliability with respect to some reasonable or normal range of conditions, not with respect to every conceivable situation. This accords perfectly with our everyday idea of reliability. My car is reliable if it starts and runs in weather conditions that fall within the normal range for where I live. I would not call it unreliable because it would not work so well at the South Pole or in the middle of the Sahara. Reliability is an incurably interest-relative notion. The standards for reliability are set by us, not by Nature. This means that there is no hope of fully 'naturalizing' epistemology by explaining knowledge in terms of reliability.

Reliability and responsibility

Any account of knowledge or justification that allows that knowing can result from meeting conditions not all of which need be known (or even believed) to be met can be thought of as having an externalist component. However, as we have seen, non-justificational analyses of knowledge are *radically* or *purely* non-justificational, thus radically or purely externalist. They sever knowledge from personal as well as evidential justification. This is a mistake.

One way to bring this out is by example.[8] Imagine, apparently conclusive evidence to the contrary notwithstanding, that a very few gifted individuals are genuinely clairvoyant. Now imagine that one of these individuals knows all about the counter-evidence and is thus sceptical about the existence of clairvoyant powers. We can also suppose that, so far, his powers have lain dormant. One day, however, out of the blue, he gets an uncannily powerful hunch about some upcoming event: the result of a horse race, say. Does he know the identity of the winner? By the standards of radically externalist accounts of knowledge, the answer should be 'Yes'. However, though intuitions can vary here, there is a powerful case for answering 'No'. The reason for answering 'No' is that it is *irresponsible* for a person to rely on a method of belief-formation that the person himself has every reason to believe to be completely unreliable, even if he is wrong about its unreliability.

It is not surprising that we should be interested in epistemic responsibility. Epistemic responsibility is an important aspect of rationality. It is important because our methods for forming beliefs go beyond the fixed cognitive equipment that animals are restricted to. Our beliefs can be made articulate and (we hope) improved. Trying to be epistemically responsible is the means to such improvement.

To see that the internal dimension of knowledge cannot simply be eliminated, we have only to return to our example and imagine that we ourselves are the person in question. We would be uneasy about relying on such a hunch, even if we found it difficult to shake: we would feel that we were going against our better judgement. Of course, over time we might notice that our hunches are surprisingly reliable. Then we could say to sceptics (including the sceptic within): 'I don't know how I do it, but I do turn out to be right a lot of the time—try me'. However, then we would be justifying our hunches by citing their reliability.

Sellars links placing a state in 'the logical space of reasons' with 'justifying or *being able to justify* what one says'. This way of insisting on the normative character of epistemic characterizations is compatible with the point that much everyday knowledge is 'grounded' in the unselfconscious exercise of recognitional abilities and reporting dispositions, and so does not involve inference from evidence. However, such knowledge is still in the logical space of reasons in that it is *open* to challenge; and if an appropriate challenge occurs, one must be able to meet it or one's entitlement to claim knowledge lapses. To have knowledge, one must always be able, when necessary, to justify what one says, even though one need not always *obtain* one's knowledge *via* a self-conscious justificatory process. Radical externalism derives much of its plausibility from ignoring this point.

At this point, we can return to Nozick's tracking analysis. Although it seems, at first sight, to be the purest of pure externalisms, the tracking analysis is so abstract that it is not incompatible with a justificationist conception of knowledge. That a given belief tracks the truth can hardly be a brute fact. For all we have seen, truth-tracking may be essentially connected with our ability to give reasons.

Go back to the steam day at the local station. My belief that such an event took place failed to count as knowledge because it was based on misleading evidence. However, suppose that I had not had a train-obsessed neighbour and that the train sounds I heard had actually been produced by the steam engines taking part in the event. Then my belief would have been a truth-tracker. But this would have been because my evidence would not have been misleading. All tracking could be like this, for anything that has been argued so far.

The involvement of truth-tracking with questions of justification and rationality is obscured by a misleading appearance of epistemic *atomism*. As stated, the tracking analysis invites the thought that whether our beliefs track the truth is a belief-by-belief affair. But it isn't. Whether a particular belief of mine will co-vary appropriately with the facts will always depend on what else I believe. The example above makes this clear: my belief about the steam day is tied to a complex array of further beliefs about steam trains, their noises, the enthusiasm some people have for them, and so on. No beliefs are *solo trackers*: they track, hence amount to knowledge, only as components in a *critical epistemic mass*. But where such masses are involved, the possibility of finding justificational relationships, if only implicit, will never be absent.

Limits of reliabilism

Perhaps the externalist should claim only that some special kinds of knowledge can plausibly be given a purely externalist analysis. These would be the cases the causal and lawlike-connection views seem to fit best: simple cases of perceptual knowledge. In fact, however, pure reliabilism fails even with respect to what seem at first to be its most favourable cases. Here we return to a point hinted at in the previous chapter: that justification is essentially connected, not simply with knowledge, but with belief itself.

The argument for this view goes back to Sellars and has, in recent years, been elaborated by John McDowell and Robert Brandom.[9] As McDowell and Brandom explain, the question that Sellars encourages us to ask first is: What distinguishes conceptual from non-conceptual activity? How does the human being who says 'That's green' differ from the parrot trained to utter the same vocables in response to the presentation of a green card? How does issuing genuine reports, or forming genuine beliefs—reports or beliefs with propositional content—differ from mere signalling, the sort of signalling that thermostats can manage, as their readings change with changes in room temperature? Sellars's answer is that the human reporter, unlike the parrot or the thermostat, has the concept 'green' and so understands what he is saying, in a way that the parrot or thermostat does not. This understanding consists in the human reporter's grasp of what follows from his reports, what is evidence for them, how they might be challenged, how various challenges might be met, and so on. Propositionally contentful utterances and genuine beliefs are, in Brandom's phrase, 'inferentially articulated'. They are essentially the sorts of things that can function as reasons and for which reasons can be demanded and given. If this is even roughly right, there must be something misleading about reliabilist 'intuitions'.

Much of the appeal of non-justificational analyses of knowledge derives from their opposition to the excessive 'intellectualism' of some traditional accounts of knowledge. The non-justificationist points out that much everyday knowledge does not appear to depend on inference from evidence. But this does nothing to show that knowledge can be detached from epistemic responsibility, thus from all aspects of justification.

More than this, the fact that knowledge does not always depend on inference from evidence is insufficient to show that epistemic responsibility can be detached from evidential justification. Here we must remember our two models of the relation between the two aspects of justification. The traditional model builds in the Prior Grounding Requirement: epistemically responsible believing is believing on the basis of adequate evidence. Its rival is the Default and Challenge model. Here a person can believe responsibly without basing his beliefs self-consciously on evidence. Nevertheless, he commits himself to providing evidence, should the adequacy of his epistemic performance be challenged. Radically non-justification epistemologies overlook this second model of the relation between epistemic responsibility and evidential justification. This is a deeply ironic result, for it shows that radical externalism trades on the very 'intellectualism' it purports to reject.

Another problem with pure externalism is that it ignores the social dimension of knowledge. Suppose that we insist on some essential connection between knowledge and evidential justification: a question that naturally arises is whether, for a belief of mine to count as knowledge, I need always to be personally in possession of an appropriate justification, or whether it is enough that some such justification be socially available. The third condition in the standard analysis is nominally neutral on this issue, though it is clear that we are ordinarily content with the weaker standard. There are obvious limits to what we can verify for ourselves, not only in specialized subjects, but in mundane matters as well. Inevitably and increasingly, we live with a division of epistemic labour, relying on other people for the justification of much that we believe.

This complicates the intuitive case for pure externalism. Granted that we allow that there can be knowledge without evidential justification, is this because knowledge has no essential connection with evidence? Or is it because we allow justification-by-evidence to be socially distributed? I think that, in a strict sense of 'evidential', evidential justification is clearly socially distributed. Indeed, one of the main functions of knowledge claims is to pass epistemic entitlements around, exploiting the fact that different people have different epistemic capacities.

If this is so, there can be a general dependence of knowledge on evidential justification, even though individuals are often justified in holding beliefs for which they cannot themselves give grounds. The demand for evidential justification would be met by the fact that grounds can be given by *someone else*. This is what goes on in the externalist example of knowledge-without-evidence: when we credit someone with knowledge using an externalist standard, we imagine *ourselves* to be aware of that person's reliability. Pure externalism thus shares another of the tradition's deepest-rooted commitments: its individualism. This, too, is an ironic outcome. Although regarded by its adherents as radically innovative, reliabilism remains deeply bound to the epistemological tradition it allegedly repudiates.

Notes

1. Gettier (1963).
2. Goldman (1967).
3. But causal or lawlike connections might still be an important ingredient in *certain special kinds* of knowledge. See Chapter 14.
4. Nozick (1981), ch. 3. Nozick's views are effectively criticized in Fogelin (1994).
5. Kornblith (1980).
6. For more discussion of this 'generality problem', see Conee and Feldman (1998).
7. Goldman (1976).
8. BonJour (1985), ch. 3. Also Fogelin (1994), ch. 3.
9. Brandom (1995) and (1998); McDowell (1995).

3

Two Ideals

Knowledge and demonstration

Rejecting radically non-justificational approaches to knowledge means staying with the standard analysis. However, the standard analysis is highly schematic and can be elaborated in various ways to produce richer conceptions of knowledge. One particularly important way of filling it in yields what I propose to call the 'classical' or 'demonstrative' conception. We have already touched on it in passing. The time has come for a closer look.

Western epistemological ideas have been decisively influenced by the Greek discovery of the *axiomatic method*: the discovery, originally in geometry, that a rich variety of results, often far from obviously true, can be deduced from a small number of primitive propositions, each of which seems self-evidently correct. On the view of knowledge that this discovery inspires, all genuine knowledge is *demonstrative*: to be known to be true, a proposition must be either immediately self-evident or deduced from such self-evident truths by a sequence of self-evidently valid steps. Anything less will yield only opinion. This is not to say that all opinions are equal. Opinions may be, in various senses, more or less probable. But they will never amount to knowledge.

The demonstrative conception of knowledge is closely linked with the Platonic demand that knowledge be infallible, and it helps to make plausible Plato's thought that knowledge and belief must have different 'objects'. To be infallible, knowledge must concern things that one cannot be wrong about. Thus, if 'appropriate justification' is taken to consist in demonstrative proof, the objects of knowledge must be universal and necessary truths, or the sorts of thing that such truths pertain to: the idealized abstractions studied by pure mathematics, for example.

Aristotle famously argues that, on pain of infinite regress, we must have knowledge of first principles: premises that serve to justify other things without themselves standing in need of justification.[1] Strictly speaking, this argument does not yield the demonstrative conception of knowledge in full detail but something more general: what is now called a 'foundational' conception of knowledge. A foundational conception of knowledge insists that justification depends on ultimate premises, today usually called 'basic beliefs'. The demonstrative or classical conception adds two further conditions: it insists that basic beliefs be self-evident, indeed necessarily true; and it requires that the inferential steps in a justifying argument be deductively valid. No contemporary foundationalist would regard these extra stipulations as automatic. The classical conception adds a lot to the thought that justification displays a foundational structure.

This talk of 'adding' should be understood conceptually, not historically. Historically, the axiomatic method furnished the model for the foundationalist understanding of knowledge. Mathematics provided the clearest example of indisputable knowledge; it did so in virtue of the demonstrative character of mathematical proof; and demonstrative proof brought a foundationalist conception of justification in its train. From a historical point of view, the modern idea of a generalized foundationalism results from the weakening of the classical ideal.

I have been referring to the demonstrative conception of knowledge as the 'classical'—we might also say 'Platonic-Aristotelian'—conception. I should note, however, that Plato was attracted to an even more demanding epistemological ideal. In the *Republic*, the demonstrative knowledge that results from mathematical reasoning is still second best. This is because the axioms from which the mathematician reasons, no matter how intuitively evident, are still taken as primitive. Exactly how to understand Plato's remedy for this unsatisfactory state of affairs is controversial. But he appears to have held something along the following lines: someone who really had knowledge would be able to see every individual thing he knew, including things that are generally taken as individually self-evident, as a necessary component in a complete and fully integrated conception of reality.

This idea, too, has had a long history. The ancient Stoics seem to have taken a similar line. Knowledge begins with basic beliefs and the inferences they give rise to; but it gains in strength as particular results begin to form an interlocking system. In the early modern period Descartes seems to have taken this position. Basic truths known by what he calls 'clear and distinct perception' are indubitable while our attention is focused on them. But such results, if they are to be usable, need to be insulated from generalized sceptical doubts. To achieve this, we show that these primitive results provide the basis for a reflective self-understanding that excludes sceptical anxiety. (In Descartes's case, this involves proving that God's benevolence precludes our being subject to massive error, a strategy that Hume dryly describes as 'making a most unexpected circuit'.) In this picture, justification operates on two levels: a basic level, at which we grasp primitive truths, and a reflective level that reinforces and stabilizes knowledge gained in the first way.

This two-level approach continues to attract adherents. It is characteristic of what is sometimes called 'modest foundationalism'. On this view, basic beliefs have an intrinsic prima facie credibility, but their epistemic status can be improved (and perhaps even occasionally downgraded) as we develop more systematic, theoretical views. However, there is also a 'single-level' version of the thought that justification supervenes on systematicity: the so-called coherence theory of knowledge. In this single-level form, the coherence theory is usually taken to be foundationalism's main (or even only) rival.

In what follows, I shall ignore these complications. When I speak of the classical or Platonic-Aristotelian conception of knowledge, I shall be referring to the demonstrative ideal, not the even more demanding conception that some philosophers, ancient and modern, have been drawn to.

The fallibilist conception

Given what I have just said, it should be clear that, in calling the demonstrative conception of knowledge 'classical' or 'Platonic-Aristotelian', I do not mean to imply that only ancient philosophers, still less only Plato and Aristotle, accept it. On the contrary, historically speaking the classical conception of knowledge is the dominant conception. In broad outline, and with some qualifications, it is accepted not only by Aristotle's medieval ('scholastic') followers, but also by such early modern philosophers as Descartes and Locke. There are strong echoes of it even in Hume, who writes in the middle of the eighteenth century. This is very striking. For not only do Descartes and Locke present themselves as radical critics of scholastic Aristotelianism, they are generally thought to stand on opposite sides of modern epistemology's great divide, Rationalism and Empiricism.

That a Rationalist should advance a demonstrative ideal of knowledge is not surprising. But an Empiricist? This seems impossible. Given the Platonic-Aristotelian conception, how can we make room for empirical knowledge? Plato is not inclined to make room for it. But for the empirically minded, this is an unattractive option.

From Aristotle to Locke and beyond, the way empiricists make room for empirical knowledge, while remaining faithful to the demonstrative ideal, is by identifying empirical knowledge with demonstrative knowledge involving empirical *concepts*: that is, concepts somehow derived (e.g. by 'abstraction') from preconceptual sensory experience. In early modern philosophy, the debate between Rationalism and Empiricism has less to do with the origins of beliefs or judgements than with the origin of 'ideas', the concepts out of which judgements are composed. Rationalists (big 'R') follow Plato in arguing that knowledge requires an extensive endowment of *innate* ideas. Empiricists deny this: they think that even the most recherché mathematical ideas can be derived from sensory experience by abstraction and idealization. This is very much the basis of Locke's attack on Descartes. But when it comes to judgements, Locke shares with Descartes the demonstrative ideal. Propositional knowledge begins with the intuitive perception of relations of 'agreement' and 'disagreement' between our ideas, and is extended by intuitively valid deduction. It is 'empirical' only in respect of the sensory origins of the ideas we combine in making judgements. The sensory origins of empirical concepts make possible knowledge that has *reference* to the empirical world but which is not dependent on empirical *confirmation*.

No contemporary philosopher thinks along these lines. Today, the demonstrative conception of knowledge is thought to apply at most to knowledge that is strictly *a priori*, the sort of knowledge that, if it exists at all, is exemplified by logic and pure mathematics. No one thinks that the demonstrative ideal can plausibly be invoked in connection with empirical knowledge, which includes all of natural science.

On the contemporary conception, empirical knowledge is doubly non-demonstrative. First of all, empirical evidence, which provides the premises for empirical arguments, is itself only contingently true: it registers facts that happen to hold but which could have been otherwise. Secondly, in most interesting cases of empirical knowledge, we want to use empirical evidence to justify conclusions that are logically stronger than the conjunction of the premises. This point is often made by saying that, in interesting empirical inferences, the link between premises and conclusion is not deductive but inductive. And because the conclusion of an inductive inference is logically stronger than its premises, such an inference never guarantees its conclusion's truth.

Putting these two ideas together, we can say that the modern conception of knowledge is *fallibilist*. This point needs to be handled with some care since, as we shall see in the next chapter, talk of 'fallible knowledge' strikes some philosophers as oxymoronic. But at this point, all I need to insist on is that the modern conception of knowledge is fallibilist in the sense that it is at home in a fundamentally fallibilist conception of *inquiry*. What I mean by this is that, while we certainly take ourselves to know all sorts of things, and commit ourselves to defending our claims to knowledge, we recognize that the possibility of error can never be logically excluded. It can always turn out that we only *thought* we knew. As fallibilists, we recognize that even what seem to be our best-grounded knowledge-claims *may* need to be withdrawn, though in advancing them as claims to *knowledge*, we are betting that they won't *have* to be.

Why did the classical conception give way to the fallibilist conception? Because 'knowledge' is an honorific term that we apply to our paradigm cognitive achievements. Today, the natural sciences provide some of the best examples of the subjection of theoretical ideas to rigorous evidential control, so that it would be absurd to be reluctant to speak of scientific knowledge. At the same time, we cannot ignore the fact that scientific theories are subject to change. Even the most successful scientific theory of all time, Newton's physics, was abandoned. Scientific knowledge does not fit the demonstrative conception, even in aspiration. It is intrinsically fallible. This is its strength: to be open to correction is to be open to improvement.

This last point is important. Logically speaking, the classical conception does not preclude human fallibility. We can always say that, although knowledge is ideally demonstrative, we often make mistakes, through logical errors or insufficient clarity in our ideas. But whereas the classical conception demands a theory of error to explain why we go wrong, given that ideally we shouldn't, the modern conception builds liability to error into the very idea of empirical inquiry. The demonstrative conception is no longer plausible *even as an ideal*.

The origins of the fallibilist conception of knowledge go back a long way. They lie, I believe, in the sceptical tradition. In antiquity, sceptics attacked the possibility of knowledge, but still needed to give some account of how they regulated their lives and opinions. Their accounts of sceptical assent are the prototypes for modern theories of empirical knowledge, even though sceptical assent was originally meant to be a substitute for knowledge proper. Only when the demonstrative ideal had loosened its grip could sceptical assent become knowledge in its own right. As we shall see, now that this has happened, scepticism has to amount to more than fallibilism, if it is to be seen as a problem.

Knowledge and understanding

The classical and fallibilist conceptions of knowledge differ in ways that go beyond fallibilism.

The classical conception is rich as well as demanding. In coming to see how a proposition follows necessarily from simple, self-evident necessities, we do not just acquire evidence *that* is it true, we see *why* it is true: indeed, we see why it could not have been otherwise. In associating knowledge with demonstration, the classical conception connects knowledge with explanation and understanding.

This points to a further way in which classical 'opinion' is very different from knowledge. Personal experience and the credible testimony of many witnesses may leave no room for doubt that various things do or have happened: for example, that the sun rises once a day. But this kind of evidence gives no insight into why the facts to which it testifies are as they are. Accordingly, it does not yield knowledge, if knowledge involves understanding and not just well-founded conviction. By contrast, given the modern conception of empirical knowledge, to know *that* something is true and to know *why* are very different matters. The modern conception of knowledge tends to sever the link between knowledge and understanding. Modern knowledge, we might say, can be *merely* factual.

Consider scientific theories: they are typically much less certainly true than the observational results they explain. On the classical conception of know-ledge, explanation and justification proceed in tandem from the antecedently more certain to the antecedently less certain. On the modern conception there is an inverse relation between explanation and justification. Justification goes from relatively certain results to relatively conjectural theories. Explanation goes the other way: from more speculative theories to relatively more secure results.

More on the value of knowledge

The classical conception of knowledge sheds light on ancient versus modern ideas about the value of knowledge. As we observed, the ancient understand-ing of knowledge is individualistic and aristocratic. These features are deeply connected. To have knowledge, not merely is it not enough to have true belief, it is not enough to have true belief formed by some reliable method. Rather, the possession of knowledge is dependent on the capacity to put the proposi-tions one accepts into proper logical order. This is even more obviously true of the full Platonic conception of knowledge, which requires a coherent overall system in which no propositions figure as ultimate starting-points. The exercise of this capacity for logical ordering requires leisure for reflection. Moreover, this reflective, theoretical dimension makes genuine knowledge very different from the tacit 'know-how' involved in practical (*banausic*) undertakings.

In Plato's ideal republic, the members of the military caste do not have knowledge, only true belief. But if justification can supervene on a belief's deriving from a reliable source, they have *justified* true belief. After all, they are educated by the philosopher-kings, who know everything there is to know. So why do the soldiers not have knowledge? Because the kind of justification they possess has no connection with understanding. At best, they are legitimately assured that what they believe is true. But they do not really appreciate why it is true. They have justified belief without reflective understanding.

These individualist and aristocratic tendencies of the classical conception of knowledge reflect the moral-practical orientation of ancient philosophy gen-erally. The philosopher aims to live according to explicit knowledge: living according to custom or inarticulate know-how is the antithesis of the philo-sophical way of life. This is yet another reason why, in Plato's utopia, the military assistants to the philosopher-kings do not have knowledge. Their lives are regulated by true beliefs. But since those beliefs rest on authority, their lives are not truly their own. The person who lives by knowledge has to know *for himself*.

Now although many modern theories of knowledge show pronounced individualist tendencies, the modern conception of knowledge is not, as such, so clearly tied to epistemic individualism. That our modern conception of knowledge should drift away from extreme individualism is not surprising. Knowledge has exploded and specialized. Nobody can master everything there is to know, not even everything there is to know within a particular discipline: Renaissance men belong to the Renaissance. Today, when we speak of scientific knowledge, we are not referring to a body of propositions that any one person knows to be true. Of course, if, like Bacon, we value knowledge for its technological effectiveness, this will not matter. The growing epistemic division of labour will be one more instance of the division of labour generally: the precondition of a highly productive and technologically sophisticated way of life.

Nevertheless, although modern epistemology has taken fallibilism to heart, the same is not so clearly true of anti-individualism. To see why this is so, we shall have to look deeply into scepticism.

Non-demonstrative inference

To further clarify the difference between the classical and modern conceptions of knowledge, let us examine more closely the idea of non-demonstrative inference. As I noted, this idea is often explained in terms of the contrast between deductive and inductive reasoning.

Consider, the following simple syllogism:

> Nikki is a husky.
> All huskies like to roll in snow.
> Therefore: Nikki likes to roll in snow.

Here, as in any deductively valid argument, it is *impossible* that the premises all be true and the conclusion false. In this sense, the conclusion *follows from* or is a *logical consequence* of the premises. Alternatively, the premises logically *entail* the conclusion. Deductive validity excludes the possibility of true premises and a false conclusion.[2]

An immediate consequence of this definition of deductive validity is that adding more premises never makes a valid argument invalid. If it is impossible for an argument's premises to be true and its conclusion false, it is also impossible for those premises *and one or more additional premises* to be all true while the conclusion is false. Notice that we could even expand the argument given above to:

> Nikki does not like to roll in snow.
> Nikki is a husky.
> All huskies like to roll in snow.
> Therefore: Nikki likes to roll in snow.

Here the premises are inconsistent: they cannot all be true. But if they cannot all be true, they cannot all be true *and* the conclusion be false. So the argument is still deductively valid. (This shows that there is more to a good argument than deductive validity. But we knew that: every proposition is a logical consequence of itself, which doesn't make 'p, therefore p' a good argument.) Because validity cannot be compromised by adding premises, deductive arguments are sometimes said to be *monotonic*. (The term is derived from an analogy with certain mathematical functions whose curves, when graphed, never go down.)

Inductive arguments behave very differently. Adding extra premises can make a strong inductive argument weak and vice-versa. Consider this:

> Just about everyone who lives in Green Bay follows the Packers.
> I have a friend who lives in Green Bay.
> Therefore: He follows the Packers.

In this case, the information given by the premises provides strong support for the conclusion, though it does not logically guarantee it. However, suppose that my friend is a recent immigrant to the United States and that a survey has shown that the vast majority of recent immigrants take no interest whatsoever in American football: this new information seriously undermines the support that the original information provided for the conclusion that my friend follows the Packers. But now suppose that my friend comes from Great Britain and that closer investigation has shown that British immigrants are an exception to the rule: they tend quickly to acquire an interest in local sports teams. Then the undermining evidence is itself undermined and the likelihood that my friend is a Packers fan goes back up.

In the case of inductive inference, new information can radically degrade the evidential value of previous information without requiring us to think that any of our previous information is false. Rather, new information can put old information in a new light, 'recontextualize' it, so that it loses the evidential force it previously had. Inductive inferences are thus *nonmonotonic*: their strength can go up and down as premises are added.

Demonstrative reasoning has two essential features: it starts from necessarily true premises and derives conclusions by following principles of deductive logic. It is natural to think that non-demonstrative reasoning differs in both respects: it starts from contingent premises and derives conclusions in accordance with principles of inductive logic, principles of 'probabilification' rather than strict entailment. But although many philosophers have seen matters this way, doing so is by no means compulsory.

If a given body of evidence logically entails a particular conclusion, it is absolutely conclusive in that it excludes every possible 'defeater' for that conclusion: that is, every possible situation in which that conclusion would be false. However, what is normally called 'conclusive evidence' does not live up to this standard. Evidence is ordinarily regarded as conclusive, not when it eliminates every conceivable defeater, but when it eliminates all *relevant* defeaters: that is, every defeater deemed, for whatever reason, to be *worth* taking seriously.

Consider here the legal standard of proof beyond a *reasonable* doubt. Not all logically possible doubts are reasonable. It is logically possible that the murder was committed by space aliens, who have cleverly concealed their existence and conspired to frame the accused. However, no jury would be expected to take such a possibility seriously. Given our background know-ledge, such a possibility is too far-fetched to be worthy of consideration. Accordingly, the prosecution's evidence is not 'inconclusive' simply in virtue of failing to eliminate it. In a concrete context of inquiry, then, evidence may *deductively eliminate* all relevant defeaters to a given conclusion, even though, considered in isolation, it does not *deductively entail* that conclusion. There is no need to postulate a special 'inductive logic' to guide non-demonstrative reasoning.

Sometimes our evidence may not even deductively eliminate a relevant alternative. Rather, it might eliminate it by making it too improbable to take seriously. But again, no special inductive logic need be involved. Such infer-ence takes place against a background of reasonable presuppositions: for example, that a sample used to gauge the incidence of a particular trait is representative of the target population. Given this presupposition, we can use deductive reasoning to give the probability that a particular member of the target population displays the trait in question.

On this view, the nonmonotonicity of non-demonstrative inference is easy to understand. The background presuppositions—often unspoken and some-times even unrecognized—that guide non-demonstrative inference are, even when reasonably made, always defeasible (i.e. subject to correction), often highly so. The degrading of seemingly strong evidence is a result of the recon-textualization that takes place when we identify and revise some presupposi-tion, either because we have run into trouble with our conclusions or acquired direct reasons for thinking that the presupposition in question is false.

Sometimes we decide that evidence is inconclusive because we discover aspects of our situation that we haven't taken into account. An expansion of the range of relevant defeaters can be informationally triggered. But it can also be economically triggered: that is, induced by considerations connected with the costs of error (compared with those of further inquiry).

Consider: you ask me whether I know when the next train leaves for the city and I tell you 'Yes, two o'clock; I just looked it up'. But then you point out that I am using last year's timetable. Since departure times are often revised, my evidence suddenly looks less than conclusive. Here, further inquiry is infor-mationally triggered by your pointing out a fact that I had overlooked: my timetable was out of date.

Now imagine, instead, that I have derived my information from the latest timetable, so that it seems clear that I really do know. However, you explain that you have an appointment that you absolutely cannot miss. Moreover, it does happen occasionally that repairs to the track require temporary timetable changes. Have I looked into whether any such changes have been announced for today? No. So do I really know that the next train leaves at two? Suddenly, things seem less clear.

In the second case, we do not imagine that either of us has hard information about delays, in the way that, in the first case, we had hard information about the timetable. Rather, it seems that when the stakes are high enough, even very remote possibilities of error become worth taking seriously. If this is right, justification, hence knowledge, has an important pragmatic dimension. Whether I can properly issue or accept guarantees depends on how important it is to get things right. Knowledge can come and go, as our standards for attributing or claiming knowledge become more or less strict. Some philosophers think that this recognizing the pragmatic aspect of knowledge yields important insights into scepticism.[3]

That what count as 'all' defeaters vary in this way is not surprising. Lots of words show this kind of interest-sensitivity. When I move to a new town, I empty my house: I take everything out of it. But I do not rip the sink from the wall, still less do I empty it in the way that an experimenter tries to empty a vacuum chamber. Or again, a surface is flat if it has no significant bumps, so both roads and billiard tables can be flat. But this doesn't mean that we could play billiards on a road surface.

We should note that recognizing the contextual sensitivity of justification does not require us to think of relativization-to-context as part of the content of a knowledge-claim. Instead, we can see knowledge as subject to what David Lewis calls 'the *sotto voce* proviso': 'S knows that p iff [if and only if] S's evidence eliminates every possibility in which not p—psst, except for those possibilities that conflict with our proper presuppositions'.[4] I take it that the proviso is *sotto voce* because an explicit relativization to context is not (intuitively) part of what is asserted in an everyday knowledge-claim, though such a claim is always entered against a background of reasonable presuppositions.

There is a lot more to be said about what makes presuppositions reasonable, and we shall be returning to this issue throughout this book.

Notes

1. *Posterior Analytics*, Book 1, 1–4, in Barnes (1984).
2. In standard philosophical terminology, to judge an argument logically or deductively valid is not to claim that the premises *are* true but only that *if* they are all true, the conclusion *must* be true also. If a valid argument also has true premises, it is said to be 'sound'.
3. See Cohen (1988), Dretske (1981), Unger (1971).
4. 'Elusive Knowledge', in Lewis (1999).

4

Unstable Knowledge

Indefeasible justification

Gettier's problem is new, much newer than the standard analysis. Our discussion in the previous chapter explains why. On the demonstrative model, justification (at least the sort of justification relevant to knowledge) depends on deductive (truth-preserving) reasoning from self-evidently true premises. This precludes the crucial presupposition of Gettier's argument: that a belief can be justified but false. It is a fairly recent innovation to extend 'knowledge' to beliefs that are well supported but not strictly entailed by the evidence we have for them. Within the abstract framework of the standard analysis, a conceptual revolution has taken place. This revolution is presupposed by Gettier's problem, which can emerge only after the classical conception of knowledge has been abandoned.

Focusing on the idea that a belief can be justified but false leads to a simple proposal, implicit in Gettier's original discussion. This is that justification will not yield knowledge if it depends on reasoning that essentially involves a false intermediate step (or 'lemma'). On this view, falsity in one's (relevant) beliefs does not necessarily destroy their justificatory power, but it does negate their capacity to yield knowledge. Smith's justified true belief that the man who will get the job has ten coins in his pocket fails to amount to knowledge because he reaches it via the false lemma that Jones is that man.

This proposal makes Gettier cases depend on a defect in someone's reasoning. However, consider the following: the sight of a candle, apparently right in front of you, leads you to believe that there is a candle in front of you; what you see is actually the reflection in a mirror of a candle standing off to one side; but you have no reason to suspect that there is anything unusual about the situation. In this case, your belief is justified and, since there is a candle in front of you (albeit behind the mirror), true. But no one would say that your belief counts as knowledge. We have a Gettier case in which no reasoning—hence no false lemma—seems to be involved.

We might respond that perception involves *unconscious* inference. You reach the belief that there is a candle in front of you by way of (unconsciously) reasoning that it looks to you as though there is a candle in front of you because there really is one. Since this is not why things appear as they do, we have our false lemma. However, it is hard to see how reflection on Gettier cases could justify positing psychologically real inferential processes.

A better idea is that the relevant reasoning is not so much unconscious as *implicit*. A certain piece of reasoning may be implicit in a claim to knowledge in the sense that, in making that claim, we commit ourselves to that reasoning's correctness. We do not have to go through it, even unconsciously. Such a commitment would be manifested by a willingness to withdraw a claim to knowledge if one's (excusable) errors were pointed out. Thus, if Smith were informed that he, not Jones, was going to get the job, he would no longer draw the same conclusion.

There is an intuitively powerful idea here: that knowledge-yielding justifications should not be undermined by improvements in one's informational state. Our new suggestion, then, is that no one counts as knowing something if there exists a true body of evidence such that, if he were aware of it, his original justification would be undermined or 'defeated'. According to this 'indefeasibility' approach, knowledge requires justification that is indefeasible, proof against undermining by the acquisition of further true beliefs.

The indefeasibility approach offers a new slant on the idea that knowledge should be infallible, offering something intermediate between the merely factive character of knowledge and the Platonic demand for absolute infallibility. Beliefs concerning contingent facts, supported by non-demonstrative reasons, amount to knowledge when those reasons are not *in fact* going to be undermined by the acquisition of further true beliefs.

Misleading evidence

Although the idea that knowledge-yielding justifications should be indefeasible is initially attractive, it is very difficult to make precise. Moreover, the difficulty is not just one of detail. Reflecting on it should make us wonder whether the thought that drives indefeasibility analyses of knowledge is really that compelling. Consideration of the indefeasibility account of knowledge provides an object-lesson in the danger of naive reliance on linguistic intuitions.

The nub of the difficulty is the fact that a person can obtain information that is correct but misleading. Such information defeats a person's justification, but would not do so if he had more information still. The classic example, introduced by Lehrer and Paxson, goes like this:

S sees a man named Tom Grabit steal a book from a library. We may suppose that S has whatever justification we like for believing that Grabit stole the book. However, we suppose that, entirely unknown to S, Tom Grabit's mother has said that Tom was not in the library, but that Tom's twin brother Tim was in the library. Let q be the statement that Tom Grabit's mother has said these things. This statement is such that if S came to have it as additional evidence, then S's justification would be lost.[1]

So far so good. There is evidence out there that undermines S's justification, which S is in no position to take into account. So although S has a justified true belief, his justification is not indefeasible and he fails to have knowledge. But now for the problem:

But suppose that Tom Grabit's mother is demented, that Tom has no twin brother, and that the mother's remarks are thus completely wrong, all of which is completely known to S.

In the situation described, the evidence that undermines S's justification is itself undermined, so that the force of S's justification is restored. Most philosophers who advance indefeasibility theories want to say that S's knowledge remains unaffected all along.

If we share this reaction, we must formulate a more qualified statement of the indefeasibility condition. Unfortunately, this challenge is remarkably difficult to meet. Complicating the intuitively appealing idea of indefeasibility only invites ever-more ingenious counter-examples, which provoke even more complicated definitions of indefeasible justification, which are met with even more elaborate Gettier stories. After a while, the consensus on how to respond to the examples breaks down and the debate stalls.

Not that this should surprise us. Concepts—epistemological concepts included—evolve to deal with a certain range of conditions. How they should be applied in any imaginable situation, no matter how bizarre, is not fixed in advance. After a point, we are legislating rather than exploring a pre-existent meaning.

Does this matter? Not obviously. The analytic problem is not interesting for its own sake. The question of how to understand the concept of knowledge is important because of the way it interacts with other epistemological concerns, methodological and demarcational. When accounts of the concept of knowledge become overly elaborate, we start to lose our sense of why we should be interested in having knowledge in the first place. Faced with some arcane situation involving multiple undermining, and with no clear interests to guide our thinking, our intuitions about what to call a case of knowledge can be expected to let us down. Accordingly, there is no reason to expect that Gettier's problem can be solved in a way that is evidently proof against all possible puzzle cases, no matter how elaborate or ingenious.

The Gettier illusion?

Most philosophers intrigued by Gettier's problem take Gettier-style counter-examples to the standard analysis to be genuine. But perhaps they have been too hasty. This is Robert Fogelin's view.[2]

To see how there might be something misleading about Gettier examples, let us begin by reminding ourselves that Gettier's problem presupposes that knowledge can be supported by non-demonstrative reasons. As we saw in the previous chapter, non-demonstrative inferences are nonmonotonic: their strength can go up and down as new information comes in. This feature of 'inductive' inference plays an important role in Gettier's problem. But it does so 'trans-personally'. We imagine *ourselves* having access to extra information that undermines the (otherwise strong) reasoning of the person whose claim to knowledge we are assessing.

The second step towards seeing how Gettier examples may not be what they seem to be is to return to the distinction between epistemic responsibility and adequacy of grounds. As we saw, the distinction is not one that we can (at the present moment) apply to ourselves. We cannot take ourselves to be epistemically responsible while recognizing that we hold a particular belief for hopelessly inadequate reasons. The distinction comes into its own from a third-person point of view. In virtue of things that only we know, we may judge that a person's grounds for a particular belief are defective, even though he is in no position to spot their deficiencies and is therefore not to be judged epistemically irresponsible.

According to Fogelin, this is the key to Gettier's problem. We have access to information that Smith lacks. Because of this 'informational mismatch', we can see that Smith is personally but not evidentially justified in his belief that the man who will get the job has ten coins in his pocket. This explains why Gettier's case *seems* to be an example of justified true belief without knowledge. In one way (epistemic responsibility), Smith's belief *is* justified. But in another (adequacy of grounds), it is not. Smith's grounds are strong only relative to his restricted informational state. Given our extra information, they are not strong at all, which is why we are reluctant to count his belief as an instance of knowledge. Combining these two reactions produces the illusion of a case of justified true belief without knowledge.

Fogelin makes his diagnosis the basis of an explicit analysis. For S to know that p, the following conditions must hold:

1.   S believes that p,
2.   p is true,
3(p).   S justifiably came to believe that p, and
3(g).   S's grounds establish the truth of p.

This list of conditions further refines the extended form of the standard analysis. The differences are that Fogelin's 3(p) contains a reference to S's 'coming to believe' that p and—the important development—that his 3(g) puts a very strong constraint on the sort of evidential justification required for knowledge. When knowledge that p is in question, grounds are inadequate if they fail to 'establish the truth' of p. Given these modifications, clauses 1 and 2 become redundant, since 1 is implied by 3(p) and 2 by 3(g). Simplifying, S knows that p if and only if S justifiably came to believe that p on grounds that establish the truth of p.

Although Fogelin offers an elegant dissolution of Gettier's problem, there is a real question as to whether his approach is fundamentally different from that of indefeasibility theorists. Fogelin's 3(g) clause demands that S's evidence 'establish the truth' of p, but what does 'establish the truth' mean here? Not that S's evidence must deductively entail that p. As Gettier himself would readily admit, this would dispose of the problem, which assumes from the outset that justificatory reasoning may be inductive. As we saw in the previous chapter, with 'inductive' evidence, no matter how strong, it is always logically possible that one's conclusion should turn out to be false. Inductive evidence 'establishes the truth' of a conclusion only subject to the presupposition of there being no further evidence which, if known, would invalidate it. This is indefeasibility all over again.

Must knowledge be stable?

Fogelin sees his analysis as very different from any indefeasibility account. In his eyes, the trouble for indefeasibility accounts of knowledge begins with the intuition that S knows that Grabit stole the book, even though there is undermining evidence in play. It is not obvious that this reaction is correct. As Fogelin points out, one's intuitive reactions to the Grabit case tend to oscillate, depending on how it is presented. If we imagine the extra information emerging piecemeal, we will see that our judgement as to whether S knows that Grabit stole the book would change over time; whereas if we imagine ourselves taking a God's-eye view, then *perhaps* we will be inclined to say that S knows who stole the book all along. There may be no stable intuitive reaction to the case as initially (under-)described.

Indefeasibility analyses of knowledge, Fogelin suggests, make a mistake akin to the 'naturalistic fallacy'. The naturalistic fallacy (for those philosophers who agree that it is a fallacy) is committed by anyone who attempts to define an ethical or evaluative term like 'good' in wholly non-evaluative terms.[3] In attributing knowledge, we positively evaluate, thus endorse, both what someone believes and his entitlement to believe it. However, instead of making explicit the endorsing component in knowledge-attributions, along the line of 3(g), indefeasibility theorists try to idealize the setting in which S forms his belief, so that his reasoning will win our endorsement. By stipulating that, when S has knowledge, he forms his belief in a setting where there is no undermining evidence, they attempt to place S in a 'Gettier-free zone': that is, in a situation where no informational mismatch of the sort that drives Gettier examples can arise. Indefeasibility theories try to describe an impossibly idealized justificatory setting, when they could have achieved the same effect more economically by explicating knowledge in terms of a straightforward endorsing clause.[4]

This criticism seems misplaced. 'Indefeasibility' and 'endorsement' analyses are not competitors. The point of analyses like those attempted by indefeasibility theorists is precisely to say something about the sorts of reasoning that will win our endorsement. Accordingly, a simple endorsing clause is no substitute for a more detailed analysis.

Comparably wavering intuitions bedevil Fogelin's own idea of 'establishing the truth'. Does evidence that 'establishes the truth' of an inductive conclusion continue to do so in the face of undermining evidence that is itself subject to undermining? Our reaction seems to depend on how we imagine this further evidence being presented. If we think of it as emerging *seriatim*, we will be inclined to say that our original evidence loses its truth-establishing power in the context of the undermining evidence, but regains it after that evidence has itself been undermined. But if we take a God's-eye view, we may be tempted to think that our original evidence was always truth-establishing, though we were not always in a position to appreciate this.

Given that our wavering intuitions establish no distinction between Fogelin's approach and the indefeasibility account, what would? The answer is: a certain way of interpreting the wavering intuitions that Fogelin describes.

We noticed early on that Plato, speaking through Socrates, demands that knowledge be stable. Indefeasibility theorists respect this requirement: they are committed to the stability of knowledge. There is a permanent fact of the matter as to whether Tom *actually knows* that Grabit stole the book. Of course, our willingness to *attribute* knowledge wavers with our information about Tom's situation. But if we deny Tom knowledge on the basis of information that is incomplete or otherwise misleading, our reaction, though justified in the circumstances, will be incorrect.

Fogelin's point about our wavering intuitions suggests another way of looking at things: that our intuitions about whether to attribute knowledge waver because knowledge itself is less than fully stable, being apt to come and go with changes in the informational environment. This thought is not evidently absurd. Information that 'establishes the truth' of S's conclusion in one context may be seriously undermined by new evidence, even though that evidence may itself be undermined in its turn. Or, even if we think that, when S's new information is misleading, his original evidence continues to establish the truth of his belief, his taking it to do so would be epistemically irresponsible, so he would fail to know for that reason. To be sure, indefeasibility theorists want to say that S knew all along, not that his belief originally amounted to knowledge, temporarily lost that status, and then regained it. And they have tradition on their side. Fogelin himself is equivocal: he refers to the 'fragility' of knowledge; but he also repudiates the idea that either knowledge or justification is context-relative. But who is right? Is knowledge unstable or isn't it? Is there even a fact of the matter?

Against infallibilism

Indefeasibility theorists are right about one thing: we do have what appear to be strong 'infallibilist' intuitions about knowledge. As more than one philosopher has pointed out, to say 'I know, though I might be wrong' sounds off-key. On the other hand, the existence of such intuitions is not conclusive. Although there is something odd about saying 'I know, though I might be wrong', it is not obvious that the oddity is a matter of self-contradiction.

Consider another oddity, first noticed by G. E. Moore: 'It is raining, but I don't believe that it is'. It could certainly be true that it is raining and that I don't believe that it is—perhaps I am engrossed in a book and am oblivious of the weather outside—so there is no logical inconsistency here. The oddity of such a 'Moore-paradoxical' sentence does not consist in what is *said* but in the *saying* of it. Saying 'It is raining' is normally a way of *expressing* one's belief. Accordingly, to go on to say 'but I don't believe it' is to take back the commitment implied by one's having uttered something, even if the qualification is not inconsistent with the content of the sentence uttered.

How about knowledge? Fogelin's remarks about the naturalistic fallacy are relevant here. As we have seen, in laying claim to knowledge, I do more than express a *personal* commitment. When I put forward a proposition as something that I know, I vouch for its correctness, thus inviting my interlocutors to rely on it as well. As Ayer says, I 'claim the right to be sure'. But this means that 'infallibilist' intuitions need to be treated with caution. To say 'I know, but I might be wrong', is to both claim and disclaim the right to be sure, as to say 'It is raining, but I don't believe that it is' is to express and disclaim belief. But in neither case is there a strict contradiction. Knowledge could be fallible; and if it could be fallible, it could be unstable. We saw in the previous chapter that standards for claiming knowledge are subject to pragmatic variation, so that knowledge might come and go. Why can't it also come and go with changes in our informational state, even when that state involves information that turns out to be misleading?

We might try to turn the performative aspect of knowledge-claims and attributions to the infallibilist's advantage. In claiming knowledge, we might say, we are not supposing ourselves to have access to an impossible God's-eye view. Rather, we are issuing a particularly strong and open-ended guarantee of the correctness of what we believe. We are betting that there is no non-misleading counter-evidence to our belief. This is true, but does not settle the issue. What are we to say of our epistemic state when we have access to misleading counter-evidence that we do not recognize as misleading? In such a situation, we would certainly be required to withdraw our knowledge-claim.

So why isn't it true to say that, so long as the situation persists, we are deprived of knowledge, which we regain when the situation is remedied?

A second point is that, even if we do have infallibilist intuitions, not all of our intuitions point this way. Fogelin's idea of looking two ways at undermining information that is itself undermined—*seriatim* and all at once—is deeply insightful. It brings out something that is often overlooked: that we also have fallibilist intuitions about knowledge. Moreover, Fogelin's own account of knowledge suggests why this is so.

On Fogelin's view, which I take to be correct, knowledge requires both epistemic responsibility and adequate grounding. Looking at the way evidence emerges *seriatim* focuses our attention on epistemic responsibility. We see that access to misleading information, which is not easily recognized as such, would make it epistemically irresponsible to hold on to our prior belief. Accordingly, if we did retain conviction, our belief would no longer amount to knowledge. However, once we come to appreciate that our extra information was misleading, we see that our grounds were adequate after all and we regain the knowledge we temporarily lost. Focusing on the epistemic responsibility aspect of justification inclines us to fallibilism about knowledge.

Focusing on the *de facto* adequacy of our grounds can push us in the other direction. Suppose that we have obtained a particular belief by way of some epistemic procedure that is in fact completely reliable. The existence of misleading evidence in no way compromises this *de facto* reliability. Accordingly, if we look at someone's belief from this external standpoint, we may be inclined to think that his belief retains its positive epistemic status, even in the presence of misleading information. However, if we keep firmly in mind the point that knowledge requires both epistemic responsibility and adequate grounding, this understanding of the sources of our conflicting intuitions clearly favours epistemic fallibilism.

What, after all, is the point of demanding indefeasibility? I agree that, with respect to beliefs that have some general or lasting significance, some measure of stability is desirable. I agree, too, that the need for stability gives us additional reasons for holding that knowledge is more than true belief. But this does not show that absolute stability is desirable.

We can reinforce this conclusion by asking whether we could ever be in a position to know that we are in possession of such a justification. Isn't Fogelin right to link the ideal of indefeasible justification with an impossible God's-eye view of our epistemic situation? Advocates of indefeasibility analyses will respond that we should not confuse the question of whether we know with whether we know that we know. Fair enough. But what this reply fails to make clear is why we take knowledge so seriously, if we are never, or almost never, in a position to know that we have it. The problem of the value of knowledge returns in full force.

The infallibilist temptation

'Ordinary language' arguments for infallibilism are inconclusive. We need to look elsewhere for the deep sources of the 'infallibilist' conception of knowledge.

Let us recall the conceptual revolution that has taken place within the abstract framework of the standard analysis of knowledge: the replacement of the classical conception of knowledge by the fallibilist conception. 'Infallibilist' intuitions are driven by more than the oddity of claiming knowledge while admitting the possibility of error. They are holdovers, I suggest, from the classical conception of knowledge, which links knowledge with demonstrative certainty. Although few if any philosophers today are tempted by the Platonic understanding of infallibility, the idea persists that knowledge demands infallibility of *some* kind. This is what makes indefeasibility analyses of knowledge the most intuitively appealing approach to Gettier's problem. To be sure, we no longer think of knowledge as a kind of super-belief that, magically as it were, excludes the possibility of error. Nevertheless, we continue to be attracted to the idea that knowledge-yielding justification must be somehow immune to being undermined by positive changes in our overall epistemic state.

This is only a suggestion. I do not know how to prove that it is correct. But if it is, indefeasibility is a temporalized version of Platonic infallibility. I explained the demand for infallibility in terms of the wish to stabilize knowledge. Unlike the statues of Daedalus, knowledge ought to *stay put*. The demand for indefeasible justification reflects this long-standing aspiration. What is not so clear is that this ideal remains reasonable after the demise of the demonstrative conception of knowledge.

It seems to me that it doesn't, particularly once we explicitly distinguish the responsibility and evidential dimensions of justification. As I have insisted, what it is responsible to believe will inevitably vary with changes in our informational environment. The demonstrative ideal avoids this by tying knowledge to 'monotonic' justification, which is never degraded by increased information. But we have abandoned the demonstrative ideal, and for good reason.

I asked whether there is a fact of the matter as to whether we should understand knowledge in some 'infallibilist' way. I think that the answer is no. In the end, it is up to us to set the conditions for knowledge, bearing in mind the goals that incline us to make epistemological distinctions in the first place. So far as I can see, the roots of infallibilism lie in the Platonic-Aristotelian conception of knowledge. Plato's desire for absolute stability is not to be detached from his thought that the proper objects of knowledge are timeless truths. Because of their roots in this older tradition, infallibilist intuitions do not sit easily with the more modest epistemological aspirations that come with our having abandoned the demonstrative ideal. There is no need to accommodate such intuitions. We should change them.

Still, whatever our detailed views about the analytic problem, one point must not be forgotten. This is that we have found no reason to suppose that knowledge can be completely severed from justification. But can we understand how it is possible for our beliefs to be epistemically justified, in an objective way? Philosophical scepticism suggests we cannot. Our next task, therefore, is to explore the challenge of philosophical scepticism. Doing so will take us to the heart of the theory of knowledge.

Notes

1. Lehrer and Paxson (1969). Approaches to Gettier's problem are surveyed in Shope (1983).
2. Fogelin (1994), ch. 1.
3. Thus, for example, an exponent of utilitarianism in ethics might claim that 'good' just *means* 'tending to promote the greatest happiness of the greatest number'. The response to all such claims is the so-called 'Open Question Argument': that even if we agree that utilitarian aims are indeed good, we still find that it *makes sense* to ask 'Is it good to promote the greatest happiness of the greatest number', which would not be so if 'good' *meant* what the utilitarian says it means.
4. I think that the analogy with the naturalistic fallacy is a bit forced. After all, indefeasibility theories, even if they idealize the setting in which beliefs amounting to knowledge are formed, still define that setting in terms of evidence. Accordingly, they are not naturalistic in the way that theories discussed in the next chapter aspire to be.

5

Agrippa's Trilemma

Philosophical scepticism

Philosophical scepticism needs to be distinguished from other outlooks often thought of as 'sceptical'. The essential feature of philosophical scepticism is a *general view* about human knowledge: in the broadest terms, the view that knowledge is *impossible*. Let us call this view *theoretical scepticism*.

In ordinary parlance, scepticism is often associated with an attitude of incredulity. The sceptic is someone who practises suspension of judgement. If he is uncomfortable with this inability to make up his mind, he will suffer from doubt or uncertainty, often regarded as the sceptic's characteristic state of mind. People have also been called sceptics because they have been suspected of not just doubting but actually *denying* important truths: there have been times when the terms 'sceptic' and 'atheist' were more or less interchangeable. These various forms of incredulity are versions of *practical scepticism*.

Philosophical scepticism may involve an element of practical scepticism, but need not; and even when it does, the theoretical and practical components may not be coextensive. Indeed, one reason for being intrigued by philosophical scepticism is that, if the sceptic is right, our urge to believe far outstrips our capacity for knowledge.

Because it involves theoretical scepticism in an essential way, philosophical scepticism must be argumentatively based. Not that the mere existence of sceptical arguments amounts to a problem. One can argue—one way or another—for just about anything, but one's arguments might be unappealing. They might involve logical errors or depend on premises we see no reason to concede. However, the best sceptical arguments are not like that. Not only do they display no obvious logical flaws, they seem to involve only the simplest and most mundane considerations. They appear to be highly 'natural' or 'intuitive', to be arguments that almost any reflective person can understand and be moved by.

This apparent 'intuitiveness' is crucial to scepticism's being such an intractable problem. If sceptical arguments were obviously dependent on arcane theoretical ideas, there would be a quick way of dealing with them. We could take the fact that certain ideas lead to scepticism as itself a decisive criticism of those ideas. Maybe this is the right approach in the end. But if so, it will take some showing.

Of course, not even the existence of powerful and intuitive sceptical arguments would present us with a problem if we were inclined to welcome their conclusions. And there are forms of scepticism that a lot of us find congenial. Thus, according to one common definition, scepticism is the opposite of dogmatism. If dogmatists are equated with theorists of any stripe, an equation the ancient sceptics were inclined to make, this is perhaps not such a benign outlook. But if we understand 'dogmatism' in our current way, as indicating a blind adherence to a fixed set of beliefs, then some degree of scepticism is an essential component of any rational outlook.

Another form of scepticism, equally benign, is indicated by the contrast between scepticism and credulity. To be a sceptic, in this sense of 'sceptic', is to take a tough-minded attitude towards standards of evidence and, as a result, to find oneself dubious about various commonly accepted claims. So, for example, the sceptically minded person is unlikely to believe, on the basis of reports in the tabloid press, that hundreds of people are abducted every year by visitors from outer space. If this were all it meant to be 'sceptical', it would be a good thing if some people were more sceptical than they are. Scepticism as either open- or tough-mindedness might be problematic at certain times and places: in Europe in the Middle Ages, in what was until recently the Communist bloc, in parts of the Islamic world, or in fundamentalist colleges. But it will not seem threatening to most readers of this book.

Two features of philosophical scepticism make it very different from such everyday 'sceptical' outlooks.

The first is its unusually wide scope. Philosophical scepticism is highly general: the sceptic wonders whether we know anything whatsoever, or anything whatsoever in certain very broad domains. This is why philosophical scepticism is formulated in terms of the *possibility* of knowledge. The philosophical sceptic does not claim merely that we *in fact* know a good deal less than we like to think (which is probably true), but rather that aspiring to knowledge is somehow *inherently* problematic. It isn't just a question of paying closer attention or working longer hours.

The second feature is its strength or depth. The most interesting sceptical arguments imply *radical* scepticism, the thesis that we never have the slightest justification for believing one thing rather than another. The important point about radical scepticism is that it is formulated in terms of justification. Knowledge is impossible because we cannot even get to the point of having justified beliefs, never mind beliefs that are well-enough justified to count as knowledge strictly so-called.

Radical scepticism contrasts with 'high-standards' or 'knowledge-specific' forms of scepticism. Many philosophers have argued, plausibly, that knowledge demands more than just some degree of justification. Some have even argued that knowledge requires certainty, in some sense of 'certainty'. Accordingly, it is possible to hold that, while we may have justified true belief, our justification falls short of the demands of knowledge. Scepticism that concedes the possibility of justification, but denies the possibility of knowledge, is what I mean by scepticism that is knowledge-specific.

The distinction between radical and knowledge-specific scepticism becomes especially clear in the light of Gettier's problem. Suppose that in the light of this problem we decide that knowledge demands indefeasibly justified true belief. The sceptic's claim that knowledge is impossible could mean that no belief is ever *indefeasibly* justified. This would be to argue for a non-radical form of scepticism, since the possibility of justified belief would still be left open. Although scepticism of this type would not be wholly without interest, it would not be all that threatening, since many important epistemological distinctions would remain unscathed. (This is why defeasibility analyses of knowledge raise the question of the value of 'knowledge strictly so-called'.) However, the sceptic could be arguing that knowledge is impossible because nothing we believe is justified, even to the slightest extent. This is radical scepticism.

In my view, non-radical, knowledge-specific scepticism is a shallow form of scepticism that is not a serious challenge to everyday epistemic practices. The reason is that, even if we saw no way of turning it aside, we could always execute what Crispin Wright has termed 'a Russellian retreat', renouncing talk of knowledge (strictly understood) in favour of talk of justified belief. Or we could decide to use 'knowledge' in a more relaxed way. The burden would then be on the sceptic to show that such a retreat would entail significant loss. By contrast, precisely because it leaves no obviously acceptable line of retreat, radical scepticism poses a much more serious threat to our ordinary epistemological outlook. Radical scepticism threatens to wipe out all significant epistemological distinctions. This result would not be so easy to live with, if it is possible to live with it at all. Generalized radical scepticism implies that, rationally speaking, we can believe anything or nothing. Or as Bertrand Russell once put it, the man who believes he is a poached egg differs from the rest of us only by being in a minority.[1] It is not obvious that anyone could take this conclusion seriously in matters of practical concern.

This is all very different from ordinary (unphilosophical) scepticism. The everyday 'sceptical' view is that most people's epistemic standards are too low or too laxly applied, not that the very idea of justification is fatally flawed. Ordinary scepticism is *demanding* and *selective*. Philosophical scepticism, as radical and general, undermines the very epistemological distinctions on which everyday scepticism depends. It is not simply different from but *precludes* scepticism of the ordinary kind.

Philosophical scepticism's radical and general character harks back to the simplicity and intuitiveness of sceptical arguments. Such arguments point to radical and general conclusions precisely because they exploit only 'lowest common denominator' features of knowledge. But for the same reason, it is hard to say how or even whether they go astray. The result is that philosophical scepticism is hard to dismiss but impossible (sincerely) to accept. It produces a kind of intellectual split personality. And this is why it is a problem.

Sceptical strategies

There are two basic families of sceptical problems, 'Agrippan' and 'Cartesian', each rooted in a distinctive pattern of argument. Some philosophers will find this claim objectionable, since it seems to ignore a third family: variations on the argument from error.

Certainly, arguments for philosophical scepticism have often made great play with the fact (if it is fact) that, even in the best of circumstances, the possibility that we are in error can never be entirely excluded. Given a demonstrative conception of knowledge, this point is potentially very damaging. Since acknowledging the possibility of error seems incompatible with laying claim to absolute certainty, if knowledge demands such certainty, we are well on the way to concluding that knowledge is impossible. However, while this knowledge-specific form of scepticism provides a strong motive for adopting a more modest, fallibilist conception of knowledge, it implies no concession at all to the *radical* sceptic. To get to radical scepticism, we need to embed acknowledgments of fallibility in a richer argumentative context, which is where my two basic families come in.

I shall begin with the Agrippan argument, not simply on account of its antiquity, but because it embodies the simplest sceptical strategy and, I am inclined to think, the most profound.

Agrippa's trilemma

The ancient sceptics distinguish various 'modes' or 'tropes': argumentative strategies for inducing universal suspension of judgement. The Agrippan argument is found in the Five Modes of Agrippa (about whom nothing is known, except that he is credited with the Five Modes), though the Five Modes simply codify a pattern of argument that occurs widely in Sextus Empiricus' account of sceptical procedures. The Five Modes are Discrepancy, Relativity, Infinity, Assumption, and Circularity.[2]

The Mode of Discrepancy makes the point that people can disagree about virtually anything. That of Relativity suggests that any claim can, perhaps should, be qualified with the rider 'according to you' (you personally, your school of thought, your culture generally, perhaps even your species).

However, we are not yet in sight of scepticism, still less radical scepticism. Sure, people disagree, but some people's views are wrong and can be shown to be wrong. And even where conclusive proof or disproof is not to be expected, some views may be better supported than others.

This is what the sceptic wants us to say. The point of the first two modes is to get us to acknowledge that, if anyone puts forward a claim as more than a personal opinion or a report on how things seem to him, he can reasonably be asked to explain why. Once this apparently innocent acknowledgment has been extracted, the Agrippan argument shows its teeth.

Suppose, then, that I make a claim—any claim. You are entitled to ask me whether what I have said is something that I am just assuming to be true or whether I know it to the case. If I reply that it is something I know, you are further entitled to ask me *how* I know. In response, I will have to cite something in support of my claim: my evidence, my credentials, whatever. But now the question can be renewed: is what I cite in defence of my original claim something that I am just assuming or something that I know? If the former, it will not do the job required of it: you can't base knowledge on a mere assumption. But if the latter, it will in turn need to be backed up, and so on.

Of course, attempts to provide justification come to a halt. But how? The sceptic will say that we just run out of ideas: either we have nothing to say, or we find ourselves going back over old ground. As an implied claim to knowledge, then, every statement I make invites a new challenge; and in the face of these constantly renewed challenges, I can do only one of three things:

1. Keep trying to think of something new to say—i.e. embark on an infinite regress (Mode of Infinity).
2. At some point, refuse to answer—i.e. make a dogmatic assumption (Mode of Assumption).
3. At some point, repeat something I have already said—i.e. reason in a circle (Mode of Circularity).

None of these gives us what we want.

With options (2) and (3), the sceptic seems on strong ground. Surely, statements offered in justification of an initial claim must themselves be justified: you can't base justifications on mere assumptions. So (2) is a dead letter. Equally, reasoning in a circle is a paradigmatically poor sort of reasoning: how can a statement support *itself*? Supposing that it could embodies a kind of pragmatic inconsistency, treating the same statement as needing support (in its role as conclusion) and as already in order (in its role as premise). So (3) is a dead letter too.

We might wonder whether option (1) is so bad. To be sure, new claims can lead to new questions, but what is so terrible about that? This reply misses the sceptic's point, which is that the regress is *vicious*. The sceptic is not saying simply that justifications *can* always be questioned further, should we find reason to question them. His conclusion is rather that no claim is *ever* justified—to the slightest degree—unless, *per impossibile*, we first run through an infinite series of prior justifications. Option (1), then, fares no better than the others. The conclusion seems to be that justification is a complete illusion.

I call the apparently forced choice between assumption, circularity, and infinite regress 'Agrippa's trilemma'. The Agrippan argument is also often thought of as 'the regress problem'. I prefer talking of the trilemma because it reminds us that the problem is to escape the regress without getting impaled on either of the remaining horns.[3] This challenge is not easily met.

Agrippa's trilemma lies at the heart of the ancient 'problem of the criterion': that is, the problem of determining what should be the standard or method ('criterion') for distinguishing between genuine knowledge and mere opinion. The Aristotelian solution to this problem is that knowledge depends on self-evidence: anything we know must either itself be self-evident or deducible by self-evidently correct steps from self-evidently true premises. The sceptical counter-move is to inquire why something's striking us as self-evident should be a guarantee of its correctness? If we ignore this question, the sceptic will say, we are just making a dogmatic assumption. But if we try to find some further validation of intuitive self-evidence, we threaten to open up the regress all over again. Finally, if we say that it is self-evident that certain things are self-evidently correct, we will be arguing in a circle. Alternatively, we could note that the demonstrative conception of knowledge places enormous weight on Reason, understood as a faculty of logical insight. But why should Reason, as opposed to sense-experience, be the arbiter of knowledge? How are we to decide: by Reason, or by experience? Whatever we do, knowledge seems to elude us.

How serious?

I have argued that philosophical scepticism is problematic only if it is intuitive, highly general, and radical. Does Agrippan scepticism meet this standard?

On the question of its naturalness or intuitiveness, the Agrippan argument's chief presupposition—that knowing differs from merely assuming or surmising and that this difference has something to do with an ability to back up or justify whatever can properly be said to be known—seems to be one of those lowest common denominator ideas that just about everyone (except perhaps extreme externalists) is ready to concede. Beyond this, the argument does not appear to be committed to any particular view about what 'back up' or 'justification' consist in. It is not, therefore, in any obvious way theoretically loaded.

The question of the generality of Agrippan scepticism is more complicated. Everyone has experienced arguments that run into an Agrippan dead end. Disputes that engage deep political differences sometimes get into a rut, with the parties shouting at each other when not going round in circles. Or imagine a debate between a devout believer, who puts his faith in divine revelation, and someone with a thoroughgoing scientific outlook, who thinks that all hypotheses need to be verified (or falsified) by systematic research involving observation and experiment. Such opponents will disagree, not just over particular facts, but over how the facts are to be determined; and how is such a disagreement to be resolved? Perhaps each disputant will dig his heels in, that is, make a dogmatic assumption. Or perhaps the believer will say that God tells him to trust revelation, leading his opponent to accuse him of begging the question. But if the scientifically minded person says that we cannot rely on revelation, because there is no scientific evidence for the existence of God, the believer will return the compliment. Perhaps, then, they should look for some third way of adjudicating their epistemological differences. But what would that be, and what would give us the right to suppose that it was more to be trusted than the criteria already at issue?

While examples like this contribute to the argument's intuitive appeal, they may suggest that the sceptic sees his problem as restricted to admittedly controversial opinions. My having posed the Agrippan problem in terms of claims, challenges, and responses might itself encourage such a reading. This impression may be further reinforced by our recalling that two of the Five Modes—Discrepancy and Relativity—explicitly call attention to differences of opinion. So it is natural to conclude that the point of the trilemma is to show that such differences cannot be resolved. On this account, the Agrippan problem may be recurrent but far from completely general.

The problem is much more general than this. As the sceptic means his argument to be understood, nothing of importance turns on the existence of actual challenges or challengers. If, in a reflective moment, I take any belief I happen to hold and ask myself why I hold it, I am off and running. The problem, therefore, concerns justified belief in general, whether actually challenged or not. The Agrippan argument applies not just to things that anyone would agree are hard to know about but to anything whatsoever, no matter how obvious. Indeed, it is especially problematic in connection with things that are so obvious that we have no idea how to argue for them in a non-question-begging way. Agrippan scepticism is not just highly general: it is absolutely universal.

Does the Agrippan argument promote radical scepticism? Historically, the argument emerged when the Platonic-Aristotelian conception of knowledge was dominant, and its characteristic applications by the ancient sceptics—for example, in posing the problem of the criterion—often take that ideal for granted. However, we must not confuse applications of the Agrippan argument with the argument itself. Although the argument was originally formulated in the context of a demanding conception of knowledge, it is not tied to that conception. The argument has the capacity to promote radical scepticism, whether or not its inventors saw it in this light. Because of this, we cannot avoid the argument simply by abandoning the classical conception for a more relaxed, fallibilist ideal of knowledge. This distinguishes the Agrippan argument from the pure argument from error. Indeed, abandoning the classical conception of knowledge for more modest epistemological aspirations is precisely what brings the distinction between radical and non-radical forms of scepticism into sharp focus.

External constraint

Given that the Agrippan problem is supposed to extend beyond matters of actual dispute, a natural reaction is that there is something artificial about it. After all, although disputes sometimes bog down or peter out through exhaustion, they can also come to a satisfactory end. When they do, it will be because whoever is on the defensive is able to cite evidence that is acceptable and convincing to all parties to the discussion. The production of such evidence is what we ordinarily call 'justification'. Claims that everyone finds too obvious to be worth discussing are not ordinarily called 'assumptions'. So what is the problem?

While the Agrippan sceptic will not dispute what we may call the *phenomenology* of everyday justification, he will caution against reading too much into it. When we say that justification proceeds from 'acceptable' claims, we really mean claims that are in fact *accepted*. This 'acceptability', which is entirely psychological and person-relative, implies no special epistemological status. The same goes for terms like 'evident' or 'obvious'. So the 'common knowledge' that terminates everyday justificational procedures can be seen, on reflection, to be nothing more than a body of common assumptions (and maybe not so common, if we broaden our imagined audience).

We can put the point like this: the reply to the sceptic just envisaged represents ordinary justification as entirely *dialectical*. But we can all see on reflection that even our ordinary concepts of knowledge and justification demand more. We connect knowledge with justification because we want to distinguish knowledge from *accidentally* true belief. Justification is supposed to establish—or increase the likelihood—that a belief is true. Justification is supposed to be *truth-conducive*. Showing that a claim follows from convictions that some or even all of us happen to share, if those convictions themselves rest on nothing at all, does not meet this requirement.

Agrippa's trilemma calls attention to the need for beliefs that meet two conditions. First, they must be non-inferentially credible: justified without deriving their justification inferentially from further beliefs. Second, given that justification cannot be seen as a purely dialectical exercise, they must be credible in a way that reflects some kind of external constraint. Empirical knowledge cannot just be a matter of bandying words about: it must have something to do with the objective world.

The demand for external constraint is not a demand merely on knowledge or even justification, narrowly conceived. Rather, external constraint is a pre-condition for our beliefs having any genuine content or meaning, for our claimings and acceptings and inferrings being more than a game with mean-ingless counters.[4] If we cannot think of ourselves as justified, in a way that involves control of our beliefs by the world, we cannot even understand ourselves as thinkers.

If this is right, Agrippan scepticism is a very deep problem indeed.

Scepticism as paradox

Agrippan scepticism is absolutely universal. However, someone might suggest that this is its weakness, not its strength. The point of giving an argument is to justify one's conclusion: so isn't it obviously self-defeating to *argue* that nothing can ever be justified?

There are three points to make about this quick way with scepticism. The first is that inconsistency is readily avoided by a little care in the formulation of the sceptical position. The sceptic can claim that the one and only thing he knows is that he knows nothing else. This claim is entirely consistent. (Socrates said that believing it made him the wisest man in Athens.) True, this version of scepticism is not absolutely universal, but it is surely wide-ranging enough to pose a serious threat to our pre-theoretical epistemic attitudes.

There is something unsatisfactory about this response, for the suspicion is bound to remain that, if argument *can* sometimes be effective, why only here? This *caveat* leads to the second point, which is that it is not clear that sceptical arguments have to produce stable conclusions, in which case no restrictions on the scope of sceptical theses may be necessary. Sceptical argumentation does its work if it produces doubt, uncertainty, or suspension of judgement. Viewed from this angle, the situation looks like this: compelling arguments seem to establish that knowledge is impossible, and so incline me to claim to know that this is so. On reflection, I see that it would be inconsistent to claim to know that I am incapable of knowing anything, which in turn inclines me to withdraw the claim. But now, encouraged by the thought that knowledge must be possible after all, I can run through the argument again, once more reaching the conclusion that knowledge is *not* possible, whereupon I reflect that it would be inconsistent . . . and so on. Similar considerations apply to sceptical attacks on justification and to relativist attacks on objective truth. Sceptical arguments do not need to lead to stable—or even credible—conclusions in order to pose problems.[5]

Another way to put this point is to say that a form of scepticism that applies to itself may be not so much self-undermining as paradoxical. The reasoning that leads to the sceptical conclusion seems to be compelling and yet no stable or credible conclusion emerges from it. In fact, this is how the Pyrrhonists treated all sceptical arguments: as intended to induce suspension of judgement, not assent to a negative, epistemological conclusion. This was because they thought that assenting to anything—including scepticism itself—would be a form of dogmatism, hence not scepticism.

Finally, we should remind ourselves that there is nothing necessarily self-defeating about assuming something to be true for the sake of refuting it. This is just the technique of arguing by *reductio ad absurdum*. We concede something for the sake of argument and go on to show that what we have conceded cannot be so. Many sceptical arguments can be seen in this light.

There is, then, no substitute for a deeper diagnosis of sceptical arguments. But I think that this would be true even if the objection in question were well taken. The problem with the argument is that it is purely dialectical. If we find ourselves drawn to sceptical arguments, it is not enough to be shown that their conclusions are unacceptable. This is something we believed anyway. What we want to know is how they go wrong and why they are, nevertheless, so seductive. Only through such understanding can their spell be broken.

The space of theories

Supposing that we decide not to throw in the towel right away, what are our choices? Assuming that an infinite regress is intolerable, we seem to have two, each defining a fundamental type of epistemological theory. The fact that the Agrippan argument seems to define the space of theories is powerful evidence for the view that the problem of scepticism plays a central role in constituting epistemology as a distinctively philosophical subject.

Perhaps the most natural response to Agrippan scepticism is to identify beliefs that are justifiably held without requiring further back-up. Perhaps some beliefs concern self-evident truths, or are in some other way beyond rational questioning. If there are such beliefs, they will bring requests for justification to a halt without being mere assumptions. Call such beliefs 'basic beliefs'. The quest for them is characteristic of *foundational* theories of knowledge and justification.

Foundationalism is under a cloud these days. But if we abandon the quest for basic beliefs, the only remaining way of avoiding a sceptical conclusion seems to be to argue that circular reasoning isn't as bad as it looks. Philosophers who take this approach point out that we do not have just one or two beliefs, and that our beliefs are not just a grab-bag of unrelated opinions. Rather, our beliefs about the world constitute an extensive and complicated *system*. The thought is thus that the members of such a system can give each other *mutual* support. This is the fundamental idea behind *coherence* theories of knowledge and justification. From this standpoint, our beliefs are not justified because they rest on a foundation but because they are systematically interconnected. Systematic interconnection is not to be equated with simple circularity.

We shall examine the strengths and weaknesses of both strategies. But first we need to introduce our second family of sceptical problems.

Notes

1. Russell (1961), 646. Russell is discussing Hume's scepticism about induction. See Chapter 17, below.
2. Sextus Empiricus (1933). Clearly, the argument builds on considerations already explored by Aristotle. As we saw in Chapter 3, Aristotle defends a demonstrative conception of knowledge by arguing that, since knowledge requires proof, and since there cannot be an infinite process of prior justification, there must be ultimate premises that are simply self-evidently true. However, though Aristotle brings in regress considerations, it is far from clear that he appreciates the sceptical problem lurking in this argument, or even that he saw himself as raising and responding to sceptical issues at all. The precise function of the Modes in ancient 'Pyrrhonian' scepticism is controversial. See Williams (1988).
3. This point is stressed by Fogelin (1994), ch. 6.
4. McDowell (1994), ch. 1.
5. This point is clearly recognized by Hume. See Hume (1976), 1. 4. 1.

6

Experience and Reality

The external world

Whereas the Agrippan argument goes back to the classical Greek sceptics, our next problem, scepticism about knowledge of the external world, is comparatively new. It receives its first clear formulation in the writings of Descartes, around 350 years ago. Despite the enormous quantity of ink spilled over it, there is still no agreed solution.[1]

It seems undeniable that we discover what is going on in our surroundings by way of our senses. We are all the subjects of a constantly changing stream of sensory experience—visual, auditory, tactile, olfactory—that puts us in touch with objects and events in our environment. However, reflection on this seemingly obvious fact leads to strange conclusions.

Our experience of the world is the end-product of a complex chain of events. Take the case of visual experience: light of various wavelengths is reflected off the surface of an object; it is focused on my retinae, inducing a certain pattern of neural excitation; impulses from the retinal neurons combine to produce a further pattern of firing in my optic nerve and eventually in the occipital region of my cerebral cortex. As a result, I am aware of a red object, say an apple, a few feet in front of me.

It seems to be a consequence of this picture that the same experiential outcome could be produced by intervention at several points in the chain. And there do seem to be odd examples of illusions produced in just this way. In 'phantom limb' cases, amputees feel pain where a limb used to be. Presumably, the nerve impulses reaching the brain are the same as they would have been if they had originated in a more normal way, so it feels just as though the amputated limb were still there. But if our awareness of the world could be produced in several different ways, why are we so sure that it is produced one way rather than another? Descartes presses this question by way of two vivid examples.

The first appeals to the fact that we have dreams. Dreams are conscious experiences that we have while we are asleep. They do not correspond in any reliable way to ongoing events in our surroundings and so do not yield knowledge of them. But there is no waking experience that could not, in principle, be faithfully mimicked by a suitably vivid dream. So how do I know that I am not dreaming right now? How do I know that I am not dreaming all the time? I can pinch myself, but maybe that is just part of the dream. In fact, it seems that any test I could propose might just be part of the dream.

Descartes does not think that the dreaming argument pushes scepticism to the limit. He thinks that the argument raises a problem about how I know particular facts about my immediate surroundings but leaves my general conception of the world largely untouched. Even in our wildest dreams, the imagination only produces unfamiliar combinations of familiar things. Descartes therefore introduces his famous thought experiment of the Evil Deceiver. Imagine an all-powerful Being bent on deceiving me, who artificially induces in me all my experiences of the world. These experiences bear no relation to reality. Not merely is the world nothing like the way I experience it to be, perhaps there is no 'external world' at all, or at least no world of physical objects.

A popular contemporary variation on Descartes's fantasy is the 'brain-in-a-vat' problem. Suppose that aliens, whose technological capabilities are far in advance of our own, capture me while I am asleep, drug me, and remove my brain, which they keep alive in a vat of nutrients. They then implant micro-electrodes in all the afferent nerve pathways to my brain. These electrodes are controlled by a supercomputer so as to exactly mimic the pattern of nerve-firing that would be produced if I were sitting at a desk, looking at a computer screen, and amusing myself with the thought of being abducted by aliens and made into a brain in a vat.

This story, though far fetched, seems perfectly intelligible. Readers may recall an episode of the television series *Star Trek*, in which the original commander of the starship *Enterprise*, who has been horribly injured, emigrates to a planet whose inhabitants have mastered this technology of 'virtual reality', so that he can live the 'life' that circumstances have taken from him. There are also films on this theme. In one, a company offers customers virtual reality holidays in the imaginary environment of their choice, and the hero ends up wondering when he is experiencing genuine, non-virtual reality and when he isn't. In the most recent, machines are keeping almost the whole human race imprisoned in vats-plus-virtual-reality, so as to make use of the electro-chemical energy humans generate (presumably more than is needed to produce and maintain them). So the question is: how do I know that I am not a brain in a vat right now? We might even say that I *am* a brain in a vat, for what after all is my skull? Perhaps the question should be: how do I know what kind of vat I am in? It is not easy to say, since anything that I experience could be part of the illusion.

Let us call these odd stories 'sceptical hypotheses'. On first encounter, they *seem* perfectly intelligible. Many philosophers would be less guarded, taking their intelligibility to be obvious. However, the question of the intelligibility of sceptical hypotheses is difficult and subtle. Perhaps we suffer from a kind of illusion of meaningfulness, so that we think we understand them better than we really do. This is an issue we will discuss later on. For now, I agree that on first hearing they seem to make perfect sense. If they don't, this will take some showing.

Even if sceptical hypotheses make sense, however, no one actually believes them, and there is no reason why anyone should. So why call them 'sceptical'? Because they are 'defeaters' of virtually all ordinary knowledge claims. They are possibilities that, if realized, make most or all of what we think we know about the world either false or unjustified.

The existence of such defeaters would not be a problem if they could easily be ruled out. But how are we to do this? Sceptical hypotheses seem to show that there are endlessly many ways that the world might be, even though my experience of it remains unchanged. Accordingly, my experience fails to provide an adequate basis for favouring my actual system of beliefs over alternatives that seem logically just as coherent. But when it comes to knowing about the world, my experience is all that I will ever have to go on. I have no magical faculty for intuiting how things are in my surroundings. My only basis for my beliefs about the world is how the world presents itself to me in experience. It looks as though my beliefs about the world, however unshakeable, are oddly groundless: *mere* beliefs rather than genuine *knowledge*.

Someone might reply that, even if sceptical hypotheses cannot be conclusively ruled out, they are still are too far-fetched to be worth taking seriously. But what does 'far-fetched' mean here, other than 'different from what I ordinarily believe'? Certainly, sceptical hypotheses are far-fetched relative to our ordinary views about the world and our place in it. But our entitlement to those views is precisely what the sceptic means to call into question.

Further problems

The problem of our knowledge of the external world is the prototype for a whole family of sceptical problems. All members of the family exhibit a common argumentative strategy. This is why I call them all 'Cartesian', even though only the problem of the external world was recognized by Descartes himself.

In the first place, take our supposed knowledge of 'other minds', the thoughts and experiences of people other than ourselves. No one will deny that our knowledge of such matters is often very imperfect. But the sceptic is suggesting something more radical: that we have no reason to think that anything we believe about such things—even that other people *have* conscious experiences—has a shred of justification. The problem here is the essential *privacy* of experience. The only thoughts and experiences we can literally *have* are our own. A politician may say 'I feel your pain'. But he doesn't literally feel *your* pain, even if he is speaking truthfully. What he really means is that it pains him to see that you are in pain. So what do we have to go on when we form beliefs about what other people think or feel? Only their outward behaviour, including of course their speech. I see you wince or grimace; I hear you groan; I conclude that you are hurting.

The inference is automatic, but does it have any rational basis? It seems not. A claim about your experiences is not logically implied by any claim about your outward behaviour. It is a logical possibility, however remote, that your inner experiences are utterly different from mine, or that you have no such experiences at all. At best, your outward behaviour is a reliable symptom of your inner states. But how could I establish this symptom's reliability? I cannot correlate your experiences with your behaviour, because your behaviour is my only clue to your experiences. For all I know, *solipsism*—the thought that I am the only person with a conscious inner life, thus the only real *person* at all—may be true.

A similar argument can be constructed with respect to beliefs about the past. Just as our only clues to another person's thoughts and feelings comes from his or her outward behaviour, our only access to the past is by way of whatever records, artefacts, and so on have survived into the present. But what makes such things indicators of how things were in the past? Someone once tried to resolve the tension between geology and Genesis by suggesting that God created the world in 4004 BC, complete with the fossil record. However, why go back that far? How do we exclude the possibility that the world sprang into existence five minutes ago, complete with delusive 'memories' implanted in the brains of its inhabitants?

What goes for the past goes for the future, or indeed for beliefs regarding any fact that goes beyond what we know on the basis of perception or memory. Although our lives depend on complex expectations about how the world generally works, the basis of these expectations is our experience of how it has worked up to now in the rather confined regions we have been able to explore. But as Hume observed, the fact that things have happened a certain way up to now is no logical guarantee that they will continue to do so. In projecting our limited experience on to new cases, we seem to take for granted some kind of 'Uniformity of Nature' principle. Unfortunately, all we know is that Nature has operated uniformly up to now. We want to infer—presumably inductively—that Nature operates uniformly, period. But if all inductive inferences presuppose the Uniformity Principle, attempts to defend the Principle itself will be circular.

In bringing up such bizarre possibilities—I am the only conscious being, the world sprang into existence five minutes ago, the laws of physics are about to undergo abrupt change—I am not suggesting that anyone does or should accept them. The question is whether there is any *reason* to ignore them? Or is it just—as Hume suggested—that sceptical worries are simply ignored, without reason? And if this is all we can say, aren't we admitting that scepticism is at least theoretically correct, hence that what we like to think of as knowledge is really assumption, however psychologically 'natural'?

Scepticism and 'pure inquiry'

Philosophical scepticism, in its most interesting form, is general, radical, and apparently intuitive. How does Cartesian scepticism measure up to these demands?

Clearly, the problem of the external world is highly general. Of course, we all agree that we are vastly ignorant about the world we live in. However, the sceptic wants to be told why *anything whatsoever* we happen to believe about the world, no matter how mundane and obvious, counts as knowledge. The same goes for the problems of other minds, the past, and induction.[2]

Note that Cartesian scepticism is additive. Putting our problems together, we reach the conclusion that we know nothing about other people, not even that there are any; nothing about the external world, not even that there is one; nothing about the future and nothing about the past. We are reduced to 'solipsism of the present moment', confined to knowledge of the contents of our own momentary mental states. This is close enough to universal scepticism.

The question of whether Cartesian scepticism is radical is subtler. To answer it, we need to expose more of the inner structure of Cartesian arguments, paying special attention to the role played by sceptical hypotheses.

Some philosophers think that Cartesian arguments exemplify an 'Argument from Ignorance'.[3] For example:

1. I don't know that I am not a brain in a vat.
2. If I don't know that I am not a brain in a vat, then I don't know that I have two hands.

So 3. I don't know that I have two hands.

This is a form of one of the oldest sceptical tropes: the argument from error. On this way of understanding Cartesian scepticism, sceptical hypotheses play the role of overlooked error-possibilities which, though far-fetched, cannot be ruled out.

Now, in everyday life, claims to knowledge are rarely, if ever, advanced on the basis of justifications that are logically impregnable. There are all kinds of ways in which our beliefs might be false, or less than conclusively justified, that we do not bother to investigate. To borrow an example from Fred Dretske, if I go to the zoo and see some black-and-white striped equines in an enclosure prominently labelled 'Zebras', I am justified in believing that I have seen the zoo's zebras. However, there are all sorts of possibilities that my evidence—adequate by everyday standards—does not rule out: for example, that the zoo's zebras have all died and been replaced with cleverly disguised mules. But as we are imagining the situation, I have no reason to suspect any monkey (or zebra) business.[4]

Extending the example, suppose that I have been made aware that zoos sometimes go in for deception of this kind. Now it is not so clear that my evidence is so compelling. Accordingly, even if the animals in the enclosure are in fact zebras, my evidence may not be sufficient for me to know this. As Robert Fogelin puts it, awareness of new error possibilities raises the 'level of scrutiny' to which a given belief or claim is subject, with the result that evidence that looked sufficient for knowledge can suddenly seem less than adequate.[5] In a court of law, a common strategy for the defence is to think up alternative scenarios, thus subjecting the prosecution's evidence to a heightened level of scrutiny.

Why is it that we do not normally expect anyone to have ruled out every possible way of going wrong before granting him knowledge? An obvious answer is that life is short. Investigation is a costly activity in terms of time, money, and opportunities forgone. Of course, when the costs of error are enormous—when checking the safety-level of a nuclear power plant or putting someone on trial for his life—we are (or ought to be) willing to invest extra resources. But in most everyday situations it would be irrational to proceed so carefully. This is the pragmatic dimension of knowledge that we discussed in Chapter 4.

Now Descartes introduces the problem of the external world in his *Meditations on First Philosophy*. The title is significant. As Descartes makes clear, 'meditation' is a form of *purely theoretical inquiry*. All pragmatic or practical considerations have been set aside: the only question at issue is whether his beliefs about the world are true. This bracketing of practical constraints raises to the maximum the standards of certainty to which his beliefs may rationally be subjected. To determine whether they really deserve to be thought of as knowledge, the 'pure inquirer' must try to eliminate every logically coherent error-possibility, no matter how outré by everyday standards. Enter Evil Deceivers and brains in vats. It begins to look as though everyday 'knowledge' is not knowledge *simpliciter* but something less exalted: knowledge-for-all-practical-purposes, say.[6]

This is an attractive account of Cartesian scepticism. It builds on something we have already acknowledged—the pragmatic dimension of everyday knowledge-attributions—and it may well answer to an important strain in Descartes's own thinking. But does it really give us a reason for taking scepticism seriously?

Pragmatists may say that it does the opposite, showing why scepticism can safely be ignored. The only knowledge worth having, they will argue, is knowledge for some practical purpose or other. In so far as we hanker after something more, this is not a problem to be solved but a neurosis to be overcome,

the historical residue of the slave-owning and aristocratic Greeks' identification of knowledge with contemplation, an identification we ought to put
behind us.[7]

I have a different objection, which is that the sceptical procedure just
sketched does not generate radical scepticism. This account of Cartesian scepticism ties the sceptic's assessment of our knowledge far too closely to a quest
for absolute certainty. Thus, even if successful, the sceptical argument shows
at most that our beliefs about the world are less than absolutely certain
and thus, to the extent that knowledge requires certainty, not knowledge.
This is high-standards, knowledge-specific scepticism in its purest form. But
radical scepticism is the thesis that our beliefs are completely unjustified,
a far stronger claim.

The fact that, in everyday life, we do not demand justifications that are
absolutely impregnable means only that ordinary justifications are fallible, not
that they are worthless. If zoos were given to faking their animals, casual
observation and a look at a label would not be such a reliable way of determining what is in the enclosure. How much less reliable would depend on the
incidence of fakery. But the fact that the animals looked like zebras and were
presented as zebras would still be *some* indication that they were really zebras.
They would not be very likely to be ostriches or snakes. So too with sceptical
hypotheses: as long as the sceptic admits that they are remote possibilities that
we may reasonably ignore in all practical situations, appealing to them will
not show that our everyday justificatory procedures are worthless, only that
they are not absolutely watertight, which we knew anyway.

To be sure, the high-standards scepticism derivable from the idea of pure
inquiry may have been significant in the heyday of the demonstrative conception of knowledge. But to contemporary fallibilists, such scepticism rattles an
unlocked door.

Underdetermination

To get to radical scepticism, the sceptic must not concede that his possibilities
are remote. He must argue that they are as likely to be true as what we
ordinarily believe. This is what he does. His point is that his bizarre stories
about Evil Deceivers and brains-in-vats are just as likely to be true as our
ordinary beliefs *given all the evidence we will ever have*. In the case of the
external world, all the evidence we will ever have comes from our sensory
experience; in that of other minds, from external behaviour; in that of the past
from presently existing documents and physical traces; in that of the future,
from the course of events up to now. In every case, he will claim, all the
evidence we will ever have radically underdetermines what it would be true or
even justifiable to believe. Like Gaul, his argument has three parts.[8]

The first step is to deny that facts about the external world (other minds, etc.) are the sort of thing that we 'just know'. Our knowledge of the external world is 'inferential', in the sense that beliefs about the external world will amount to knowledge only to the extent that they can be justified by appropriate evidence. This evidence is provided by perceptual experience: that is to say, by how things look, sound, smell, taste, and feel to us. The sceptic seems on strong ground here and his sceptical hypotheses reinforce his position. If the ex-commander of the *Enterprise*, safely envatted, cannot 'just see' that his 'reality' is only virtual, how are we supposed to just see that ours isn't?

The second step is to argue that there is no logical connection between experiential evidence and beliefs about the external world. Sceptical hypotheses play a crucial role here too. The brain-in-a-vat story, if intelligible, gives an account of the external world wildly at variance with what we normally believe, but logically consistent with all the experiential evidence we will ever have. If this point is granted, no amount of information about the course of experience will ever logically entail that the world is one way rather than another. Indeed, strictly speaking, no such information will ever logically entail that there *is* an external world, in anything like the way we normally imagine. There is no *deductive* route from experience to facts about the world.

All that remains, then, to take us from the evidence of the senses to knowledge of the external world is some kind of *inductive* inference. As we know, this kind of inference is highly problematic in its own right. But forget that for the moment. Even granting the legitimacy of inductive inference, can it help us here?

We might suppose so. The evidence for inductive inference is observed correlation. Because we have observed that smoke generally goes with fire, we are entitled on a subsequent occasion to infer the existence of fire from the presence of smoke. Smoke is a *reliable indicator* of fire. In the same way, our experiences are reliable indicators of objective states of affairs. If it looks to me as if I am sitting in front of a computer screen, this is generally because I am in just that situation. Of course, it is logically possible that this experience should result from some other source: it might be an unusually vivid dream, a hallucination, or even (worst case) the result of some ghastly simulation experiment being carried out on me without my knowledge. But these are abnormal cases: experience remains a reliable, if less than perfect, indicator of how things objectively are.

On reflection, we see that this won't work at all. Inductive inference depends on establishing correlations, which we can do only when we have *independent access* to the facts to be correlated. When we see smoke in the distance, we can verify its association with fire by going closer. But we cannot get closer to the world than our sensory experience of it. Experience is not like a curtain that we might draw aside to see what is going on behind. To suppose that we can correlate our experiential states with states of the external world is to imagine that we have some independent way—that is, some way independent of experience—of gaining access to facts about the world, and that is precisely what we do not have. There is no analogy to the case of smoke and fire.

We have been led to a second, apparently fatal trilemma. To be rationally justifiable, our beliefs about the external world (other minds, etc.) must be either immediate, deductively inferable from immediate knowledge, or inductively so inferable. But they cannot be any of these things. Accordingly, they cannot be justified at all. This is radical scepticism.

Connections

Cartesian scepticism is general and radical. But is it also intuitive? To give this question more bite, let us briefly compare our two fundamental forms of scepticism, Agrippan and Cartesian.

Cartesian problems can involve Agrippan elements in the following way: once we accept the problem in its own terms, we fall into the Agrippan traps of assumption or circularity. Consider external world scepticism. Once we agree that knowledge of the external world depends on sensory experience, we find ourselves needing bridge principles to link experience with objective reality. But such bridge principles—for example, to the effect that certain experiences are reliable indicators of certain objective states of affairs—themselves involve knowledge of the external world, which is what we were trying to justify in the first place. Similarly with induction. To rationally extend our beliefs beyond what we have actually observed, we need a principle that itself goes beyond what we have actually observed. Some philosophers have concluded that the Uniformity Principle is an indispensable 'postulate' of empirical reasoning. But 'postulate' is just a polite word for 'assumption'.

The fact that the Cartesian sceptic can exploit Agrippan tropes should not lead us to imagine that Cartesian problems are just the Agrippan problem all over again. Cartesian problems remain underdetermination problems. They arise because (i) beliefs of a certain type (say beliefs about the past) seem to depend for their justification on beliefs of some quite distinct type (e.g. beliefs about currently available documentary, archaeological, and other relevant evidence), and (ii) the available evidence, no matter how extensive, is always compatible with competing hypotheses, some of them quite bizarre. We fall into circularity or assumption in our attempts to get our inadequate evidence to point one way rather than another.

Do these partitions of our beliefs into problematic and (at least relatively) privileged classes make Cartesian scepticism theoretically loaded, compromising its claim to be intuitive? Not obviously. Surely, whatever we know about the external world comes from our sensory experience; whatever we know about the past comes from traces that have survived into the present; whatever we know about the future comes from our knowledge of past trends; all we know about another person's inner life is what is revealed by outward behaviour. What more does the sceptic need from us?

Reflection on the character of Cartesian problems as underdetermination problems suggests another important way in which Agrippan and Cartesian scepticism come into connection. Agrippa's trilemma encourages us to look for beliefs that cannot sensibly be subjected to demands for justification. However, any such beliefs must belong to fairly restricted kinds. Thus to many philosophers, beliefs about how things appear to us—experiential beliefs—have seemed to be the most plausible candidates for the role of things that we 'just know' and which therefore stop the regress of justification, when empirical matters are at issue. But if is this is how we try to escape from Agrippan scepticism—in effect, by identifying a *restricted foundation* for empirical knowledge—we run right into scepticism of the Cartesian variety. The philosophical sceptic can thus follow a two-pronged strategy: deploy Agrippan scepticism to edge us into looking for a restricted basis for knowledge; then bring in underdetermination arguments to show that, once we have accepted such a basis, we shall find ourselves permanently confined to it.

More on the space of theories

In our discussion of the Agrippan problem, we saw how the structure of the Agrippan argument defines the space of epistemological theories that might salvage the idea of justification from the sceptic's attack. This provided backing for my claim that scepticism, while not the only problem that the theory of knowledge tries to deal with, plays an especially significant role in philosophical epistemology. In an exactly analogous way, the Cartesian trilemma appears to define a space of possible theoretical responses. This capacity to define the range of theoretical options convinces many people that sceptical problems lie at the heart of philosophical epistemology.

The first possibility is to deny the evidential gap. According to this 'direct realism', knowledge of the external world is not always and everywhere inferential. Certainly, we do think of ourselves as often 'just knowing' various things about our surroundings, without depending on elaborate inferences. So perhaps there is hope here, at least in connection with some Cartesian problems.

Moving to the second stage of the argument, perhaps we were too hasty in conceding that there are no deductive links between experiential and worldly knowledge. Perhaps, in some way or other, external world propositions mean what they do because of evidential links with human experience. This 'appeal to meaning' can take various forms. But its basic idea—that external reality cannot be an unimaginable 'something we know not what', wholly alien to human experience—has considerable intuitive appeal.

The third and final option is to challenge the sceptic's identification of induction with extrapolation from observed correlations. Since we do seem to go in for more complicated forms of inductive inference than the sceptic's argument appears to allow for, this 'inductive approach' cannot be dismissed out of hand either.

Not every strategy is plausibly applied to every problem. Still, none is an evident non-starter. We shall examine them all.

Does it matter?

A common reaction to the problem of the external world is that it doesn't matter whether sceptical hypotheses are true or not. If I am a brain in a vat, or a victim of the Evil Deceiver, everything in my experience will be the same. So far as I am concerned, my virtual reality is as good as the real thing.

This response raises interesting questions about the value we place on truth. Would anyone really choose to be stupid and gullible, so stupid and so gullible that, while his 'friends' despise him and view him simply as a source of amusement, he never catches on? Is such a life really 'just as good'? Is it made better by the person's inability to appreciate his situation for what it is? Or does this make it the more contemptible? When the starship commander gets to brain-in-vat planet and embarks on his virtual life with his virtual (in reality dead) lover, how do we feel about his future? He never really acts, never really accomplishes anything: it only seems to him that he does. He has no friends and no children that will outlive him: such things are all part of the illusion. Perhaps we think that, given his misfortunes, this shadow of a life is good *for him*. But this is pity bordering on contempt.

Similar remarks apply to problem of other minds. Does anyone really think that it would be alright to be the only conscious being in a world of automata, provided that the automata continue to manifest familiar behavioral reactions? I doubt it.

Notice, finally, that even if we were to turn aside from the problem of the external world on 'What does it matter?' grounds, we would still be faced with the problem of induction. If the course of Nature changed dramatically the next instant, we should know all about it. But do we take this possibility seriously? Any moment, Sartre's Roquentin thinks, my tongue could turn into a lizard. Anyone who seriously entertained such thoughts would suffer paralysing anxiety. That this is not our permanent state shows that we dismiss sceptical possibilities: not because it doesn't matter whether they are realized but because we are convinced that they are not. In some way, the possibility of their being true is not on the horizon. What we want as philosophers is to understand how we might be entitled to our natural certainty. Is it just a psychological fact? Do we know more than the sceptic allows? Or are we fated to live with an outlook that resists reflective understanding?

Notes

1. *Meditations on First Philosophy*, in Cottingham *et al.* (1984). On the novelty of Descartes's problem, see Burnyeat (1982) and Williams (1998).
2. On the essential generality of the sceptic's interests, see Barry Stroud, 'Understanding Human Knowledge in General', in Clay and Lehrer (1989).
3. e.g. DeRose (1995).
4. Dretske (1970).
5. Fogelin (1994), 93 f.
6. This account of Cartesian scepticism is given by Bernard Williams (1978).
7. This pragmatist line is associated especially with Dewey (1984).
8. This analysis of the pattern of Cartesian argumentation is due in all essentials to Ayer (1956). For a detailed defence of Ayer's analysis, see Williams (1996a), esp. chs. 2, 5.

7

Foundations

The goals of theory

What should we demand of an epistemological theory purporting to solve the Agrippan problem?[1]

The first desideratum is that the theory offer a coherent and plausible account of its basic ideas, showing how they indeed yield a solution. This means blocking the regress without covertly lapsing into assumption or circularity. While such a requirement may seem too obvious to be worth stating, it proves extremely difficult to meet. Closely examined, many theories fail to meet it.

A second requirement is that the theory explain how we can have a workably extensive body of knowledge. The Agrippan sceptic's suggestion that no belief or judgement is ever justified is formally contradicted by the thesis that there is at least one justified belief. But establishing this minimal thesis would not be a satisfactory response to Agrippan scepticism. Descartes famously argued that it is impossible rationally to doubt that one is thinking or that one exists, since doubting is a form of thinking and one has to exist to be deceived (*Cogito ergo sum*). However, if this were all Descartes was able to salvage from the sceptical wreck, he would not have accomplished very much. Not everything we believe need be justifiable, but enough must be.

Finally, it is not enough to show that knowledge is logically or 'theoretically' possible. While a theory of knowledge may involve a degree of idealization or 'rational reconstruction', it should show how knowledge is within the grasp of creatures more or less like ourselves. Knowledge should be humanly possible.

The foundationalist's dilemma

Foundationalism and the coherence theory are generally taken to represent the two main strategic approaches to the Agrippan problem. Typically, they are distinguished by what they imply about the *structure* of epistemic justification.

Foundationalist theories claim to identify basic beliefs (or perhaps some even more primitive form of awareness, such as experiences themselves), which provide stopping-points for chains of justification. Such beliefs (or other states) are justified without deriving this positive epistemic status from any further beliefs. They are *intrinsically* credible. In this picture, a system of justified belief is like a building: there is a bottom level—a foundation—on which all the upper storeys stand. By contrast, coherence theories make justification a matter of the interconnections between beliefs. An individual belief derives its credibility from its playing a role in a larger system of beliefs. One might think of a system of beliefs as like a space station, held together by its internal structure and wheeling along through space without *resting* on anything. Or one might use the analogy of an ecosystem, in which organisms, by playing their distinctive roles, keep each other going. Where the foundationalist sees an *architecture* of knowledge, the coherence theorist sees something like an *ecology*, with beliefs occupying interdependent niches.[2]

Let us call the foundationalist's structural thesis *structural foundationalism*:

(STF) (i) There are basic beliefs, beliefs that are *in some sense* justifiably held without resting on further evidence. (ii) A belief is justified if and only if it is either itself basic or inferentially connected, in some appropriate way, to other justified beliefs.

Notice that clause (ii) makes use of the idea of justified belief. This may strike some readers as circular. In fact, it isn't. Rather, structural foundationalism treats the class of justified beliefs as specifiable recursively. To specify a class recursively, we being by identifying a basis: anything in the basis is a member of the class in question. We then introduce one or more generating relations: other things can get into the class by standing in an appropriate relation to already accredited members. Thus, starting with the base members, we add whatever is appropriately related to them. Then we add whatever is appropriately related to our expanded collection, and so on. Finally, we stipulate that nothing else is a member. (This is why I have 'if and only if' in clause (ii) of (STF).)

For a simple example, consider the natural numbers (0, 1, 2, 3 . . .). The basis is 0 and the generating relation is that of being the immediate successor of a number. So 0 is a number; so is its immediate successor (call it '1'); so is 1's immediate successor (call it '2'); so is 2's immediate successor, and so on. Nothing else is a number.

Foundationalists treat the class of justified beliefs in exactly this way. There are basic beliefs (specified some way or other) and there are justification-transmitting inferential connections (deductive, inductive, etc.) A belief is justified if and only if it is either itself basic or can be reached by a succession of accredited inferential moves from some initial collection of basic beliefs, just as a number is either 0 or generated from 0 by repeatedly finding immediate successors.

This structural thesis is important. But it does not fully characterize traditional foundational epistemologies, which embody what I call *substantive foundationalism*:

(SUF) (i) and (ii) as above. (iii) There are certain kinds of beliefs (or other conscious states) that by their very nature—that is, in virtue of their content—are fitted to play the role of terminating points for chains of justification. These beliefs (or other states) are epistemologically basic because *intrinsically credible* or *self-evidencing*.

Where structural foundationalism says only that justification comes to an end with some beliefs or other, substantive foundationalism makes the much stronger claim that there are beliefs of certain broad kinds, identifiable by their distinctive content, with which justification always comes to an end.[3]

In saying that basic beliefs are basic in virtue of their distinctive content, I am not insisting that their content be sufficient to make them justified. The point is rather that only beliefs with a certain kind of content have the potential to be basic. So, for example, many foundationalists have held that one important source of basic knowledge is our 'immediate awareness' of our own thoughts and sensations. Thus my belief that I now have a headache is foundationally justified by my having a headache: not the content of my belief but the fact that it points to. I need not deny this. My point is simply that, for substantive foundationalists, basic beliefs can be sorted into kinds on the basis of their distinctive content: for example, as beliefs about immediate experience. So the difference between structural and substantive foundationalism is like that between 'All roads lead somewhere' and 'There is somewhere (Rome perhaps) to which all roads lead'. Substantive foundationalism implies structural foundationalism, but not vice versa.[4]

What is the appeal of the stronger thesis? One factor is that structural foundationalism, treated as a *purely* structural thesis, is not obviously responsive to Agrippan scepticism. The Agrippan sceptic claims not to challenge the phenomenology of everyday justification, conceding that ordinary justification involves citing evidence that no party to the discussion is *in fact* prepared to challenge. But he sees this 'justification' as merely dialectical, thus vulnerable to the Mode of Assumption. A foundationalist response to the Agrippan sceptic needs basic beliefs that are not simply *unchallenged* but *unchallengeable*. Perhaps not absolutely unchallengeable, but at least not automatically challengeable and thus at least *prima facie* justified.

While correct as far as it goes, this cannot be the whole story. Presenting foundationalism and the coherence theory as the two main theoretical strategies for dealing with the Agrippan problem, while illuminating theoretically, is historically off-key. Foundationalist ideas pre-date Agrippa's trilemma. (As we have seen, they are strongly evident in Aristotle, whose concern with sceptical problems is much less certain.) As for coherence theories, though we may find coherentist elements in Plato's epistemological theorizing, pure coherentism—understood as a clear alternative to foundationalism—is a relatively recent invention, belonging (at the earliest) to the nineteenth century. The choice between foundationalism and the coherence theory did not spring into being as an immediate consequence of Agrippan scepticism.

That foundationalist ideas pre-date Agrippan scepticism suggests that they have at least some appeal independently of their anti-sceptical potential. This is just as well: wanting there to be terminating judgements does not guarantee that there are any. Foundationalism would never have been plausible had there not been an example of knowledge apparently conforming to the foundationalist ideal. The deep (or at least original) source of foundationalism's appeal lies in the axiomatic method. Axiomatized theories—such as Euclid's presentation of plane geometry—offer a compelling example of foundationalism in action.

The geometrical model, however, is problematic as a model of knowledge in general, and not just because it encourages a demonstrative—hence extremely restrictive—conception of knowledge. Euclid's geometry is an example of a finitely axiomatized theory: it involves a fixed number of proper axioms (together with a few definitions and general principles). This gives the theory a certain independence of epistemological theory. Because its basic assertions can be displayed for the reader's inspection, their self-evidence can be directly experienced, case by case, and so does not need to be explained. However, a general theory of knowledge must allow for an expanding stock of basic beliefs. Accordingly, a generalized foundationalism demands that we identify one or more *kinds* of basic belief or judgement. This is substantive foundationalism, which from now on is what I shall have in mind whenever I speak of 'foundationalism' without qualification.

According to substantive foundationalism, evidence for the truth of belief of a given non-basic kind *must*, in the last analysis, be sought in beliefs belonging to some more basic, 'epistemologically prior' kind. These epistemological kinds cross-cut and are more fundamental than ordinary subject-matter divisions. They correspond to what Descartes called 'the order of reasons'.

Viewed in this light, beliefs and judgements stand in natural relations of epistemic priority and fall into natural epistemological kinds. These relations and kinds are natural in the sense that they are fixed and permanent. They exist independently of our interests and decisions. They define 'our epistemic position', a framework of constraints within which all our knowledge-seeking activities are fated to take place. Substantive foundationalism is thus committed to what I call 'epistemological realism'. This is not realism as a position within epistemology (the view that there is a real world out there which, in favorable circumstances, we can learn a lot about) but rather a kind of extreme realism about the subject-matter of epistemological theory.

The dominant strain of foundationalism today is empiricism, in one form or another. Modern foundationalists have almost invariably taken it that some basic beliefs must be empirical: in fact, perceptual. Most have taken it that basic perceptual beliefs have to do with the contents of experience—how things appear to us—experience, or experiential beliefs, thus being epistemologically prior to beliefs about the external world.

The second limitation that must be overcome, if the geometrical model is to be extended to knowledge generally, concerns the connection between basic and non-basic knowledge. The individual steps in Euclid's reasoning are meant to be self-evidently deductively valid. Again, this gives geometry a certain independence of epistemology. (Indeed, it was not until the work of Frege, at the end of the nineteenth century, that logical theory progressed to a point where mathematical reasoning could be represented as formally valid.) But a generalized foundationalism, especially a version that has abandoned the demonstrative conception of knowledge, cannot restrict itself in advance to deduction as the only warrant-conferring form of inference.

These points suggest two problems for foundationalism. The first is to explain how it is that some beliefs manage to be genuinely basic, in the foundationalist's strong sense of intrinsically credible. Call this 'the problem of the basis' or 'the problem of security'. The second is to explain the inferential connections between one's chosen basis and a workable superstructure of empirical knowledge. Call this 'the problem of the superstructure' or 'the problem of adequacy'.

There is an obvious tension between the two problems. The more ambitious a claim, the less our assurance of its truth: only beliefs or judgements that are fairly modest in their assertional content are plausible pretenders to the role of intrinsically credible basic beliefs. Accordingly, the quest for security puts the foundationalist under pressure to accept a severely restricted basis for knowledge. But the more restricted the basis, the more challenging the task of recovering a workable superstructure. This is the foundationalist's dilemma: to define a basis for knowledge modest enough to be secure but rich enough to be adequate. This problem offers the critic plenty of room for manoeuvre.

Sources of knowledge

Prior to the nineteenth century, virtually all philosophers concerned with knowledge were foundationalists of one sort or another. But they tended to approach questions about the epistemic status of various kinds of beliefs by investigating their origins, rather than by talking, as I have done, about the structure of justification. So is my account of foundationalism misleading?

A good way of casting light on this issue is to further investigate the distinction between *a priori* and *a posteriori* knowledge. This distinction is generally explained in terms of dependence and independence with respect to observation. What kind of 'dependence' is at issue here?

Traditionally, this question has been answered in terms of how the different types of knowledge can (or must) be acquired: particularly in terms of which faculties—the senses or reason—need to be exercised in their acquisition. *A priori* knowledge can be established by the use of Reason alone. By contrast, to find out whether there a squirrel on my lawn right now, I *have* to go and look ('use my senses'). Or if I don't go myself, I have to get someone else to look for me. There are many ways to learn particular facts about the world—through testimony, by reading books, and so on—but for such information ever to have got into circulation, at some point somebody had to go and see for himself. This dependence on observation as its *ultimate source* is the hallmark of *a posteriori* knowledge.

Some philosophers argue that the traditional focus on the origins or sources of different kinds of knowledge was always misguided: that the correct way to distinguish between *a priori* and *a posteriori* knowledge is not in terms of how the two types of knowledge *originate* but rather in terms of how they are *justified*. *A posteriori* knowledge is knowledge that involves beliefs that require support from observational evidence. By contrast, *a priori* knowledge, as in pure mathematics, depends solely on logical intuition and reasoning. Observation is irrelevant.

There is something initially appealing about this view. We acquire beliefs in all sorts of ways, which need not line up in any neat way with important epistemological distinctions. A mathematician looking at the petals of a flower may be stimulated to have some new thoughts about symmetry. Her experience may be powerful enough to convince her of the correctness of her new ideas. And they may even be correct. Still, whether they count as knowledge will depend on her providing proofs. Similarly, a scientific hypothesis might come to us in a dream. But what converts it from speculation to knowledge is confirmation by experimental evidence.

However, there is less disagreement here than first appears. Although whether a belief amounts to knowledge has traditionally been linked to its sources, those sources have themselves been understood in ways that make them relevant to questions of justification. Knowledge is belief from *reliable* sources; and to trace a belief to a reliable source is to justify it. Recognizably reliable sources are thus *authoritative*. This is a perfectly commonsensical view. If we know that our informant is generally truthful, we will be justified in believing what he tells us. If an expert on English furniture tells us that the chair is a Chippendale, we will take his word for it. And so on.

Traditionally, Reason has been conceived on the model of a hyper-reliable informant. In generating mathematical knowledge, Reason operates in two ways. The most basic mathematical truths are grasped by a kind of pure rational insight: they are self-evident because they literally 'stand to reason'. Less obvious truths are deduced from these self-evident beginnings by individually obvious steps. Reason, when operating properly, leads us to a grasp of necessary truths and so cannot misinform us. To trace a belief to Reason is thus to provide it with impeccable credentials and so to justify it. There is no tension between treating theories of knowledge as theories of justification and the traditional tendency to understand different kinds of knowledge in terms of their distinct, authoritative sources.

Rationality

Since there are many versions of foundationalism, foundationalists can diverge in their epistemological views. Nevertheless, there are certain general ideas that go naturally with a foundationalist conception of knowledge and justification.

Let us begin with the problem of rationality. According to an immensely influential view, it is always irrational to hold beliefs that are not adequately justified. Call this a strongly *justificationist* conception of rationality. This conception is deeply embedded in the foundationalist outlook. Indeed, it is hard to say which is the chicken and which the egg. Foundationalists feel the need for a strong response to scepticism because scepticism attacks justification, without which there is no rationality. With a different conception of rationality, we might not feel the need for such a strong response to scepticism.

I must stress that I am thinking here of substantive foundationalism. As we know, Agrippan scepticism is compatible with structural foundationalism. The Agrippan sceptic does not deny that everyday 'justification' generally comes to a halt with beliefs or claims that no party to the discussion feels the need to deny. His point is that this 'common knowledge' is no more than conveniently shared assumptions. Furthermore, there is no reason why any given dispute *must* so terminate. In many cases, we may not share enough assumptions to bring a dispute to a mutually satisfactory conclusion, in which case our dispute will bog down and may stay bogged down indefinitely. To a philosopher attracted to a strongly justificationist conception of rationality, this is intolerable, for it implies that there we have no guarantee that important disagreements can be rationally adjudicated. This explains why purely dialectical justification is distasteful to so many philosophers: it seems hostage to contingent agreement. In the absence of such agreement, disputes will be resolved by non-rational means: rhetorical devices, or worse still, force.

Even if extensive disagreement is acceptable, the Agrippan sceptic's tolerance for structural foundationalism is a standing invitation to relativism. By contrast, substantive foundationalism holds out the promise of a neutral basis for the (in principle) adjudication of all disputes, or all that are genuinely significant. This promise is an important source of foundationalism's appeal.

Epistemic risk

Moving on, what does foundationalism look like as a method of inquiry? Some philosophers, Descartes perhaps, have used the foundationalist picture of justification as a literal method: a procedure to be followed in building up a correct system of beliefs. So understood, foundationalism amounts to a counsel of extreme caution: we are to add to our stock of beliefs only such beliefs as we can infer, by evidently warrant-conferring procedures, from a secure basis of primitively evident beliefs. This should make us wonder whether a strongly justificationist conception of rationality is really so rational. Of course, we should like to know the truth: however, avoiding errors and maximizing our number of true beliefs are not the same thing. Methodologically speaking, foundationalism is dramatically tilted towards error-avoidance. Perhaps we would do better in the long run if we loosened up and took more epistemological risks. Our mistakes might be more than offset by extra discoveries.

Contemporary philosophers do not usually interpret foundationalism in procedural or genetic terms. They recognize that we are all acculturated into a complicated system of beliefs and that no one does or could construct such a system from the ground up. Foundationalism is neither a psychological account of how such systems are acquired, nor a set of prescriptive rules governing their construction, but an account of their justificational structure. Foundationalism reveals constraints to which a belief-system must conform to count as justified, hence rational.

From this standpoint, the naive problem of method—how should we conduct inquiry—is ill-stated. Epistemologically speaking, what matters is not where ideas come from but how they can be verified (or falsified). This understanding of foundationalism goes naturally with a sharp distinction between 'contexts of discovery' and 'contexts of justification'. There are no strict rules for thinking up new ideas, only rules of thumb. But there are strict criteria of justification. So although wild ideas can be entertained, they cannot be retained if they fail to find adequate support. Accordingly, the non-genetic understanding does not affect foundationalism's bias towards error-avoidance.

Empiricism and the *a priori*

In principle, substantive foundationalism can take either rationalist or empiricist forms. However, in recent times the dominant form of foundationalism has been empiricist. For modern foundationalists, at least some basic beliefs must be empirical.[5]

This brings us to what I called the problem of unity: are there fundamentally different minds of knowledge, associated with different methods of verification? Empiricist foundationalists think that there are. They want to allow for both demonstrative knowledge, as found in pure mathematics, and empirical knowledge, as found in the natural sciences. This puts them under pressure to recognize at least two sources of basic knowledge: some faculty of rational or logical intuition, by which we recognize primitive logico-mathematical truths and the validity of elementary inferences; and some forms of primitive experiential knowledge, which give us an expanding database of contingent information.

Since this database is apt to be highly restricted, we are not going to be able to make a workably extensive system of empirical knowledge out of its deductive consequences alone. This pushes foundationalists towards recognizing two forms of warrant-conferring inference: deductive and inductive. As we shall see, foundationalists are required to regard both sorts of inference as *a priori* valid.

How should empiricists understand the *a priori*? To address this question, we need to review (and introduce) some distinctions:

1. A Priori *versus* A Posteriori. *A priori* knowledge is independent of empirical justification or verification. *A posteriori* (or empirical) knowledge depends on experience or observation. Virtually all contemporary epistemologists regard scientific knowledge, which depends on experimental confirmation, as *a posteriori*. (Historically the *a priori/a posteriori* distinction has been closely associated with that between the innate and the learned. The very idea of the *a priori*, as that which can be known prior to experience, encourages this assimilation, which should nevertheless be resisted.)

2. *Necessary versus Contingent.* A necessary truth is one that holds 'in all possible worlds'. Truths of pure mathematics and elementary logical truths have almost (though not quite) universally been held to be necessary. Two and two don't just happen to make four: no other result is so much as possible. (Of course the word 'two' might have had a different meaning, but that is beside the point.) Anything that is not necessary is contingent: contingent truths are those that happen to obtain but might not have. I happen to sitting at my desk right now. But I might have decided to take a walk or have done various things that would have placed me elsewhere. Early modern Rationalists thought that some fundamental principles of the natural sciences are necessary. Today, however, virtually all philosophers agree that science deals exclusively with matters of contingent fact.

3. *Analytic versus Synthetic.* Analytic truths are truths that hold by definition or in virtue of meaning. They are 'conceptual' truths. (Analytic falsehoods are statements that are—perhaps implicitly—oxymoronic.) Anything that is not analytic is synthetic. 'Bachelors are unmarried males' is analytic. 'Bachelors tend to die before married men' is synthetic. Anyone who understands an analytically true statement must recognize that it is true: there is no gap here between understanding and knowledge. On the other hand, analytic truths convey no information about the world. By contrast, knowledge of synthetic truths is clearly 'substantial' in that it is not guaranteed simply by understanding the meaning of one's terms.

These are distinct contrasts: the first is epistemological, the second metaphysical, and the third semantic. How they line up is an interesting question. It has been characteristic of empiricism in its more radical forms to say that they are coextensive. That is: a truth is *a priori* knowable if and only if it is necessary; and a truth is necessary if and only if it is analytic. On this view, there is no *a priori* knowledge of substantial or factual matters, so that attempts to demonstrate factual truths *a priori*, such as the Ontological Argument for the existence of God, must be deeply misguided. Kant saw this as Hume's challenge to philosophy, understood as the quest for *a priori* knowledge of fundamental truths. How is *a priori* knowledge of synthetic truths so much as *possible*? Of course, perhaps it isn't. Empiricists are sure that it isn't.

The reason behind the empiricist outlook is not far to seek. It is plausible to hold that whatever is necessarily true must be knowable *a priori*. Experience can only tell us how things are, not how they must be. At the same time, empiricists are suspicious of the idea that purely *a priori* procedures can tell us anything about how the world actually is. The solution is to explain necessity in terms of analyticity. To be sure, there are statements that cannot be false: but this is because their truth is guaranteed by our linguistic conventions. There is no *a priori* insight into external reality. Modern empiricism is characterized by a linguistic doctrine of necessity. A consequence of this doctrine is a deflationary attitude towards *a priori* knowledge. Though there is such knowledge, it is not really 'substantive' or 'factual'. It merely reflects our linguistic conventions.

The plausibility of this epistemological standpoint owes a lot to developments in mathematics and science. For Rationalists, geometry was always the paradigm of rational knowledge. Epistemologically and metaphysically, it seemed on a par with arithmetic: *a priori* and necessary. At the same time, by revealing the structure of space, it seemed to tell us important truths about the real world. However, the development of non-Euclidean geometries calls this paradigm into question. From a purely mathematical standpoint, there are all kinds of geometrical spaces. Which mathematical theory best describes real space is an empirical issue, not decidable independently of physical considerations. The development of non-Euclidean geometries contributes powerfully to the appeal of the empiricist idea that pure mathematics is a wholly conceptual form of inquiry.[6]

Because they continue to be widely recognized, it is important to mark these distinctions. However, none is beyond controversy and not everyone accepts the empiricist position.[7] But I have a different question, which is whether some (or even all) of these distinctions have outlived their usefulness. For foundationalists, who are constrained to take the *a priori/a posteriori* distinction seriously, it is important to determine how the lines should be drawn. For others, the significance of this task is much less clear.

Drawing lines

This brings us to the problem of demarcation. Not only does foundationalism suggest a sharp internal boundary between *a priori* and *a posteriori* knowledge, it produces an almost irresistible impulse towards fixing external boundaries. Some things we like to think we know resist justification on the restricted basis to which the foundationalist's quest for security forces him to retreat. Such things will fall outside the province of knowledge.

Some philosophers connect questions of justification with questions of meaning. Thus logical positivists put forward the Principle of Verification, according to which a statement is not meaningful unless it is possible to explain what would count as verifying or falsifying it. Truly interminable disputes are not just pointless: they have no real content. Positivists saw most 'philosophical' disagreements in this light. But philosophical theses are not alone in falling outside the charmed circle of knowledge, hence of genuine meaningfulness. By foundationalist standards, moral claims—indeed value-judgements generally—cannot plausibly be regarded as empirically grounded. Positivists tended to accord them 'emotive' meaning. They make no literal or factual claims, which might be true or false, but express our attitudes of approbation or disapproval. This is sometimes called the 'Boo–Hooray' theory of moral judgement. Value-judgements are not really judgements: they are cheers or jeers.[8]

The ideal of clarity

We have seen that empiricist foundationalism has pronounced demarcational tendencies. But it has certain unifying tendencies too. Because foundational-ism purports to be a fully general theory of epistemic justification, it is unfriendly to the idea of a plurality of methods. At best, foundationalists will recognize different ranges of data.

Some philosophers have held that there is a fundamental methodological distinction between the natural and the 'human' sciences (*Natur-* and *Geisteswissenschaften*). In physics or chemistry we seek to explain events by bringing them under laws; and we test putative laws experimentally. In history or anthropology we want something different, a kind of interpretative understanding (*verstehen*). We want to get a feel for past circumstances or exotic ways of life 'from the inside'. This is more a matter of sympathetic imagination than experimentation.

On the whole, the empiricist outlook has not been friendly to such ideas: hence the tendency for empiricist psychology to take behaviouristic forms. But it is doubtful whether classical Rationalism should think much better of them. This is not surprising: it is not easy to assimilate notions like *verstehen* to the foundationalist model of verification. But this is not all. There is a tendency, deeply entrenched in the foundationalist outlook, to place a high value, not only on securely grounded knowledge, but also on absolute conceptual clarity. 'Clear and distinct ideas' was Descartes's epistemological ideal, and 'Define your terms' remains a characteristically foundationalist slogan. These demands—for epistemic security and conceptual clarity—are two sides of the same coin. The meaning of a basic statement or belief must be absolutely self-contained: its meaning cannot shift, depending on whatever context of further statements or beliefs it comes to be embedded in. This kind of variability would be incompatible with the requirement of intrinsic credibility. Epistemically and semantically, foundationalism is *atomistic*. As for non-basic statements, each of these must have a precisely delimited meaning all of its own. Only thus will it stand in definite relations to some specifiable range of basic evidence. Foundationalists therefore distrust metaphor. Metaphorical description, by its very suggestiveness and open texture, resists association with precisely and individually delimitable verification-conditions. For the foundationalist, this automatically degrades its cognitive value.[9]

Some will conclude that the demarcational consequences of foundationalism are reason enough for seeking another approach to epistemology. However, we should remember that foundationalism promises significant rewards for the costs it exacts. Can it deliver them?

Notes

1. My discussion here is heavily indebted to Fogelin (1994), ch. 6.
2. Ayer (1956) treats the full range of sceptical problems within a broadly foundational perspective. In post-war American philosophy, the most significant defender of foundationalism is Roderick Chisholm. See Chisholm (1982).
3. In Williams (1992), I make the same distinction using the terminology of formal versus substantive foundationalism. This terminology was introduced by Ernest Sosa and I have changed my terms because Sosa's distinction is very different from mine. For Sosa, substantive foundationalism contrasts with the coherence theory while formal foundationalism contrasts with what he calls 'epistemic pessimism'. Formal foundationalism (in epistemology) says that

   (i) every belief with a certain non-epistemic property F is justified, (ii) if a belief bears relation R to a set of justified beliefs then it is itself justified, and (iii) every belief is justified in virtue of (i) or (ii).

   In effect, formal foundationalism is the view that the class of justified beliefs can be specified recursively, by identifying a basis and a generator: elements you start with and a procedure for generating further elements from them (plus what you add as you go along). The epistemic pessimist is the philosopher who doubts that any such 'interesting' specification of the class of justified belief is possible. My notion of structural foundationalism is weaker, since it does not require that the class of basic beliefs be specifiable in wholly non-epistemic terms, still less that it be specifiable (as Sosa sometimes seems to suggest) in non-normative terms. By contrast, my notion of substantive foundationalism is stronger, involving as it does the commitment to content-based classifications of basic beliefs. I am not sure whether our different ways of dividing up the territory reflect deep disagreements. I adopt mine with an eye to setting up the contextualist epistemology I present in Chapters 13 to 15. For Sosa's views, see his essay 'The Foundations of Foundations' and his justly renowned 'The Raft and the Pyramid', reprinted as chapters 9 and 10 of Sosa (1991).

4. I am indebted to Ernest Sosa for forcing me to clarify this point.
5. Rationalism has not had a very good press at all in recent philosophy. But for an intriguing defence of traditional Rationalism, see BonJour (1998).
6. BonJour (1998) argues forcefully that empiricists, whether 'moderate' or 'radical', have no good account of *a priori* knowledge. He is also willing to take a Rationalist stance towards geometry as providing *a priori* knowledge of the structure of space.
7. For an important discussion of why these distinctions should not be thought to line up, see Kripke (1980), Lecture 1.
8. For the positivist outlook, see the essays in Ayer (1959).
9. For a critical discussion of the foundationalist ideal of absolute clarity and a penetrating critique of foundationalism generally, see Elgin (1996).

8

The Problem of the Basis

Intrinsic credibility

Foundationalism aims to bring demands for justification to an absolute stopping-point with epistemologically basic beliefs. In its traditional form, foundationalism requires basic beliefs to be *intrinsically* credible: justified independently of all inferential connections to further beliefs or factual pre-suppositions. I say 'in its traditional form' because one might try to combine a foundationalist picture of the structure of justification with a pure reliabilist account of basic knowledge. In this 'externalist' version of foundationalism, basic knowledge would be non-inferential but not independent of external facts (concerning the reliability of various cognitive processes). Since we have already found reason to reject pure reliabilism, traditional foundationalism is what we need to examine here. We shall take up the question of what we can learn from the reliabilist alternative in Chapter 15.

The idea of intrinsic credibility entails an *atomistic* view of justification. Indeed, it entails an atomistic conception of meaning and understanding. If a belief can be justifiably held in the absence of any further beliefs, *a fortiori* it can be held (justifiably or not) in such conditions. The foundationalist's commitment to intrinsic credibility is thus a commitment to *encapsulated* knowledge: knowledge that is independent, justificationally and semantically, of any further knowledge.

Since intrinsic credibility is credibility that attaches to a belief independently of all external factors—even factors concerning what else a person believes—it must somehow depend only on content: what a basic belief means or is about. For the foundationalist, *content determines (epistemic) status*, in the sense that only beliefs with a certain kind of content are even candidates for playing the role of basic beliefs. Foundationalism is committed both to a content-based theory of epistemic justification and to an atomistic account of content. How content, or meaning, might be constituted, given the foundationalist's semantic atomism, is a question we shall discuss in due course.

Traditionally, foundationalists have insisted that basic beliefs be rationally indubitable or (a slightly weaker notion) incorrigible: exempt from rational correction. One way for a judgement to be indubitable, *prima facie* consistent with the content theory, is to take as its object a proposition expressing a simple necessary truth. It would be absurd to think 'I know exactly what it means to claim that two plus two equals four, I'm just not sure that its true'. Because the falsity of such a proposition is inconceivable, you cannot have a clear grasp of its meaning and be in doubt as to its truth. However, this is not a good model for a generalized foundationalism, which is supposed to apply to *empirical* knowledge of *contingent* truths. The foundationalist needs to explain how indubitability or incorrigibility can attach to propositions that are not necessarily true.

Descartes's famous 'I think' and 'I exist' perhaps fit the bill. If I am in a position to think such thoughts, they must be true. But since I might never have been born or might have been, at this moment, in a state of dreamless sleep, it is not a necessary truth that I exist or that I am thinking. However, such 'pragmatically self-verifying' propositions seem too specialized to serve as models for foundational judgements generally. Here our second success condition—that an epistemological theory ought to salvage a usably extensive body of knowledge—makes itself felt. For the foundations of empirical knowledge generally, we need a form of *perceptual* knowledge that is non-inferential in the foundationalist's demanding sense.

Appearance and reality

Most modern foundationalists have sought basic empirical knowledge at the level of experience: our awareness of how things appear to us or, more generally, in our immediate knowledge of our own mental states, including all occurrent thoughts and feelings. Their thought has been that, although we can always go wrong in judgements about how things objectively are, we cannot go wrong about how they *seem* or *look* to us to be or how we *think* they are. Not even the Evil Deceiver or scientists running brain-in-vat experiments can deceive us here. They may systematically deceive us about how things are, but the deception depends on our awareness of how things appear to be. The whole point of the brain-in-vat experiment is to simulate normal experience, which means that the sceptical scenario concedes that experiential information is not subject to the same kind of doubt as knowledge of the external world. Experiential knowledge is basic by virtue of being the 'highest common factor' in 'veridical' and 'non-veridical' perception.[1]

There is already something disturbing about this line of thought. We saw that Agrippa's trilemma can be seen as revealing the need for some kind of external constraint on our thoughts and beliefs. In a way, empiricist foundationalism respects this demand. Our experiences just come to us: we have no control over how things appear to us. Our beliefs, in so far as they are subject to experimental control, are subject to a kind of external constraint, with the

result that justification is more than dialectical. But is this constraint sufficiently 'external'? Looked at from another angle, it seems not. It seems too
subjective: not constraint by objects in the world but constraint by our experiences of objects (objects which, pending a refutation of Cartesian scepticism,
may not even exist). But setting this problem aside, let us see how far we can
get with the foundationalist's basic ideas.

There seems to be something right in the claim that we cannot be wrong
about how things appear to us. 'Looks' or 'appears' talk cannot be iterated. I
can say 'This tie looks green to me, but the light is a bit funny in here so
perhaps it is really blue'. But I can't say 'This tie looks as if it looks green to
me, but perhaps it really looks blue'. What would such a claim even mean?

While this is suggestive, we must go carefully. One reason why 'looks' talk
does not iterate might be that it is a *guarded* form of reporting on how things
are. I find myself inclined to report that the tie is green but, realizing that the
lighting is not ideal, I am reluctant to commit myself. I express this diffidence
by saying that the tie looks green, rather than that it definitely is green. Once I
have withheld commitment, there is no further guardedness for additional
'looks' talk to express, and so such talk cannot be iterated. To be sure, this is
not the last word on perceptual appearing. Still, it is clear that there is much
more to the foundationalist idea of basic knowledge than is obviously justified
by the logic of ordinary 'looks' talk.[2]

Against acquaintance

What, according to foundationalism, does empirical knowledge ultimately
rest on? Does it rest on beliefs or judgements about experience? Or does the
foundation of empirical knowledge consist in our experiences or sensations
themselves? Foundationalists have been tempted to say 'in a way, both'.
Experiential judgements are the most basic form of judgement; but their
epistemic status as absolutely non-inferential depends on a more fundamental
kind of awareness, below the judgemental level. Thus, I know that I have a
headache simply by having one; or I know that something looks red simply by
virtue of being in the appropriate state, a state in which redness is present in
my visual experience. In this spirit, Bertrand Russell wrote of 'knowledge by
acquaintance'.[3] For reasons we shall come to, this is more than a casual temptation: foundationalists are under strong theoretical pressure to take this line.

I remarked in Chapter 1 that our epistemological tradition has tended to
take propositional knowledge as its primary focus and to treat such knowledge
as theoretically fundamental. Now I have to enter a caveat. Philosophers like
Russell, who see empirical knowledge as resting on knowledge by acquaintance, think that even the most rock-bottom propositional knowledge rests on
something more basic still.

What are we acquainted with? Typically, foundationalists take experience to involve the 'immediate' presence to consciousness of a special kind of mental particular: a sensation or sense impression. Such things are immediately present or 'given' in the sense that we know about them simply by having them. To stress this feature, the particulars we 'sense', the objects of acquaintance, have often been called 'sense-data', though this terminology is no longer as popular as once it was. The point of saying that the sensing of sense-data involves 'immediate' presence to consciousness is that this form of awareness is not mediated by any kind of representation, including the sort of conceptual representation involved in linguistically articulated thought. The reason for insisting on such absolute immediacy is that representation seems always to involve the possibility of misrepresentation. But our awareness of our own thoughts and sensations is supposed to be error-proof; for it is by being error-proof that it underwrites the non-inferential judgements that occur at the next level up.

This approach to the foundations of knowledge is fraught with difficulties. One problem stands out immediately: how could merely having experiences or sensing sense-data justify anything? However basic knowledge is understood, it must be capable of standing in logical relations to whatever judgements rest on it. For example, it must be capable of being consistent or inconsistent with them. But this means that even basic knowledge must involve propositional content and so cannot consist in a mere relation to a particular. Sensing a sense-datum is no more knowing anything than is standing next to a lamp-post. For this reason, some philosophers reject the idea that experience—if experiencing is sharply distinguished from judging or believing—can justify anything.[4]

We may baulk at this: surely experience makes an essential contribution to our knowing about the world around us. No doubt it does, in some sense. But if we are to treat experience as the foundation of knowledge, experience must itself be understood to involve propositional content: the sort of content expressed by complete sentences. We cannot understand experience in terms of the mere presence of a particular, even a mental particular, and hold on to the idea that experience constitutes a form of knowledge, capable of playing a justificatory role. This does not mean that, in experiencing the world, we are always muttering sentences under our breath. It does mean, however, that the content of experience, if it is to have any epistemological significance, must be propositional in form. This amounts to rejecting any sharp distinction between experiencing and judging or believing.

Foundationalists have tended to vacillate on this point. Many foundationalists have contrasted the givenness of experiences or sense-data with any kind of judgement. Russell's 'acquaintance' is supposed to be a direct relation to a sense-datum, conceived as a sensory particular: for example, a red patch in one's visual field. This account of experience gains an air of intelligibility from its analogy with ordinary talk about acquaintance with people and places:

knowing the Prime Minister, knowing Manhattan, and so on. But the analogy
is superficial. Russellian knowledge by acquaintance is supposed to be prior
to—thus independent of—all propositional knowledge, which Russell refers
to as 'knowledge by description'. Knowing people and places is nothing
like that. It is impossible to 'know Manhattan' without knowing anything
whatsoever *about* Manhattan.

Acquaintance with sense-data is supposed to be a form of non-
propositional knowledge. This is what I claim we cannot understand: how
something can be non-propositional and yet knowledge. Knowledge provides
evidence, grounds for further inferences. But only that which can be true or
false—thus prepositionally contentful—can confirm or refute. Under pressure, Russell tends to write of our being acquainted with sense-data *as* red,
square, or whatever. But how is this different from being aware *that* something
in one's visual field is (or appears) red or square? It looks like an attempt to
have things both ways.

There are, of course, ways in which the richness and complexity of perceptual experience exceeds our capacity for precise verbal expression. Some
philosophers regard this as a decisive reason for crediting experience with
non-conceptual content (perceptual content, say), just as Russell urges. But we
should not make too much of our verbal limitations. True, we can discrimin-
ate many more shades of colour that most of us remember the names for. But
even here, we are aware that the precise shade of blue in the curtains is
different from that in the carpet. The main point stands: only where there is
propositionally articulable content can there be relations of justification.[5]

Someone might object that this argument assumes an excessively 'intellectualist' conception of justification, according to which justification is
entirely dependent on logical relations among propositions (or the propositional contents of beliefs and other mental states). But there are other ways
in which experiences might be relevant to justification: for example, they may
serve (causally) as reliable guides to our environment, so that the policy of
relying on them (except where there is reason to think that appearances are
deceptive) is justified by its consequences (and not by any intrinsic feature of
the experiences themselves).

I have a lot of sympathy with this line of thought. But it is no defence of
traditional foundationalism, which itself takes an 'intellectualist' conception
of justification for granted. Challenging that conception will lead us
eventually to epistemological views profoundly at variance with traditional
foundationalist ideas.[6]

The ambiguity of 'experience'

The idea of non-propositional knowledge represents a reaction to a deep
tension in empiricist foundationalism, a tension clearly identified by Wilfrid

Sellars. According to Sellars, the classical empiricist conception of 'experience' conflates two ideas:

(1) The idea that there are certain inner episodes—e.g. sensations of red or of $C^\#$ which can occur to human beings (and brutes) without any prior process of learning or concept formation; and without which it would in some sense be impossible to see, for example, that the facing surface of a physical object is red and triangular; or hear that a certain physical sound is $C^\#$.

(2) The idea that there are certain inner episodes which are the non-inferential knowings that certain items are, for example, red or $C^\#$, and that these episodes are the necessary conditions of empirical knowledge as providing the evidence for all other empirical propositions.[7]

The first idea concerns the sort of 'awareness' or 'experience' that we enjoy simply in virtue of being conscious or 'sentient' beings. The second idea concerns the sort of awareness that is involved in knowledge properly so-called: the sort of knowledge that involves the ability to make propositionally articulable claims. Robert Brandom calls the two types of awareness 'sentience' and 'sapience'.[8] So in Brandom's terms, the traditional empiricist conception of experience as the foundation of knowledge involves a mistaken attempt to reduce sapience to mere sentience.

Talk of sensing sense-data is derived from familiar talk about sensations: headaches, tickles, itches, and so on, the kind of awareness or consciousness we share with animals and prelinguistic infants. The capacity for experience in this sense, the sense captured by the first idea, is indeed primitive, unacquired. However, the sort of knowing involved in the second idea is not plausibly regarded as primitive in this way. Knowing that x is F—for example, that there is something red and triangular in my visual field—requires familiarity with systems of classification, systems that bring 'particulars' under 'universals'. It therefore depends on training in the use of such systems, training that results in our knowing where the boundaries of various descriptive categories lie. It depends on learning a language.

If we want to think of conceptual abilities as independent of the social process of language learning, we must think that such abilities—at least those relating to basic observable facts—are innate. This is something that empiricists have been reluctant to claim. However, this reluctance threatens them with self-contradiction. Sensing a sense-datum, call it 's', is supposed to be sufficient for one's non-inferentially knowing that s is (say) red. But while the ability to sense sense-data is supposed to be unacquired, the ability to know facts like 's is red', which presupposes conceptual mastery, is not.

To say that merely having sensations is not sufficient for knowledge is not to say that it is irrelevant. Experiences can certainly be involved in *causal* relations to beliefs and judgements, as when my having a certain visual experience causes me to exclaim 'How blue the sky is today'. But causal relations are not what the foundationalist needs. A foundationalist can allow that causal explanation is sometimes epistemically relevant, in that it can excuse me from charges of epistemic irresponsibility. If I hold certain strange beliefs as the result of a brutal regime of indoctrination or brainwashing, I will not be held epistemically accountable in the usual way. But no foundationalist can allow that a purely causal explanation of my holding a belief is sufficient to justify it, on pain of undermining the case for manifestly credible basic beliefs. If causal relations were sufficient for justification, there would be no need to detour through experience. We could say that we have basic, non-inferential knowledge when we stand in appropriate causal relations to objects or events in our external surroundings. This is what contemporary externalists do say. Foundationalists appeal to experience because they want experience to involve a kind of knowledge. However, what they give with one hand they take away with the other by treating that knowledge as 'non-propositional'.

This is not surprising. Propositional content involves conceptual or descriptive content, and description is inseparable from the possibility of misdescription. It seems, then, that propositional content is inseparable from the possibility of error. If this is so, no judgement, however modest, is absolutely indubitable. So if basic experiential knowledge has to be indubitable, there is no such knowledge.

This is another reason why foundationalists have been attracted to the idea of non-propositional knowledge. In thinking of relations like acquaintance as absolutely 'direct' or 'unmediated', philosophers like Russell mean to exclude even the 'mediation' involved in bringing an object under a concept: that is, describing it or thinking of it in some definite way. But this very tactic embodies a tacit recognition that descriptions can apply or not. It is true that by eschewing all description, we avoid the possibility of getting things wrong, but only because we also give up the possibility of getting them right. If you refuse to play the game, you can't lose. But you can't win either.

The content problem

We have been led to what we may call 'the content problem'. The problem is to show how basic beliefs can be indubitable without losing all content, thus ceasing to be beliefs. In my view, it is insoluble.

Basic judgements must be synthetic—answering to contingent facts—yet indubitable. Many attempts to explain how this is possible employ the idea that basic judgements involve a strongly demonstrative element. Thus the content of a typical basic experiential belief would be something like '*This* is (or appears) red *now*'. In thinking 'This', we engage in a kind of 'mental pointing', a deliberate focusing of attention on some aspect of our current experience.[9] Such judgements, while not analytic, are *like* analytic judgements in that anyone who has mastered the rules for the use of demonstratives and elementary descriptive terms, and who uses those terms in a fully mindful way, cannot judge mistakenly. The only sort of mistake that can be made is a slip of the tongue, or its mental equivalent, thus a 'verbal' not a 'factual' error. Considered misjudgement is impossible.[10]

Behind this account of basic knowledge lies a certain picture of meaning and understanding. In this picture, two sorts of rules or 'definitions' determine the conceptual abilities that go with understanding a language. Some words get their meaning by *discursive* definitions: definitions that link words with other words. Such definitions state analytic truths, such as 'A bachelor is an unmarried male'. But not all words can get their meanings this way. Some meanings must be established by *ostensive* definitions, which set up rules or conventions linking words with extra-linguistic reality. Ostensive definitions apply first and foremost to objects and qualities that we can grasp directly in experience: we learn what things are properly called 'red' by being presented with examples. Of course, the redness in question must be 'phenomenal' or 'experiential': the highest common factor redness that is present to consciousness when something looks red, whether or not it really is red. With this restriction in place, it is clear that one cannot understand a term like 'red', the meaning of which is fixed by direct correlation with something consciously present, and make mistakes when mindfully applying it in basic demonstrative judgements.

We have gone right back to the doctrine of acquaintance. The model of meaning and understanding just presented postulates a kind of grasping of red things as red that is prior to any mastery of linguistic or conceptual systems of classification. The possibility of empirical knowledge depends on there being what Sellars calls 'self-authenticating, non-verbal episodes'. It is questionable whether we even understand this idea.

Still, assume that we do, to some extent. The fact remains that basic demonstrative judgements are not purely demonstrative, but contain a descriptive term, and this threatens to leave the content problem untouched. Foundationalists emphasize the demonstrative element in basic judgements because they want to tie basic knowledge to an immediate knowledge of present facts. They want to do this because they admit that, if a judgement has implications for what must obtain in other situations, it cannot be immune from error and cannot really be *intrinsically* credible. But description in and of itself carries such implications. In thinking of something as 'red', I am assimilating it to the class of objects that I would have thought of as red on other occasions. Foundationalists meet this objection by postulating a 'non-comparative' or 'purely phenomenological' use of terms like 'red'.[11] However, if this use is absolutely non-comparative—devoid of all implications for further applications of the concept—how does 'This is red' differ from 'This is this'? Once more, we have lost all empirical content.

Here we come to the heart of the content problem. The foundationalist's basic judgements have to be 'stand alone' judgements in a very strong sense: judgements that we could entertain, and which would amount to knowledge, without our knowing or even believing anything else. This is what genuinely *first* principles have to be like, and it is this conception of 'first principles' for which Sellars coined the pejorative description 'the Myth of the Given'. The key point is that the foundationalist's epistemic atomism commits him to a kind of semantic atomism: an atomism about meaning and understanding. The difficulty is to see how any judgement could be wrenched out of all inferential connections to further judgements and retain any content at all.

The reliability problem

The quest for certainty forces foundationalists to make their candidates for basic judgements ever more modest in content. But so long as content persists, the possibility of error remains. Eventually, the temptation arises to eliminate propositional content altogether. The price of giving in to this temptation is epistemic irrelevance.

Perhaps the demand for strict indubitability is too strong. Maybe foundational beliefs can be epistemically privileged without being strictly indubitable. One suggestion is to distinguish more precisely between indubitability and incorrigibility. Incorrigible beliefs, we might say, could in principle be false, though we could never be in a position to correct them. This is still a striking epistemological asymmetry: incorrigible beliefs serve as the touchstone for accepting or rejecting other beliefs while remaining themselves immune to correction.

This won't work. If we can go wrong in our basic judgements, how can our errors systematically fail to create problems in our inferential superstructure? If incorrigibility is supposed to be different from absolute indubitability, the difference ought to make a difference. But if errors at the basic level have consequences higher up, why shouldn't they be retrospectively detectable? It is not clear that there is a workable notion of incorrigibility, distinct from strict indubitability.

If we abandon incorrigibility, we begin to drift away from foundationalism towards a coherentist model of justification. In retrospective self-correction, we are trading off our basic against our non-basic beliefs, trying to find an optimum balance. This kind of mutual adjustment is central to the coherence theory's account of empirical justification. This suggests that it is difficult to give up the requirement of strict indubitability for basic beliefs while remaining faithful to foundationalism.

It may not be impossible. According to 'modest foundationalists', the intrinsic credibility attaching to basic beliefs only amounts to *prima facie* justification, which may be inferentially overridden in the context of a developed belief-system. A basic belief is thus always justified unless there is some special reason to suspect that it might be false. This is all we need to block the regress of justification; and it spares us the need to defend an impossible ideal of empirical certainty.

Modest foundationalism offers an attractive prospect, but will it really work? The *prima facie* credibility of basic beliefs is still supposed to be intrinsic. So it must somehow belong to the nature of basic beliefs, however picked out, to be right most of the time. If they are no more likely to be correct than any other beliefs, we lose the basic/non-basic distinction altogether. The question is, what sort of truth is it—necessary or contingent—that beliefs with the defining feature of basic beliefs are more likely to be right than wrong? This is the reliability problem.[12]

Since we are in search of foundations for empirical knowledge, some of our basic beliefs must be empirical. But it is hard to see how it could be a necessary truth that particular empirical beliefs are highly truth-reliable. On the other hand, if our reliability in certain matters is an empirical fact, the sceptic will want to know why we should accept it. As a general claim, he will say, it will need inductive support from particular observations. If these observations differ from the sort of observations whose credibility we are trying to explain, we will need to know why they should be trusted, reopening the regress of justification. If they are the same, we will simply be reasoning in a circle: assuming our reliability in certain matters to underwrite that very reliability. And if we say that it is just obvious that we are reliable reporters on our thoughts and sensations, the sceptic will point out that we are simply making an assumption. Agrippa's trilemma reasserts itself.

One reply is that the reliability problem assumes that the foundationalist is committed to a person's being able to justify the reliability of his basic beliefs. This might be resisted. Maybe it is enough that a person *be* reliable in certain matters. Maybe it is unreasonable to insist on his always being able to account for his reliability. In other words, a foundationalist might deny the K-K thesis, opting for an externalist approach to basic knowledge. This is the externalist version of foundationalism I mentioned at the beginning of this chapter.

From all that has been said, it should be clear that externalism can hold no appeal for a philosopher sensitive to the concerns of traditional foundationalism. It is not just that this kind of reliabilism obviates the need to give 'experience' a distinguished role in empirical knowledge. Rather, to explain non-inferential justification in terms of *de facto* reliability is to abandon altogether the foundationalist quest for a fixed class of intrinsically credible basic judgements. The boundaries of non-inferential knowledge would be fixed by what, as a matter of empirical fact, we find ourselves capable of being trained to respond to. An epistemology like this might contain an element of formal foundationalism, but it would not be substantively foundationalist. (I shall explain all this further in Chapter 15.)

I laid down three explanatory goals for a theory of justification: to give a coherent account of its basic ideas, explaining how they defeat the fatal trilemma; to show how the theory allows for a workably extensive system of justified belief; and to show how knowledge is humanly possible. There is a strong case for thinking that foundationalism falls at the first hurdle.

Notes

1. This formulation is due to McDowell (1994).
2. Sellars (1997), 32 ff.
3. Russell (1969), 113.
4. Davidson (1986).
5. For an important recent discussion of the issues broached here, see McDowell (1994).
6. This objection is urged by Sosa (1980) in the context of responding to what he calls 'the Coherentist Critique of Foundationalism'. I agree with Sosa that coherentists have no business complaining about the intellectualist conception of justification: they are themselves fully committed to it.
7. Sellars (1997), 21–2. The following discussion is deeply indebted to Sellars. For more details on the Sellarsian attack on the appeal to the Given, see Williams (1999a).
8. Brandom (1994).
9. Pollock (1974), 74. A classic early statement of this view is by Schlick (1934).
10. In his essay 'Basic Propositions', in Ayer (1954), Ayer endorses the impossibility of mistake at the basic level. However, he changed his mind: see Ayer (1956), 61 ff.
11. See Chisholm (1982), 141 ff.
12. My argument here is much influenced by BonJour (1985), 30 ff.

9

Reduction and Inference

Out of the frying pan

Supposing that a foundationalist could solve the problem of security; could he solve the problem of adequacy? Could he retrieve a workable edifice of empirical knowledge?

The foundationalist picture of a hierarchy of broad classes of beliefs, ordered by general relations of epistemological priority, leads straight to a variety of underdetermination problems. In other words, foundationalism escapes Agrippan scepticism only at the cost of exposing us to various forms of Cartesian scepticism. The problem of adequacy is the problem of how to deal with scepticism in its Cartesian form.

Let us focus on the problem of the external world. The Cartesian sceptic argues that, although knowledge of the world rests ultimately on experiential knowledge, there is no justifying inference—deductive or inductive— connecting what we know on the basis of experience alone with our beliefs about objective reality. This leaves the foundationalist three options. He can:

1. argue that knowledge of the external world is not necessarily inferential but can be 'direct' or immediate. This is the strategy of direct realism;
2. argue that further reflection reveals logical or conceptual links between experiential knowledge and beliefs about the external world. This is the approach of reductionism and the criterial theory;
3. argue that the sceptic underestimates the resources of inductive inference. This is the inductive approach.

We shall examine all three strategies.

Direct realism

In the form in which I am about to discuss it, direct realism does not take issue with the foundationalist picture of knowledge: it simply claims that the foundations can be set at a higher level than the sceptic allows.

It is obvious right away that, with respect to some Cartesian problems, this strategy is not even minimally plausible. Barring telepathy and precognition, the direct realist approach has no purchase on the problem of other minds or the problem of induction. Conceivably, we might claim that memory puts us in direct touch with the past, though this too has a whiff of the supernatural about it. And in any case, even granting personal memories the status of direct knowledge, we would still be left with an impossibly restricted basis for historical knowledge generally.

The direct realist's most promising theatre of operations is the problem of the external world. Obviously, he cannot plausibly claim absolute certainty for his basic beliefs: we do make mistakes. Still, we also think of ourselves as often 'just knowing' this or that about objects in our surroundings. I know that there is a computer screen in front of me because I can see that there is. It isn't a matter of inference. But in what sense isn't it a matter of inference?

Here we must bear in mind that, *as a version of substantive foundationalism*, direct realism is committed to the existence of non-inferential knowledge in a very strong sense of 'non-inferential'. The direct realist is not just saying that, in everyday situations, our opinions about what is going on around us are generally made off the cuff and accepted without special scrutiny. Rather, direct realism credits certain observational beliefs with intrinsic credibility. Such beliefs constitute foundational knowledge, knowledge that we could have on its own, in isolation from collateral knowledge of the world and our relations to it.

It is doubtful that we ever think of perceptual knowledge as absolutely non-inferential in this way. The problem is not just that we do not credit ourselves with unqualified reliability: our reasons for regarding ourselves as fallible matter crucially here. The extent to which we regard ourselves as trustworthy observers is determined by empirical considerations: it has nothing to do with intrinsic credibility, even if the credibility is only *prima facie*. We realize that we are more or less reliable, depending on a wide range of environmental and psychological conditions. We are good at taking in facts about familiar objects, relatively close to hand, in good light, when we are wide awake and not distracted . . . and so on. If the world were different, or we were different, our reliability as perceivers would be different. We might be better at spotting some things, worse at spotting others. Ordinary cases of 'just knowing' or 'just seeing' are embedded in an extensive body of collateral knowledge about the world and our place in it, not encapsulated in the way that foundationalism demands. (We shall see in Chapter 15 that this embedding is nevertheless compatible with the existence of observational knowledge that is genuinely non-inferential.)

Reductionism

The next possibility to explore is that there are logical links of some kind between privileged and problematic beliefs. According to reductionism, statements from the problematic class can be translated into logically complex statements from the privileged class. Thus, according to *phenomenalism*, talk about the physical world is really just shorthand for logically complex claims about sensory experiences: claims about the experiences we do or, in various conditions, would have.[1] External objects are, in this sense, 'logical constructions' out of sense-data, actual and possible. Precursors of modern phenomenalism include Berkeley, who identifies objects with collections of 'ideas', and J. S. Mill, who defines external objects as 'permanent possibilities of sensation'.

Like direct realism, reductionism is probably at its best in connection with the external world. With respect to the problem of other minds, the analogue of phenomenalism is logical behaviourism, the thesis that talk about someone else's thoughts and sensations is just a roundabout way of talking about behaviour and behavoural dispositions. However, it is difficult to believe that when I describe someone as being in great pain, *all* I mean is that he is disposed to groan or grimace and to quieten down when given an analgesic. Such behaviour is a symptom of pain, not the pain itself. Similarly with respect to the problem of the past. Surely, talk about the past is more than shorthand for talk about documentary and other evidence existing *in the present*.

These implausibilities notwithstanding, reductionist theories give voice to a powerful idea: the verificationist conception of meaning. On this view, meaning and understanding cannot be detached from verification in the way that the sceptic supposes. The sceptic wants to argue that the world could be wildly different from the way we normally take it to be, even though our experience, the ultimate basis of all empirical knowledge, remained unchanged. Accordingly, we can understand all sorts of stories about how the world might be but can never know how it really is. The phenomenalist replies that we only *think* we understand this suggestion. In fact, we have no clear conception of a 'reality' somehow 'behind' our experience. The world-as-we-experience-it— the world we can find out about—is the only world we can even conceive. The distinction between the objective and the merely apparent features of the world must be one that we draw within our experience. It cannot be a contrast between experience and an ineffable 'reality'.

O. K. Bouwsma once offered a cute variant on Descartes's tale of the Evil Deceiver. In his first attempt to deceive someone, call him 'John', the Deceiver turns the world (victim included) into paper. Naturally, John sees through the ruse: he makes crinkling noises when he moves, is highly inflammable, easily folded up, and so on. So the Deceiver embarks on a series of improvements, eventually getting to the point where the 'deception' is absolutely undetectable. But now where is the deception? What is John deceived *about*? In the world as he experiences it, everything remains the same; and what other world do we care about? What other world is there? What other world can we even imagine?[2]

It is easy to feel sympathy for philosophers who resist the sceptic's attempt to create an unbridgeable gulf between 'experience' and 'the world'. Nevertheless, reductionism expresses this resistance in the form of a bold theoretical programme that is impossible to carry through. It is not just that no one ever *has* reduced an external-object statement to a conjunction of experiential statements: no one *can*.

Laws of experience

The phenomenalist wants to treat external objects as logical constructions out of experiences. However, one of our most salient beliefs about external objects is that they exist independently of being perceived. The bookcases in my study do not cease to exist when I turn my attention to the computer screen. Indeed, there are countless things that no one will ever see.

The phenomenalist deals with this problem by claiming that translating an external-object statement into experiential (or 'sense-data') statements will involve liberal use of *conditionals*. I believe that my bookcases exist when I am not looking at them: what I mean by this is that *if I were* to turn around I *would* get the appropriate as-of-bookcases experiences.

The conditionals in question here are *subjunctive*. Unlike indicative conditionals, which say what follows if such and such *is* the case, subjunctive conditionals say what *would* be true if such and such a condition *were* to hold. In many cases, the relevant conditionals will be *counterfactual*: their antecedents will be false. My bookcases have continued to exist while I have been typing these words. During this time, I have *not* turned to look at them. But if I *had*, I would have enjoyed perceptual experiences of the relevant kind.

Subjunctive conditionals are connected with *natural laws*. When I say that the match would have lit had I struck it, I am relying on there being certain physical and chemical laws having to do with friction, heat, and combustion. Similarly, what the phenomenalist needs for his conditionals to work is that there be laws of experience. Since the phenomenalist wants to reduce *all* external-object talk to experience-talk, he needs *purely* experiential laws: lawlike regularities logically analogous to the laws of physics but concerning only relations between experiences, without reference to physical events.

No one has the faintest idea as to whether there are any such regularities. It is true that we think of experience as being regular and predictable; but what we mean by this is that we can predict the sort of experiences we will have *in particular physical and physiological conditions*. If I swivel round in my chair with my eyes open, if nothing falls on my head knocking me unconscious, and so on, then I know how things will appear to me: my bookcases will come into view. But these experiential regularities are object-dependent, whereas the phenomenalist needs object-independent regularities concerning experiences alone. The trouble is, such regularities are vulnerable to disruption by every

blink of the eye, turn of the head, lapse of attention, change in the environment, and so on indefinitely.[3]

Although this may not be a knock-down proof that no such regularities
exist, it is certain that they would be so complicated that no one knows, or
even could know, that there are any. We lack the ability to track experience at
the level of detail phenomenalism requires. If verifying an external-object
statement were dependent on verifying its phenomenalist translation, knowledge would be humanly impossible, even if the phenomenalist programme
were feasible in principle.

A second point is that the phenomenalist has not really followed through
on his promise to display a logical link between experiential evidence and
external-object statements. Given a phenomenalist translation, the simplest
particular claim about an external object implies various *general* claims about
experience. At most, phenomenalism would reduce the problem of the
external world to the problem of induction. This would not be a negligible
achievement. But it would not be a complete answer to scepticism either.

Semantic mass

Is the phenomenalist programme of sentence-by-sentence translation of
external-object claims into experiential equivalents feasible even in principle?
It seems not. The problem is that single external-object statements do not
have *any* experiential consequences. By itself, the existence of my bookshelves
implies nothing about my experience, *unless further facts concerning the
external world are taken for granted.*

In committing myself to the unperceived existence of my bookshelves, I
commit myself to supposing that, if I were to swivel round in my chair, I
would enjoy such and such experiences. Of course, this conditional won't do,
since this talk about swivelling round involves unreduced reference to events
and objects in the external world. The problem for the phenomenalist is that
such reference is ineliminable. If it is night and there is a sudden blackout, I
won't get the usual experiences; if as I swivel the roof falls in and knocks me
unconscious, I won't enjoy any experiences at all, except perhaps briefly seeing
stars. If someone has slipped a hallucinogen into my coffee, my bookshelves
may appear to melt: *and so on indefinitely*. No external-object statement, *taken
alone*, has any particular experiential implications.

This problem is not unique to phenomenalism. Consider logical behaviourism. According to a logical behaviourist, talk about mental states is roundabout talk about behaviour. Not only actual behaviour: just as external objects
can exist unperceived, mental states can exist without being acted upon. You
believe that it is going to rain this morning. This belief *might* show itself by
your remembering to take an umbrella when you go out. But of course, you
might stay home, so that you get no chance to express your belief in action.

Like the phenomenalist, then, the logical behaviourist has recourse to subjunctive conditionals. He analyses mental states in terms of behavioural dispositions: what you *would* do if appropriate circumstances *were* to present themselves.

This leaves him with the same problem: an ascription of a particular mental state does not appear to have any behavioural consequences, not even dispositional consequences. You believe that it will rain this morning: does this mean that if you were to go out you would take your umbrella? Yes: if you care about not getting wet, if you intend to walk rather than drive, if you are not in such a hurry that you forget, and so on . . . There is no prospect of appealing to such dispositions to effect a reduction of the mental to the behavioural, since the relevant behavioural dispositions associated with a given mental state are themselves conditional on further mental states.

Once more, foundationalism is frustrated by its epistemic and semantic atomism. For the foundationalist, knowledge rests on encapsulated items of basic perceptual knowledge. Accordingly, if the link with non-basic knowledge is reductive, the reduction must be carried out on a sentence-by-sentence basis, and this is what cannot be done. While many beliefs indeed depend for their justification on confirmation by experience, they have no experiential consequences they can call their own. They have definite experiential consequences only as members of groups of beliefs with critical semantic mass, and even then only subject to vague *ceteris paribus* qualifications. Sentence-by-sentence translation into basic experiential statements is a non-starter.

The criterial theory

The 'criterial' view is less ambitious than strict reductionism. It holds that it belongs to the 'logic' of physical-object statements to be responsive to experiential criteria. In other words, it belongs to the meaning of a physical-object statement that certain experiences count for or against it. Similarly, it belongs to the logic of statements about the inner life of another person that certain outward expressions constitute good evidence for the ascription of particular states. Without such public criteria, we would not even be able to think of other people—and perhaps not even ourselves—as having an inner life.[4]

The criterial theory respects the fundamental idea behind reductionism: that understanding a claim is importantly connected with grasping what counts for or against it. But it avoids the impossible task of showing how full-scale translations of, say, physical-object into experiential statements might proceed. And it has the added advantage of not committing us to thinking that, in speaking of someone's inner life, we are *only* talking in a roundabout way about his outward behaviour. There must be some truth in this. Nevertheless, *as a defence of foundationalism*, the criterial view is a failure.

We are invited to suppose that it is analytically or conceptually true that certain experiences give me good reason to think that there are two bookcases in my study. At the very least, this must mean that having such experiences is a reliable indicator of the presence of bookcases. But just as no single statement about objects in the external world strictly entails that I would have such and such experiences if such and such conditions were to obtain, no single statement entails anything about what experiences are reliable indicators of its truth. At most, we can say that such relations of reliable indication hold 'other things being equal' or 'in normal conditions'. But since these qualifiers point to an indefinite range of further empirical presuppositions, this shows that no analytic evidential connections hold between any single statement about an external object and any definite body of experiential knowledge. The holistic character of the relation between worldly and experiential commitments is as much a problem for the criterial theory as it is for strict reductionism.

Are there analytic truths?

Reductionism and the criterial theory lean heavily on the notion of analytic or conceptual truth. I have been arguing that the connections postulated by these approaches between experiential evidence and statements about the world are not plausibly viewed as analytic. But an even more fundamental problem is that the analytic–synthetic distinction is dubious in itself.

Suspicion of the analytic–synthetic distinction is much associated with Quine.[5] Quine's point is not just that the distinction is vague, like the red–orange distinction, but that it should be rejected altogether. In Quine's eyes, the analytic–synthetic distinction reflects false theoretical views about meaning, just as the witch/non-witch distinction reflects false views about supernatural powers. The fact that adepts of such views think that they can recognize cases is neither here nor there. Nobody is really a witch; and no statement is really analytic.

One reason for being suspicious of the analytic–synthetic distinction is that it depends on an obscure notion of absolute synonymy. It is supposedly a hallmark of analytic truths that their denials are self-contradictory. However, the self-contradiction is not explicitly logical. Compare the tautological sentence 'All male siblings are male siblings' with the allegedly analytic sentence 'All brothers are male siblings'. Denying the first results in the formally self-contradictory claim 'Some male siblings are not male siblings'. But denying the second yields only 'Some brothers are not male siblings'. To be sure, we can turn this latter sentence into an explicit contradiction by substituting 'male siblings' for 'brothers'. The justification for the substitution is that 'brother' and 'male sibling' have 'the same meaning'. But do they? *Alle menschen wirden bruder*: all men will be brothers, though presumably not male siblings. The reply will be that Schiller is not using 'brother' in the 'literal' sense. But what sense is that? The sense that makes 'Brothers are male siblings' analytic? We are not getting anywhere.

The notion of synonymy needed to explain the analytic–synthetic distinction is not the everyday notion of 'having the same meaning'. That notion is highly contextual and interest-relative. No one denies that *for certain purposes* (legal proceedings involving a disputed will, say) 'brother' can be *treated* as meaning 'male sibling'. But 'brother' stands in complex relations to other words: there are blood brothers, lay brothers, brothers in arms, and brothers under the skin. Prescinding from all purposes and interests, there is no way of deciding when words 'mean the same thing'. Here we see another instance of foundationalism's stake in encapsulated 'meanings'.

Analytic truths are often explained as 'true by definition'. However, the notion of definition is as context-sensitive and interest-relative as that of sameness of meaning. For expository purposes, a scientific theory can be sorted out into definitions and empirical postulates; but if the theory runs into trouble, modifications can be made anywhere. Moreover, this kind of sorting into definitional and empirical elements can be done for theories that are comprehensively false (like witch-theory), so being 'analytic-in-a-theory' does not mean being analytically true. Being designated a 'definition' confers no privileged epistemological status, no immunity from revision. Yet explaining epistemic privilege is the main reason for accepting the analytic–synthetic distinction in the first place.

It is no accident that the examples used to introduce the analytic–synthetic distinction often involve quasi-legal terms like 'bachelor' or 'brother', for which it is at least *prima facie* plausible that there is a single criterion of applicability. Even here, as we just saw, it is doubtful that matters are so simple. But for other terms, particularly natural kind terms like 'gold', the idea of definitionally fixed meanings is not even *prima facie* plausible. Natural kind terms involve 'law-cluster' concepts: we identify gold by a cluster of physical and chemical characteristics, none of which is absolutely essential. Maybe we will rethink the periodic table so radically that we no longer count gold as a metal.

I do not deny that the analytic–synthetic distinction has a certain *prima facie* plausibility. It does seem that certain proposition are 'meaning-constituting' in the sense that, if anyone denied them, it would be doubtful that he understood them. If you understand what it means to say that $2 + 2 = 4$, you see that it is true. To say of such a proposition, 'I know what it means, it just doesn't seem very plausible to me', would be (at best) a bad joke. Our acceptance of this and other elementary propositions fixes what we mean by '2', '4', and ' + '. In this way, it is claimed, truth-by-virtue-of-meaning explains *a priori* knowledge.

Quine denies that there is any principled way of sorting things we accept into those that are 'meaning-constituting' and those that are empirical. To be sure, if someone denies something crashingly obvious, there will always be a question of whether he understands what he is saying. But this provides no reason for supposing that some propositions are true by virtue of meaning alone. Furthermore, even if we agreed on which propositions are (in a common-sense way) meaning-constituting, we would still not have an explanation of *a priori* knowledge because, as already remarked, there is no automatic connection between a proposition's being meaning-constituting— 'analytic-in-a-theory'—and its being true. After all, we can understand theories that we know to be false. So while, if we like, we can say that part of what we mean by 'phlogiston' is that it is a substance released by combustion, our commitment to such meaning-constituting claims about phlogiston remains merely conditional. If there is such a substance as phlogiston, it is released during combustion; but since there is no such thing, it is false that phlogiston is released during combustion. We can understand 'phlogiston' without supposing that any claims belonging to the phlogiston theory of combustion are true.[6]

Quine is right about scientific concepts like phlogiston. Postulates governing their use can be meaning-constituting and nevertheless not true. *A fortiori*, they are not true by virtue of meaning alone. But what about logic and mathematics? Quine would say that, since logic and mathematics are both used in science, they too are in principle open to revision. All that matters is getting a theory that is optimal with respect to empirical adequacy and theoretical simplicity. In this sense, even logic is responsive to empirical considerations. It has been suggested that, in quantum mechanics, a revised logic might be part of the best overall theory. Of course, this suggestion may prove unfruitful. But then again, it may not. Not even logic is unrevisable in principle.

Suppose that we did revise logic in the interests of improving quantum theory: would we have to give up using classical logic in non-scientific contexts, such as courts of law? Surely not. Noting this, Paul Horwich suggests that we might end up with two logics: an *a priori* logic involving our familiar concepts of 'not', 'or', and so on, and an *a posteriori* logic involving technical variants of familiar logical notions.[7] However, there is another way to look at the situation: that theories do not have to be unqualifiedly true to be practically preferable in many (or most) contexts. Geocentric astronomy is good enough for navigation, Euclidean geometry for surveying, and Newtonian physics for aiming rockets at the moon. Everyday indispensability does not distinguish logic from more obviously empirical theories.

The doctrine of analytic truth and the doctrine of acquaintance are part of the same theoretical package. Foundationalist empiricism recognizes two source of meaning: some terms derive their meanings ostensively, by correlation with whatever is 'directly presented' in experience. Given this stratum of primitive, encapsulated meanings, other terms can be introduced. This may be by explicit term-by-term definitions; or it may be by rules for the use of whole sentences, rules that thus implicitly define the terms that these sentences contain. As 'purely conventional', such definitions and rules are true in virtue of meaning alone, hence knowable *a priori*. We have just seen that the second component in this package—analyticity—is in no better shape than the first.

Induction and explanation

We come finally to the inductive approach. Anyone who adopts this approach will concede to the sceptic that simple induction is no help with the problems in hand. But there are more sophisticated forms of inductive inference, notably what is sometimes called 'inference to the best explanation'. On this view, inductive inference is not a matter of reading off hypotheses from observational data. Rather, given a range of data to explain, we formulate various hypotheses, selecting the best in the light of various epistemic desiderata: for example, empirical adequacy and theoretical elegance.[8]

So conceived, inductive justification is far from algorithmic. If competing theories perform well with respect to different criteria, it can be difficult to pick a winner. Sometimes we have to choose between empirical and theoretical virtues: a clumsy and complicated theory may fit the data better than a simple and elegant one. In such a case, we might even go with the less empirically adequate theory, trusting that its empirical performance can be improved over time. But a choice can be justified without being uniquely justifiable.

That inductive inference is not always inference to a uniquely best explanation does not mean that there are no cases in which clear winners emerge; and it is clear that our ordinary ways of understanding the world are far better than the sceptic's trumped-up alternatives. At best, sceptical hypotheses cover the same experiential data. They have no predictive superiority and are vastly inferior theoretically. Even if logically coherent, Descartes's Deceiver hypothesis is thin and underdescribed, compared with our usual account of how experience arises. (Why does he do it, and how?) It is a worse explanation and may be justifiably dismissed.

There is something in this: sceptical hypotheses *are* thin and underdescribed. Moreover, this kind of inductive approach avoids commitment to sentence-by-sentence evidential connections. In adopting the 'hypothesis' of an external world, we are elaborating a whole theory with respect to the course of experience. There is no reason to expect individual statements in the theory to have specific experiential consequences.

These advantages notwithstanding, the inductive approach, as a defence of foundationalism, shares deep theoretical commitments with its rivals. To see this, we need only ask what the 'hypothesis' of the external world is supposed to explain. The answer, which goes back to Hume, is the *coherence* of our experience. Our experience is not a phantasmagoria, but displays predictable patterns. This is what makes it justifiable to trace experience to our causal interactions with an external world of persisting objects. But this takes us back to square one. The coherence of experience is just its conformity to purely experiential laws. In the relevant sense of 'coherent', no one has the slightest idea whether experience is coherent or not.

Someone might reply that this objection misunderstands inference to the best explanation. In particular, the objection takes for granted an impossibly rigid distinction between observation and theory. In science, observations are not any random facts that investigators happen to have registered. Observations are selected on the basis of theoretical commitments, which means that other facts may be rejected as irrelevant. It used to be thought necessary to explain the exact number of the planets and not just their motions, but after Newton this idea was abandoned. More than this, observations often cannot be made at all unless a certain theoretical orientation tells us how and where to look. For centuries, astronomers puzzled over various irregularities in the behaviour of the planets or 'wandering stars'. But irregularities only count as such given background expectations as to what 'regular' behaviour would consist in. In these and other ways, observation is 'theory laden'. Maybe the same is true with respect to the coherence of experience: we need to think in terms of an objective world in order to appreciate the ways in which experience is stable and regular.

In considering this sophisticated defence of the inductive approach, we must remember the current context of our discussion, which is foundationalism. The whole point of foundationalism is to insist on the absolutely basic character of experiential knowledge. From a foundationalist standpoint, it must at least be possible to identify the facts that the external world 'hypothesis' is supposed to explain independently of adopting the hypothesis. Once we treat our belief in an external world and the recognition of certain regularities in experience as part of a single explanatory package—each component gaining credibility from the other—we have abandoned foundationalism in favour of some form of coherence theory.

Can the coherentist approach succeed where foundationalism fails? That is our next question.

Notes

1. Ayer was one of phenomenalism's best-known and most faithful advocates, although he spent much of his career modifying and weakening his phenomenalist commitments. See 'Phenomenalism', in Ayer (1954), and Ayer (1956), 118–32.
2. 'Descartes' Evil Genius', in Bouwsma (1969).
3. My critical line is inspired by Sellars's essay 'Phenomenalism', in Sellars (1963).
4. See e.g. Pollock (1967). The 'descriptivism' defended in Ayer (1956) strikes me as a related view. The appeal to criteria is closely associated with certain followers of

Wittgenstein, though there is much controversy over what Wittgenstein had in mind. For an argument to the effect that Wittgenstein did not embrace what I here call a criterial epistemology, see John McDowell, 'Criteria, Defeasibility and Knowledge', in McDowell (1998).

5. 'Two Dogmas of Empiricism', in Quine (1961). The analytic–synthetic distinction is the first dogma, reductionism the second. An important reply to Quine is Grice and Strawson (1956). Harman (1969) is still the best exposition of Quine's views about meaning. For recent defences of ideas closely related to the classic logical empiricist approach to analyticity and *a priori* knowledge, see Peacocke (1993) and Boghossian (1996). Peacocke and Boghossian are critically discussed in Horwich (1998*a*), ch. 6.

6. See Horwich (1998*a*) for the best recent discussion of this and related points.

7. Ibid. 146 n.

8. On inference to the best explanation, see Harman (1973), ch. 10. These ideas about inductive inference are applied to Cartesian scepticism in Vogel (1990).

10

Coherence

Radical holism

Whereas foundationalist theories of justification are *atomistic*, coherence theories are *holistic*. For the coherence theorist, there is not question of a belief's being justified all by itself, as the foundationalist's basic beliefs are supposed to be. To be justified, a belief must fit into a justified system; and the system is more or less justified depending on how well it 'hangs together' *considered as a whole*.[1] This reference to whole systems is crucial. Coherence theories do not claim merely that the epistemic significance of a given belief must always be assessed in the context of some further commitments. Rather, they insist that the justification of individual beliefs depends on certain properties of total belief-systems. Coherence theories are *radically* holistic.[2]

The difference between foundationalism and the coherence theory is sometimes explained in terms of two competing models of justifying inference. The foundationalist conceives justifying inference on a *linear* model, in which justification proceeds from given 'premises' to 'conclusions' by justification-transmitting rules. The coherence theorist's holistic model of justification is decidedly *non-linear*. While the beliefs that comprise a given system will be logically interconnected in various ways, these connections are not in themselves relations of justification. Rather, the density of such interconnections contributes to the coherence of the system. Justification, which depends on coherence, is primarily a property of the whole system. Individual beliefs are justified derivatively in virtue of belonging to a coherent total view.

The coherence theory's radical holism can be obscured by a tendency for coherence theorists to think of 'coherence' in two ways. Sometimes a belief is said to be justified if it fits in—*coheres with*—a suitable background system. Since, in this sense, a foundationalist insists on a justified belief's cohering with the relevant set of basic beliefs, this *relational* coherence does not distinguish the coherence theory from foundationalism. The coherence theory's distinctiveness arises from tracing the epistemic status of the background system to the way the entire system fits together. This *systematic* coherence implies radical holism.

Because they are radically holistic, coherence theories reject even formal foundationalism. This seems to create tension with the phenomenology of justification. Ordinarily, disputes are resolved by finding evidence that is acceptable to all parties, not by assessing anyone's total system of beliefs.

The coherence theorist has a reply to this: ordinary justification, which involves bringing *specific* evidence to bear on a *specific* disputed claim, is *local* rather than *global*. However, specific evidence is only the tip of the iceberg. When such evidence is found credible and relevant, this is always in virtue of a shared system of background beliefs. Usually, as its name suggests, the background system operates tacitly and, in matters of local justification, is simply assumed to be in order. However, when a dispute proves intractable, we may need to make some aspects of the background system explicit, so as to locate the source of the disagreement. More important still, if we are to cope with scepticism, we cannot rest content with a mere assumption that our beliefs at large are justified. The coherence theorist's task is thus to explain what it is for our submerged system to be 'in order', to explain the global justification that local justification takes for granted.

Objections

A recurrent criticism of holistic approaches to justification is that they allow any belief, no matter how absurd, to be 'justified' by surrounding it with suitable supporting beliefs. These can be as absurd as the original belief, for all that matters is that the beliefs in the system support *each other*. Accordingly, there is no distinction between a 'reasonable' belief-system and the delusions of a logically adept paranoid. As one critic famously puts it, a coherence theorist 'must consider arbitrary fairy stories to be as true as a historical report, or as statements in a textbook of chemistry, provided the story is constructed in such a way that no contradiction ever arises'. But since we can 'arrive at any number of consistent systems of statements which are incompatible with one another', the coherence theory 'fails altogether to give an unambiguous criterion of truth' and is therefore 'logically impossible'.[3]

Not everyone will see this line of thought as an objection. It can just as easily be taken as an argument for relativism. Once we abandon foundationalism, the argument will go, we must admit that there is no *external* standard by which to evaluate different belief-systems. If there are different ways of viewing the world, each of which hangs together internally, there are no grounds for saying that one is more justified, or even more true, than another. But while a vaguely coherentist epistemology sometimes lies behind relativism, whether the coherence theory as such is committed to relativism is another question. Most of its philosophical defenders deny that it is.

The charge of 'logical impossibility' depends on framing the objection in terms of truth. However, contemporary coherence theorists respond that they are advancing a theory of justification, not truth. Truth is not a matter of degree: either the cat is on the mat or it isn't. But my belief as to the animal's whereabouts may be more or less justified. So while incompatible views can't all be true, there can be circumstances in which they are more or less equally justified. No theory of justification is committed to giving a criterion that is 'unambiguous' in the sense of always picking a winner.

To be sure, some theorists hold that truth, as well as justification, should be explained in coherentist terms. But they do not identify truth with whatever degree of coherence is present in a person's current system of beliefs. Rather, they explain truth in terms of *ideal* coherence or coherence at the limit of inquiry. It is not so obvious that this fails to yield an 'unambiguous' criterion.

While well taken, these points do not dispose of the difficulty. Since the aim of a theory of justification is to articulate constraints on what we can justifiably or rationally believe, no such theory can allow a person to be justified in believing anything whatsoever. Even if there is not always a unique best system, some systems must be better than others. Failing this, there will be no defence against sceptical hypotheses involving Evil Deceivers or brains-in-vats. The worry behind the argument from fairy stories is that the coherence theory cannot satisfy even this minimal requirement.

On closer inspection, the argument resolves itself into at least two objections. The first is that, since coherence reduces in the end to logical consistency, and since there is no limit to the number of consistent systems of statements, there is no limit to the number of 'justified' systems. Call this the 'many systems' objection. The second is suggested by the contrast between science and fairy stories. In what sense are the latter 'arbitrary' while the former are not? The answer, surely, is that fairy stories are *simply* made up. By contrast, scientific views, even if they originate in wild flights of fancy, stand or fall with *empirical evidence*: facts about the world, ascertained by observation. The coherence theory, because it makes justification supervene exclusively on belief–belief relations, fails to allow for empirical constraint: constraint *by the world*. Call this the 'isolation objection'. Exploring these objections will give us a clearer view of how the coherence theory is supposed to work.

Coherence and explanation

With respect to the many systems objection, an obvious first move is to reject its identification of coherence with mere logical consistency. Thus coherence theorists often claim that coherence is more than 'absence of conflict' between beliefs: it also involves 'positive connections'. These connections may include logical entailments but also, perhaps, relations of inductive confirmation, weaker than strict entailment but stronger than consistency. To indicate this kind of epistemological connectedness, coherence theorists often speak of our system of beliefs being held together by 'inferential connections' between its elements. But many theorists also lay great emphasis on the existence of *explanatory* relations: our beliefs should not just be compatible, they should hang together theoretically. However, on a standard view of explanation, confirmation is the inverse of explanation. Newton's laws, together with certain initial conditions, predict and explain the movements of the planets. In turn, the details of those movements confirm Newton's laws. Identifying coherence with explanatory coherence therefore implies epistemological connectedness as well.

We can relate these ideas to the distinction between local and global justification. The logical, epistemological, and explanatory relations between individual beliefs are precisely what we exploit in 'linear' local justification, where we back up a given belief by citing other beliefs. However, these belief–belief relations are also significant holistically in that, the denser they are, the more a given system is a genuine system and not just a ragbag of unrelated opinions. With richer internal connections, a belief-system is more coherent, thus from a global standpoint more justified.

Coherence theorists typically emphasize a second way in which coherence goes beyond mere consistency: scope or 'comprehensiveness'. A system is more coherent the more it takes in, the greater the range of facts it records, explains, and allows us to anticipate. This is an important corrective to the emphasis on systematicity. Obviously, one way to keep one's outlook tightly integrated is to narrow one's view, ignoring or denying inconvenient facts. But this would not be a rational procedure and would not produce an optimally coherent system of beliefs. The goal of inquiry is to understand as much as possible. This means taking in as much as possible and integrating it as best we can, using the fewest theoretical primitives, minimizing reliance on *ad hoc* hypotheses, establishing connections between our views on various topics, and so on. According to coherence theorists, we are always tacitly modifying our total view, 'making it more complete, less *ad hoc*, more plausible'.[4]

Many coherence theorists also insist on a principle of conservatism: faced with a problem in our belief-system—for example, a previously overlooked contradiction—we look for the least change that will remove the difficulty. However, conservatism is better seen as a consequence of the comprehensiveness requirement than as an independent aspect of coherence. Keeping our belief-system as comprehensive as possible means engaging in damage-limitation when problems arise. For example, we avoid taking on board beliefs that would force us to jettison large chunks of an otherwise functional system. Not that we *cannot* take such beliefs on board: epistemological conservatism is not blind traditionalism. We can accept some loss of comprehensiveness for a large gain in theoretical integration, provided that the loss is not so great that the system becomes less usable. The coherence theory is 'conservative' only in that the need for a useful system gives comprehensiveness a certain priority over integration.

If the coherence theorist is granted these points, a lot of steam goes out of the many systems objection. In its 'fairy story' version, the objection does not even deal with workably comprehensive belief-systems, concentrating rather on individual stories or theories. Clearly, a system that included rich historical and scientific beliefs would be much more comprehensive than one that didn't, so such lore cannot simply be disregarded. But with such a system in place, no 'arbitrary fairy story' would be locally credible. Even to make such stories consistent with a workable system of scientific beliefs we would need a large number of *ad hoc* postulates explaining why fairy-doings are exempt from natural laws. With these hypotheses in place, the fairy-believer's system might perhaps be somewhat more comprehensive than that of his scientific critic. But it would also be much more *ad hoc*, thus on balance less coherent.

These ideas are readily extended to paranoid delusions and sceptical hypotheses. Take Descartes's Evil Deceiver story: it offers no positive advantages over our normal view. There is nothing that it explains that our standard view leaves out. On the contrary, to the extent that we could believe it at all, we could still only get through life by relying on the Deceiver's *simulacra* of ordinary facts. Like the paranoid's delusions, this sceptical hypothesis can accommodate—after the fact—anything that our ordinary view turns up. But it does not allow us to anticipate anything that our standard view does not. At the same time, while offering no gains, the hypothesis entails clear losses. We don't know *why* the Deceiver is up to his tricks. Of course, we could speculate, but nothing in the story suggests elaborating it one way rather than another. A Deceiver-based world-view would be more complicated, more *ad hoc*, but no more functional. Sceptical hypotheses, even if logically possible, may justifiably be dismissed. In this way, the coherence theorist sheds light on the feeling that sceptical hypotheses, if not conclusively eliminable, are nevertheless idle.

This coherentist argument avoids the objections that sink the foundationalist's appeal to inference to the best explanation. That appeal requires holding that experience is 'coherent' in the sense of subject to purely experiential regularities. For the true coherentist, by contrast, our beliefs about the world and about experience are part of a single, integrated system. The true coherentist's appeal to explanatory coherence does not presuppose that there are facts to be explained that we can identify independently of all more 'theoretical' views. Rather, recognizing relevant facts and elaborating theories to explain them are two aspects of a single process: making our total view as coherent as we can.

Coherence and observation

Let us now turn to the isolation objection: that the coherence theory, by reducing justification to belief–belief relations, 'cuts justification off from the world'. Because our discussion so far has only enriched our understanding of the relations the coherence theorist has in mind, it does nothing to alleviate this worry. But what worry exactly? It is all too easy to become haunted by a vague picture of our belief-system's floating clear of reality, like a helium balloon cut loose from its moorings. We need a sharper formulation of the objection than this.

A better way to frame the objection focuses on the thought that genuine justification must involve some element of external constraint. This is not just a point about knowledge narrowly conceived, but about meaning. If justification were purely dialectical, our 'beliefs' would be no more than counters in a self-contained game. They would not be about the world at all.[5]

Granted that empirical knowledge must be responsive to what goes on in the world, how can this be? Events in the world can *cause* us to have various beliefs, but causation is not justification. Justification requires logical rather than causal relations. This is the point of the slogan that only a belief can justify a belief. How, then are we to distinguish empirical knowing from the weaving of fantasies? Indeed, how are we to distinguish genuine believing from making moves in a self-contained game? Appeal to comprehensiveness and systematicity don't help, for they require only that our fantasies be more elaborate than the average fairy story: that the game be complicated. What we want is for our belief-system to respond to input from *outside*.

The coherence theorist does not deny the importance of external input. We have, he will say, all kinds of *cognitively spontaneous beliefs*: for example, those beliefs that we think of as 'perceptual'. (These beliefs need not be thought of as *sotto voce* verbalizations: they may be carried by experiences, so long as experiences are thought of as involving propositional content.) But these spontaneous beliefs are subject to assessment in the light of a complicated array of general beliefs about our abilities as observers. Each of us knows that his reliability as an observer is apt to vary. We do better in good light, stone-cold sober, than at dusk having downed one aperitif too many. For the coherence theorist, we need both spontaneous beliefs and epistemic beliefs to regulate them. Call this the 'rationalized input requirement'. This is a *material* constraint on coherence, supplementing the *formal* constraints discussed in the previous section.[6]

It is important to see that, for the coherence theorist, input *must* be rationalized. There would be no need to appeal to coherence if we allowed that external constraint could be the result of cognitively spontaneous beliefs that are merely *in fact* reliably caused by the circumstances they represent. To allow this would be to desert the coherence theory for an externalist version of foundationalism. For a coherence theorist, our causal relations to the world are epistemically relevant only to the extent that they are represented in our belief-system or total view. Epistemic or 'reliability' beliefs are an essential component in the coherentist's theoretical package.

The need for epistemic beliefs further explains why the coherence theory does not encourage blinkered adherence to entrenched views. We might think that, given the desirability of comprehensiveness, it is always rational to reject observations that undermine successful theories. Indeed, it *can* sometimes be rational to do this. For example, if one group of investigators gets experimental results that run counter to a successful theory, but which resist replication, we may be entitled to conclude that their experiment went wrong, even if we are not sure how. But the coherence theory does not license general insouciance about observational evidence. Dismissing otherwise irreproachable observations, because it amounts to an implicit rejection of vitally important epistemic beliefs, can do *more* damage to our belief-system than jettisoning long-standing theories. We cannot make a policy of ignoring consistently replicable results *solely* on the ground that they threaten some favourite views.

The presence of reliability beliefs in belief-systems gives particular observations much more weight than we might have supposed. This is important for the coherence theorist because it undermines one of the foundationalist's strongest and most appealing intuitions: that there is an asymmetry between theory and observation. Because observation has more power to undermine theory than theoretical commitments have to discount observation, we may feel that there must be something to the foundationalist's idea of epistemic priority. Recognizing entrenched epistemic beliefs allows the coherence theorist to simulate the observation–theory asymmetry without committing himself to the idea that perceptual beliefs enjoy an absolute epistemic privilege.

Where foundationalism postulates a fixed observational vocabulary, the coherence theory allows our theoretical views to modify our ideas about what is observable. This is a plus. Armed with enough theory, we can see electrons in a cloud chamber. Special training enables some people to see things others miss: it takes skill to use a microscope. Conversely, we can become sceptical of past observation-claims. Where the witch doctor sees spirits, we may find the effects of hallucinogenic plants. Where some see 'recovered memories', closer investigation reveals irresponsible therapists working on distressed and suggestible patients. Reliability beliefs are no more absolutely privileged than the perceptual beliefs they regulate. However systematically significant, they are open to revision.

The isolation objection is not immediately fatal to the coherence theory.

The coherentist outlook

At first sight, the coherence theory offers a very different picture of justification. Where foundationalism is atomistic, the coherence theory is holistic. Foundationalism is committed to encapsulated knowledge; the coherence theory precludes anyone's having only a single justified belief. Foundationalism takes seriously the idea of building up a system of justified beliefs one element at a time, starting with a first item of knowledge. For the coherence theory, a belief-system must be acquired more or less whole.

The coherence theory's holism is semantic as well as justificational. The foundationalist picture sees meaning on a 'definitional' model. Primitive terms get their meaning by being defined 'ostensively'; others can then be defined discursively. The meanings of individual terms, or words, is primary; that of sentences is derivative. By contrast, the natural way for a coherence theorist to understand meaning is functionally or inferentially. A belief derives its meaning or content from its inferential connections to other beliefs—connections that reflect its inferential role in a larger system of beliefs—rather as a connecting rod is the engine-component it is in virtue of how it works together with other components to constitute a functioning engine. Sentences, which express the meanings of complete judgements or beliefs, are primary; word-meanings are abstractions from patterns of sentence-use.

Like foundationalism, the coherence theory is committed to a strongly justificationist conception of rationality. At the same time, the coherentist model of justification—hence of rationality—is less constraining than its foundationalist rival. For the coherence theory, justification always involves a trade-off between systematicity and comprehensiveness. In theoretical matters, given the importance of epistemic beliefs, particularly those governing observation, this will often take the form of weighing theoretical neatness against empirical adequacy. Secondly, because the coherence theory accepts that beliefs are always, if only implicitly, evaluated in large groups, there is never a unique solution to a problem. If, in testing a particular theory, we find our expectations disappointed, there will be different ways of making adjustments to our beliefs so as to iron out our difficulties. Maybe our theory is false in its fundamentals; maybe there are problems with ancillary theories, concerning our experimental set-up; maybe the apparatus malfunctioned; or maybe we just misread the dial. Sometimes further tests offer guidance, though sometimes they don't. Most importantly, in no case is there a meta-criterion telling us exactly how much weight to give to the different factors in coherence or which beliefs to revise in order to accommodate recalcitrant observations. The coherence theory is compatible with a range of epistemological temperaments, all equally rational.

Does this mean that the coherentist outlook is relativistic after all? Not obviously. Relativists see individuals or 'cultures' as trapped in self-enclosed systems. Sophisticated forms of the coherence theory challenge this picture. Coherentism, because of its insistence on rationalized input, offers an essentially *dynamic* view of belief. Belief-systems change under pressure to accommodate input that those who hold them do not fully control. Also, the theoretical environment changes with the emergence of new ideas; and no one can anticipate all the ways in which original thoughts may provoke revisions in how we see the world. Accordingly, belief-systems are not stable enough to constitute the self-enclosed systems or 'perspectives' of the dogmatic relativist. At any given time, there will be issues that nobody knows how to resolve. But we cannot conclude from this that they are intrinsically irresolvable. This is a plausible defence, though not the last word.

The coherence theory is unfriendly to many of foundationalism's favourite *demarcational* ideas. A coherence theorist cannot recognize any fundamental distinction between the 'demonstrative' and 'inductive' sciences. Everything, even mathematics and logic, owes its acceptability to its playing an important role in the overall economy of our belief-system. In consequence, there is no deep, principled distinction between *a priori* and *a posteriori* knowledge. In principle, anything we accept can be modified, if this would make our overall belief-system function better.

The distinction between the necessary and the contingent is also problematic. As we shall see, coherence theorists are under pressure to give a coherentist account of truth, as well as of justification. Roughly, truth becomes idealized justification. This view does not encourage a 'two sorts of truth' position. Older coherence theorists sometimes put this by saying that all truths are necessary, but their point is best taken as a way of resisting the necessary/contingent distinction.

This epistemic conception of truth has often been connected with the idea of degrees of truth. For foundationalists—or for advocates of the correspondence theory of truth generally—a belief or proposition is either true or it isn't. While justification can come in degrees—a belief can be more or less justified—truth is all or nothing. But if truth is understood epistemically, it loses this all-or-nothing character. Some readers may find this an implausible consequence of holism: surely, either the cat is on the mat or it is somewhere else. How can simple factual claims be more or less true? However, we should remember here that holism affects our understanding of meaning as well as our conception of knowledge. On the functionalist or inferentialist understanding of meaning that the coherence theorist adopts, enlarging and revising the inferential connections between our beliefs changes their meanings. As our beliefs evolve, our concepts evolve too. Our beliefs become truer as the concepts they involve become more adequate. We don't mean by 'tree' quite what our animist forebears meant by the word they used to talk about oaks, limes, and beeches. So even their simple factual claims, being inferentially freighted in ways we regard as misguided, were not wholly true. This is not a self-evidently foolish view

From what has just been said, it should be clear that holism is hostile to the analytic–synthetic distinction. We may choose on occasion to regard some things we accept as 'true by definition' or 'true in virtue of meaning', thereby distinguishing them from empirical or factual commitments. But this designation confers no epistemological privilege. If a definition combines with other views to generate problematic consequences, it is as open to revision as anything else.

So much for the foundationalist's main internal boundaries. What about external boundaries? Foundationalism, in its dominant empiricist form, tends to downgrade 'value-judgements' of all types as not really expressions of knowledge. For the coherence theory, matters are not so clear cut. Consider an influential account of how we achieve a considered moral outlook: we attempt to formulate general principles in the light of reactions to particular cases. But once in place, our tentative principles may modify our intuitive judgements. The quest for a considered moral outlook is a search for 'reflective equilibrium' between general principles and particular judgements, with both categories open to revision. This looks very like a particular application of how the coherence theorist understands reasoning generally. It is not at all clear that a coherence theorist does or should recognize deep distinctions between empirical or 'scientific' and moral reasoning.

However, while the coherence theory is hostile to tying demarcational concerns to overly rigid conceptions of empirical reasoning, it is not so obviously inimical to demarcational projects as such. It is compatible with 'explanationist' approaches to demarcation.

A belief-system is more coherent the fewer independent sub-systems it contains. Coherence is also increased by epistemological self-understanding: our understanding of why we accept the things we do. Indeed, given the crucial role of epistemic beliefs, some measure of such understanding is an indispensable component of a coherent view. Now in some cases, the things that my beliefs are about play an indispensable role in the best explanation of why I believe it. If I look out of my window and notice my dog on the lawn, the fact that my dog is on the lawn plays an indispensable role in the best explanation of why I believe that he is. Moral judgements may be different in this respect. I regard a certain type of behaviour as utterly heinous. Is this best explained by the fact that such behaviour is utterly heinous? Or do other factors—my upbringing, my temperament, local customs—sufficiently explain my view, without bringing in moral facts at all? If they do, we may be able dispense with irreducible moral facts. This will increase the coherence of our overall view by reducing the number of independent sub-systems and increasing our epistemological self-understanding. Whatever the merits of this idea, it is not excluded by a coherentist outlook in epistemology.[7]

Notes

1. A coherentist approach to knowledge (and truth) is evident in British Idealism. See e.g. Bradley (1914) and Blanshard (1939). There are clear coherentist elements in Quine (1961), though whether he is a fully paid-up coherence theorist is a difficult question. The same goes for Davidson: see his 'A Coherence Theory of Truth and Knowledge'

(1986), in Lepore (1986), but also his 'Afterthoughts' (1987), in Malachowski (1990). Harman (1973) and (1986) develops a number of coherentist ideas in very interesting ways. A recent sophisticated defence of the coherence theory can be found in BonJour (1985). Lehrer is another prominent contemporary coherence theorist, or is widely regarded as defending a coherence theory: see his 'Knowledge Reconsidered', in Clay and Lehrer (1989). However, Lehrer's views have pronounced affinities with what I call 'contextualism'. (See Ch. 14 below.) Bender (1988) is a useful collection of critical essays on the views of BonJour and Lehrer.

2. This claim is mildly tendentious, since some philosophers use 'coherentist' to describe any epistemological outlook that is not (substantively) foundationalist. I think that my usage is both historically correct and, because it allows for a clear distinction between coherentism and contextualism, theoretically well motivated. My picture of the coherence theory owes a great deal to BonJour who, it seems to me, is admirably clear about the theory's fundamental aims and commitments.

3. Schlick, in Ayer (1959), 212–16.
4. Harman (1973), 159.
5. McDowell (1994), Lecture 1.
6. This response is essentially BonJour's. See BonJour (1985), ch. 6. BonJour, in turn, is drawing on ideas from Sellars (1997). For a more extended treatment of the coherence theory of justification, see Williams (1996a), ch. 7.
7. Harman (1977), ch. 1.

11

The Myth of the System

Do we have a total view?

The coherence theory looks like an attractive alternative to foundationalism. It builds on ideas that are direct responses to foundationalism's fundamental problems; and it offers a way of taking justification and rationality seriously without pressing them into a rigid mould. On closer examination, however, these advantages disappear. The coherence theory is radically holistic: it ties justification to the comprehensiveness and systematicity of our whole system of beliefs or total view. How clearly we understand this talk of total views is questionable in the extreme.

There is something fishy about the coherentist image of a 'web of belief'. On this picture, a proposition is either in the system or out of it. This seems unrealistic. We have different styles of acceptance. For example, we might accept a certain theory as a promising working hypothesis, though we would not say that we believe it to be true. Like much traditional epistemology, the coherence theory places too much emphasis on belief as an all-purpose attitude of acceptance. Belief is a rather special normative attitude: a relatively unrestricted form of commitment. Not everything we accept (in some circumstances, or for some purposes) is something we unqualifiedly believe. It is not clear that we have a single acceptance-system, active in all contexts of inquiry.

A coherence theorist may deny that he treats belief in a simple all or nothing way. An important aspect of the coherence theory is that beliefs have different degrees of entrenchment. Some beliefs, because of their centrality and wide-ranging explanatory or inferential significance, cannot be rejected without severe damage to the system at large. Since such damage is prohibited by the comprehensiveness requirement, beliefs like this enjoy a high degree of immunity to revision. By contrast, beliefs that are only loosely integrated into the system can easily be rejected or modified. Because beliefs vary widely in their functional importance, the fact that a belief is either in the system or out of it does not imply a uniform acceptance-status.

This is true but does not really meet the objection. Differences in styles of acceptance cannot be assimilated to differences in degrees of entrenchment.

Take the case of accepting something as a working hypothesis or for the sake of argument. In its appropriate context, a proposition accepted in this way may be treated as definitely correct in the sense that it is (temporarily) exempted from scrutiny. In context, it may be deeply entrenched without being, in any unqualified way, believed. Indeed, we may accept something as a working hypothesis even when our long-term purpose is to falsify it. Karl Popper thinks that, in science, we are always subjecting our hypotheses to potentially falsifying tests. For this reason, he holds that 'belief' is a poor term for our attitude towards even the most successful scientific theories. Anyway, if there really are different styles of acceptance, and if an item's acceptance status varies from context to context, there may be no yes-or-no answer to the question of whether a given item is in or out of the system.

To be sure, some things we know play a role in larger, functionally useful systems of commitments: there is a distinction between useful knowledge and mere information. But this distinction does nothing to encourage us to think in terms of a single super-system or total view, rather than a congeries of relatively independent sub-systems.

Coherence theorists often speak of a belief-system's being held together by 'inferential' or 'explanatory' connections. But the idea of such relations tying our beliefs together into a single system is evidently fictional. I could lose an enormous amount of my scattered historical knowledge without much impact on what I know of physics or mathematics. Our 'belief system', if we should talk this way at all, shows a considerable degree of *modularity*: we don't have a single system, but an indefinite number of sub-systems that are at best loosely connected. These sub-systems are always to some degree porous. Developments in the physical sciences—new methods for dating ancient arte-facts or for mapping the traces of vanished settlements—may lead to serious revisions in our historical views. But developments like this can be understood without invoking the idea of a total view.

A coherence theorist will see modularity as an indication that our present system of belief is not as coherent as it ought to be. The drive for greater coherence is what keeps inquiry moving. However, while it is true that know-ledge is sometimes advanced by bringing together fields of investigation that were hitherto separate—the rapprochement between the biological and phys-ical sciences has given us molecular biology—this point gives little support to the ideal of total integration. Even in the sciences, progress can take the form of proliferation as much as that of integration or reduction; and in any case, there is more to life than science. Why should political theory ever have much to do with quantum physics, or pet care with parliamentary history? No reason. The coherence theory builds in a metaphysical bias towards monism: the idea that everything we know should somehow form one massive 'com-plete theory of everything'. It ignores the fact that the progress of knowledge also creates new forms of inquiry, capable of standing on their own two feet.

These objections are just preliminary skirmishes, intended to suggest that coherentist metaphors are less than compelling. There are more theoretical problems to be dealt with.

Logic and inference

According to coherence theorists, belief-systems are held together by 'inferential' and 'explanatory' connections. It is far from clear that the existence of such connections is compatible with radical holism.

Recall that the coherence theory is supposed to embody a non-linear model of justifying inference. On this model, although the beliefs in a given system will be interconnected in various ways, these connections are not directly justificational: that is, they are not relations in virtue of which one particular belief or set of beliefs justifies some further particular belief. Interconnectedness among its components, together with its comprehensiveness, determine a system's degree of coherence. Justification, as coherence, is therefore primarily a property of whole systems. Individual beliefs inherit their justification from belonging to a coherent total view. On this model, inference is not the passage from beliefs to other beliefs along lines of inferential connectedness: it is the holistic selection of a particular total view over less coherent alternatives. All justifying inference, even so-called local inference, is implicitly holistic, that is, global.

As Gilbert Harman has argued, if there were such a thing as genuinely linear inference, it would follow so-called 'rules of inference', such as Modus Ponens:

> If P then Q.
> *P.*
> ∴ Q.

Because we often do seem to make inferences in accordance with this rule, it is tempting to read the rule as saying that given 'P' and 'If P then Q' one may (or perhaps must) infer 'Q': a paradigm of linear inference. But according to Harman, it is a mistake to read this or any other logical inference-rule this way. We must remember that an equally good 'rule of inference' is Modus Tollens:

> If P then Q.
> *Not Q.*
> ∴ Not P.

This rule offers a sharp reminder that inference is not always either a matter of drawing the deductive consequences of beliefs one already has or of accepting beliefs that one's current beliefs inductively support. If we find that our current beliefs imply absurd conclusions, we should revise our current beliefs. Modus Ponens may simply provide an occasion to apply Modus Tollens:

nothing in logic tells us which rule to apply in particular circumstances. These 'rules of inference', then, are really rules of entailment. They tell us that a certain conclusion follows logically from the given premises. They do not tell us what to infer from what, if 'inference' is understood as the process of adding to or subtracting from one's system of beliefs.[1]

The fact that premises may need to be re-examined in the light of what they imply appears to support the coherence theorist's view that, even when inference seems to proceed linearly, we are really evaluating the comparative acceptability of whole systems of beliefs. When we accept the logical consequences of some particular beliefs, we are not really 'inferring' conclusions from given premises. Rather, we are judging that continuing to accept the beliefs in question, together with the newly recognized consequences, gives a more coherent end-result than rejecting one or more of those beliefs so as to avoid their implications. Linear inference requires premises that never need to be re-examined, no matter where they lead us: foundationalism in its strongest form.

For a philosopher who accepts this line of thought, it makes no sense to think of belief-systems as coherence theorists often want to think of them: as held together by inferential connections. For there to be inferential connections linking beliefs to other beliefs, our belief system would have to be structured so that some beliefs function as fixed points, while others are more or less up for grabs. This is exactly what coherence theorists, as radical holists, deny.

Explanations and interests

When coherence theorists speak of a total view's being held together by explanatory coherence, they have the following picture in mind. Our belief-system or total view contains a myriad of beliefs about particular matters of fact and a smaller, though still extensive, array of general or theoretical beliefs that explain or make sense of them. The greater the range of particular facts we can explain, and the smaller the number of primitive theoretical commitments we employ in explaining them, the greater the explanatory coherence of our system at large. However, as we just saw, at the global level our beliefs are held together only by logical relations, particularly implication or entailment (and logical relations of confirmation or probabilification, if there are such). Thus the coherence theorist needs explanation to be intelligible in terms of such relations.

There is an account of explanation to hand. According to the 'deductive-nomological' ('D-N') model, which used to be standard, an event or state of affairs is explained by showing that the statement that it occurred or obtains is deductively entailed by one or more natural laws together with statements concerning the surrounding conditions. Schematically:

(E) $L_1, L_2, \ldots L_n$ (Law-statements)
      $C_1, C_2 \ldots C_k$ (Statements of conditions)
      _____   (Deductively entail)
      E   (Statement that the event to be explained occurred.)

For example, given Galileo's law of falling bodies and information about how long a stone has been in falling towards the Earth, we can deduce—thus explain—the distance the stone has travelled. On this account, explanation is close to being a logical notion. To characterize explanation, we need only the logical concept of entailment and the (supposedly) near-logical concept of a natural law. But although it promises coherence theorists just what they need, the D-N model is problematic. Few philosophers, if any, defend it today.[2]

One objection is that the conditions laid down by the D-N model are not even necessary features of explanation. For example, we can explain particular events by other particular events without invoking laws. The garage window broke because it was hit by a cricket ball. No doubt, physical laws are involved in cases like this; but I don't have to know what they are in order to explain how the garage window got broken. Furthermore, even if I did know, I still wouldn't be able to give a full-dress D-N explanation since I would never be in a position to determine all the relevant conditions: the precise strength of the glass, the mass, velocity, and angle of impact of the ball, and so on.

Someone might reply that my explanation is still D-N, but vague and approximate. If a ball hits with *sufficient* force a *sufficiently* brittle object, that object will shatter; in this case the force and so on were sufficient, therefore . . . But this statement of laws and conditions adds nothing to what we already know: that in this case, the ball broke the window. At most, it indicates a commitment to there being laws, though we may not know what they are.

This all seems correct to me. Still, it may not be such a fundamental criticism, since it allows that the D-N model may be a correct account of *ideally complete* explanation. A more interesting line of attack is that the D-N model does not state sufficient conditions for explanation: that is, that we can have a D-N 'explanation' and still not have an explanation (or have only a *very bad* explanation—the line is not a sharp one).

Here is a simple example, adapted from Hilary Putnam.[3] You notice me working in my office at six p.m. and wonder why. The following explanation is proposed:

No object could have exited Williams's office in Δt seconds (a very small time interval) without exceeding the speed of light, which is physically impossible.
  Williams was in his office at Δt seconds to 6 p.m.
  Therefore:
  Williams was in his office at 6 p.m.

Putnam would say that this a very bad explanation and perhaps not an explanation at all. The 'explanation' cites things you can be presumed to know already; and if, knowing these things, you still feel the need for an explanation, they must not address what you want explained. Most likely, you wanted to know what I was up to: you wanted an intentional rather than a physical explanation. This gets us somewhere, for it acknowledges that there are different kinds of explanation; but not all the way, since it allows that the explanation given above is a good one, just not the sort that was wanted.

The deep problem with the D-N model of explanation is that to 'explain an event' is always to explain it *as described in a particular way*. We never just 'explain an event': we explain something *about* it, focusing on some features and ignoring others. In our original example of the falling stone, highlighting the stone's speed of descent tacitly projects us into a context where the focus of interest is the physics of motion: the question is why the stone is *falling*. If the question had been why a *stone* is falling rapidly towards the Earth, the explanation might have been that the castle's defenders had to resort to dropping stones on the attackers' heads, having run out of boiling pitch. What counts as a good explanation depends essentially on interests and background knowledge. Explanation is context-sensitive in ways that 'logical' accounts, like the D-N model, fail to capture.[4]

Someone might reply that the fact that we typically focus our explanatory demands on certain aspects of a given situation is only of pragmatic significance and has nothing to do with the *logic* of explanation. Some things—like my failure to exit the office at warp speed—do not 'call for explanation' because we already know what the explanation is. The explanation is *contained in* our background knowledge. It is not, however, *relative to* a context of interests and presuppositions.

This response underestimates the contextual sensitivity of explanation. Consider again 'explaining' my presence in my office by the physical impossibility of my exiting within the stated time constraints without exceeding the speed of light. Putnam's intuition—that this is a very bad explanation, if it is an explanation at all—needs correction. The correct response to this example is that we have *no idea* whether it presents an explanation, still less whether the explanation is good or bad. The reason that the example strikes us as a bad explanation is that we effortlessly project ourselves into the sort of context in which questions about my staying in my office would typically come up; and in such a context, the appeal to physical impossibility would be completely beside the point. But explanations like this are not always beside the point. Suppose that I were charged with a crime: if I could establish that, just before the crime was committed, I was so far away that getting to the scene of the crime would have been physically impossible, I would have a watertight alibi. This would be a very good explanation for why I was not the criminal. Abstracted from a context of questions, interests, and background knowledge, a D-N 'explanation' is *just a deduction*. But to move to the level of our total view, where all beliefs are up for grabs, is automatically to abstract from all particular contexts of explanation, which depend essentially on there being all sorts of things that are not in question. At the level of a total view, explanation disappears.

Foundationalism in disguise?

While the coherence theory claims to articulate a distinctive, 'non-linear' conception of justifying inference, it may not be the radical alternative to foundationalism that it purports to be.

Let us return to the isolation objection: the thought that the coherence theory cannot allow for genuine external constraint. We met this objection by allowing for rationalized input: 'cognitively spontaneous' beliefs regulated by various epistemic beliefs. However, this apparently innocent talk of 'cognitive' spontaneity masks a crucial ambiguity. We might give it a purely psychological reading: cognitively spontaneous beliefs are conceptually structured experiences, or inclinations to judge, that arise without any conscious process of inference. But this isn't what we want: not every spontaneous thought or daydream is something that amounts to 'input' constraining our belief-system. So perhaps we should say that sufficiently vivid or powerful experiences or inclinations to judge are what matter. This is the ambiguity I just spoke of. Our input from the world is supposed to be more than psychologically vivid: it is supposed to be epistemically, hence normatively, significant, that is, something that we *ought* to take account of and which we can be criticized for ignoring. But then the question is: what is the source of this normative significance? If it is intrinsic to experiences or perceptual beliefs, we have abandoned the coherence theory proper for modest foundationalism: the view that basic beliefs have intrinsic *prima facie* credibility that can be strengthened, and occasionally undermined, by how their incorporation into belief-system at large affects overall coherence. But if they have no intrinsic credibility—if their epistemic significance is wholly derivative from our epistemic beliefs—all constraint is ultimately dialectical: a matter of how beliefs fit together, with no constraint that is seriously external to our way of looking at things. To avoid collapsing into foundationalism, the coherence theory must stay true to its radical holism, thus giving up on the idea of external constraint.

Even taking this line may only put off the evil day. According to radical holism, no beliefs are epistemically privileged. There are no fixed points: in any inferential situation, everything we believe is (theoretically) up for grabs. But if everything is up for grabs, even our criteria of coherence, there is simply no saying—at the time, anyway—why we make one inference rather than another. Coherence theorists are hostile to the idea that any knowledge is *a priori*: even basic logical principles have to pay their way by contributing to the smooth functioning of a total view. Nothing is immune from revision. But at the very least, this has to be an oversimplification. Belief-systems derive their degree of coherence from the character of the logical relations between their component beliefs. Furthermore, a basic feeling for logical relations is the prerequisite for following any justificatory or evaluative procedure, including the application of criteria of global coherence. How, then, can everything be up for grabs?

This question is particularly pressing with respect to the criteria of coherence themselves. Why not subject them to the same questions that get directed against logical rules? Supposedly, we cannot see inference as regulated by rules like Modus Ponens because the question always arises as to why we accept the consequences of prior beliefs, in accordance with the rule, rather than revise those beliefs because their consequences are unacceptable. But the same goes for whatever principles regulate the selection of total views. We can always ask why we apply these particular criteria of coherence, or trade off competing criteria in the way we do, rather than modify our epistemic principles in order to hold on to a particular combination of beliefs. We had better not answer this question by appealing to a further set of meta-criteria: to do so will open a new regress.

Coherence theorists avoid these problems by implicitly assigning the criteria of coherence a special status. When they deny that any beliefs are epistemically privileged, they really mean any 'first-order' beliefs, beliefs about the world. The criteria of coherence—which embody 'second-order', epistemic beliefs about what makes the beliefs in a system more likely to be true—function as the fixed points by reference to which first-order acceptance is regulated. These epistemic beliefs thus enjoy a *foundational status*. In so far as this status is assigned *a priori*, the coherence theory represents a rationalistic—'top down' as opposed to 'bottom up'—variant of foundationalism.

This complicates the coherence theorist's attitude to 'linear inference'. The criteria of coherence prescribe revisions to total views: for example, they tell us that, if one modification to our belief-system increases its comprehensiveness, without loss of integration, while another reduces both, the system resulting from the first modification is more coherent and is to be preferred. This example of reasoning involves a straightforward application of Modus Ponens. The coherence theory is therefore not unqualifiedly hostile to linear inference: it excludes it only at first order. While there is nothing strictly contradictory in this view, it is oddly unmotivated. Once any element of epistemic privilege or linear inference is admitted, the question arises as to why its role should be so restricted. Why not allow it a larger role, given that doing so would let us stay closer to the phenomenology of everyday justification?

Knowing what we think

The epistemic beliefs implicit in acceptance of the criteria of coherence are not the only locus of epistemic privilege in the coherence theory. To apply these criteria we need to know what all our beliefs are and how they hang together.

This seems unrealistic. No one has the faintest idea how *many* beliefs he has, or even how to go about counting them. This isn't just because we have so many beliefs that we wouldn't know where to begin, though this is perfectly true. Rather, we lack clear criteria for individuating beliefs—that is, saying when beliefs are the same and different—without which there is no possibility of counting. Asking how many beliefs I have is like asking how many drops of water there are in a bucket: who's to say? I believe that my dog is in the garden right now; do I *also* believe that he is not in the house, not in the basement, not in Siberia? Or are these beliefs somehow included in the original belief? This is an odd question. With respect to beliefs, we do not normally have any use for fine-grained criteria of individuation. Unless we become captured by the coherentist image of 'our beliefs' as a finely articulated, complexly inter-related network—a 'web of belief'—I doubt we shall ever have any use for them.

Even if we had a clearer conception than we do of how our beliefs constitute a genuine totality, this totality would be completely unsurveyable. No one has a clue what his actual belief-system looks like *as a whole*, still less how it stacks up against the incalculable number of alternative systems that would result from the endlessly many ways in which his existing system might be modified. The coherence theory is impossibly idealized. It makes human reasoners like Leibniz's God, who conceives (in the minutest detail) every world there could *possibly* be, choosing to create the best.

But waiving this difficulty, what is the epistemological status of our supposed self-knowledge? As the author of the most comprehensive recent version of the coherence theory recognizes, the coherence theory must pre-suppose two things: that everyone has a primitive sense of what his beliefs are and how they hang together; and that he is entitled to presume that this sense is more or less accurate. Coherentist justification proceeds under a *Doxastic Presumption.*[5]

In an everyday sense, we all do know what we believe: that is, if asked for our opinion on a definite subject, we can give it if we have one to give. But this is a world away from what the coherence theorist has is mind. For his pur-poses, 'knowing what I believe' means having a sense of the extent and struc-ture of my total belief-system. I have no such sense; and even if I did, I have no idea how I should estimate its accuracy. The Doxastic Presumption is *completely* unwarranted. Why not *Doxastic Assumption*?

Of course, the word 'presumption' is carefully chosen. If our supposed knowledge of our own belief-system is allowed to be questionable, it will need to be backed up by some justifying inference. This can hardly be coherentist: such an inference would require us to estimate the coherence of our beliefs about our beliefs. We would then have to presume these beliefs to be more or less accurate, or else produce a meta-meta-argument about the coherence of our beliefs about our beliefs about our beliefs . . . and so on without end. Invoking a 'presumption' is meant to prevent any such regress getting started. In effect, it confers *foundational status* on the relevant kind of self-knowledge.

Epistemologically basic beliefs concerning the content and structure of our total view are regulated by equally basic epistemic principles. The coherence theory is foundationalism in disguise.

Notes

1. Harman (1986), chs. 1–2, App. A.
2. For discussion of the D-N model by one of its leading advocates, see Hempel (1965).
3. Putnam (1978), 42.
4. The case for the interest-relativity of explanation is developed by Garfinkel (1981).
5. BonJour (1985), 81–2.

12

Realism and Truth

Losing the world

Our objections to reductionism, although decisive, may not get at what is really unsettling about reductionist strategies. The real problem with (say) a phenomenalist analysis of external-object talk is that, even if it could be carried through, it would not salvage our pre-theoretical aspirations towards knowledge of the external world. At best it would provide us with a pale simulacrum of such knowledge. For phenomenalists, the world is not something to which experience gives us access. Rather, talk about the world is just a roundabout form of talk about experience. Phenomenalism cannot satisfy our aspiration to knowledge of an objective world.

There is a logical aspect to this worry. According to the phenomenalist, to say that there are two bookcases in my office, even though the room is currently unoccupied, is to say that *if* you or I were to be in my office we *would* be having such and such experiences. However, simple statements about the external world do not feel the least bit 'iffy'. The statement that there are two bookcases in my office is straightforwardly categorical: true if there are two bookcases there, false otherwise.[1]

Phenomenalism is a form of idealism, the doctrine that thought and reality are really one and the same. The problem with idealism is that it flies in the face of common-sense *realism*. From a realist standpoint, the facts of the world do not depend on what anyone does or would experience. Human beings have existed for only a brief moment in the universe's history. Much has happened that we will never know about. Much would have happened even if human beings had never evolved. It is not easy for an idealist to respond to this thought in a satisfactory way. This is what I was hinting at when I suggested that empiricist foundationalism does not really offer enough in the way of external constraint on our beliefs.

Phenomenalists, or idealists generally, will reply that realism is mistaken or even incoherent. They will claim that realist prejudices are the source of sceptical anxieties. There is something to this. Sceptical arguments, particularly Cartesian arguments, do seem reflect a commitment to realism. The sceptic presents experience as a guide to an independently existing reality:

the only guide we have and, unfortunately, one that is completely inadequate. Phenomenalism calls in question the sceptic's conception of reality. Phenomenalism is anti-sceptical in virtue of being anti-realist. This is its strength, but also its weakness. The sceptic claims that we know nothing about the world: our knowledge extends no farther than experience. The phenomenalist tells us not to worry. Of course we know all sorts of things about the external world, because the external world is only a logical construction out of experience. This solution to scepticism is not easy to distinguish from scepticism itself.[2]

One lesson to learn from all this is the importance of what I call the apparent 'naturalness' of sceptical problems. To concede that sceptical arguments are natural or intuitive, is to give the sceptic a tremendous dialectical advantage. If realism leads to scepticism, and if realism is the common-sense or 'default' position, any anti-sceptical strategy that challenges realism will be *revisionary*: it will not really salvage what we thought of, pre-theoretically, as knowledge of the world. On the contrary, it will implicitly concede that our pre-theoretical epistemic aspirations are incurably paradoxical, which is why they must be changed. Any such change will inevitably involve large concessions to scepticism.

Truth and correspondence

Realism is generally taken to have important implications for our understanding of truth. According to realists, whether a proposition about the world is true depends on the way the world is, whether the proposition 'corresponds to the facts'. Realists therefore insist on distinguishing sharply between a proposition's being true and our being justified in taking it to be true. Sceptics, too, insist on this distinction, though they treat it as the entering wedge for a much more radical assault on the possibility of knowledge.

The correspondence theory of truth has attracted severe criticism. One focus of attack is the notion of correspondence itself. Talk of correspondence naturally calls to mind pictures or mirror-images. We do indeed speak of pictures as being 'true to life'. But the correspondence theory is supposed to explain the truth of beliefs or judgements or propositions, the content of which is expressed by complete sentences. Sentences are not pictures, at least in any straightforward way.

We might think that explaining correspondence is not quite so difficult for early modern philosophers, like Descartes, who discuss knowledge in terms of ideas. Ideas include sense-experiences as well as conceptually articulated thoughts; and we can, perhaps, form a vague conception of what might be meant by supposing our ideas to correspond to the world. We think of our experience as something like a private picture-show, and we ask ourselves whether the events on the screen (our experiences) accurately reflect what is going on outside the cinema (in the external world).

On reflection, this doesn't help. Knowledge requires judgements—thoughts or beliefs that can be true or false. Such thoughts demand propositional content: the sort of content that is expressed by complete sentences. Whatever the merits of thinking of experience as picturing the world, a picture doesn't say anything unless we read something into it. Even for Descartes, knowledge arises when we make judgements about the extent to which our experiences mirror the world. Whether or not we think of ideas as mental pictures, and whether or not we take the linguistic turn, the problem for the correspondence theory is to explain what makes judgements true.

Another problem for the correspondence theory is to explain what thoughts (or propositions or sentences) correspond *to*. The usual answer is *facts*. The trouble with the appeal to facts is that, in general, we have no way of indicating what fact a sentence, when true, corresponds to other than asserting the sentence. Thus the sentence 'Snow is white' is true iff it corresponds to the fact that snow is white. Saying that a thought or sentence corresponds to the facts looks more like another way of saying that it is true than a genuine explanation of what its being true amounts to.

There are sophisticated contemporary versions of the correspondence theory that avoid both mirror-imagery and naive appeals to facts. But examining them would take us too far afield. Moreover, I do not think that examining them would yield epistemologically significant results, at least so far as scepticism is concerned. The reason is that the 'realist' presuppositions of sceptical arguments are very minimal. Sceptical arguments do not depend on metaphysically charged conceptions of truth.

Deflating truth

For traditional theorists of truth, the nature of truth may be difficult to explain, but that truth has a nature is something they take for granted. Just as a scientist might want to explain what it is that makes some substances acidic, so a philosopher will want to explain what makes true sentences (propositions, beliefs, etc.) true. However this preconception has been challenged by proponents of so-called 'deflationary' accounts of truth.[3]

An early version of such an approach to truth is the redundancy theory, according to which 'It is true that Caesar was murdered' *means no more than* that Caesar was murdered. Any difference is entirely 'stylistic': for example, we may use 'It is true that . . .' to speak more emphatically. Because it stresses the use of 'true' in performing such special speech-acts, this approach is sometimes also called the 'performative' theory.

More recent views, such as Quine's disquotational theory, do not claim that 'p' and 'It is true that p' are synonymous. Rather, what matters about 'true' is given by certain logical equivalences. Thus:

'Snow is white' is true if and only if all snow is white; 'Grass is green' is true if and only if all grass is green . . . and so on.

Appending 'is true' to a quoted sentence is just like cancelling the quotation marks ('disquotation'). Notice that while, on the redundancy theory, to think of truth as *any* sort of property is, in Ramsey's words, just 'linguistic muddle', on the disquotational theory we *can* see truth as a property, a complete theory of which is given by the appropriate equivalences. Of course, we cannot write this 'theory' down, since it will have infinitely many axioms. But since these axioms share a common structure, we can indicate more or less what they are.[4] These axioms capture all there is to the idea of 'correspondence'.

For deflationists, the function of truth-talk is expressive. As Quine puts it, 'true' offers a way of replacing talk about the world with logically equivalent talk about words. Moving to the level of talk about words ('semantic ascent') gives us new things to generalize over: that is, linguistic objects, sentences. This move to the 'meta' level allows us to express agreement and disagreement with sentences that we cannot specify. One type of case is where we do not know exactly what these sentences are, as in 'What the President said is true'. Another is where there are too many of them. We want to assert all instances of logical laws, like the Law of the Excluded Middle. We can accomplish this with the aid of semantic ascent: every sentence of the form 'p or not p' is true.

This may seem trivial; and deflationary theorists are often suspected of belittling the concept of truth. In fact, however, the generalizing power of truth talk adds enormously to our language's expressive powers. It allows us to express general cognitive goals, such as seeking truths and avoiding false-hoods. It allows us to acknowledge our fallibility by saying that even our best-supported theories may be false: we do not have to list them. The capacity for generalization of this kind is indispensable to reflection on inferential and methodological commitments. And the ability to engage in such reflection is integral to human rationality.[5]

Truth and verification

The deflationary approach to truth has a good claim to capture all there is to the idea of truth as 'correspondence' or 'fitting the facts'. It is 'realist' only in what it does *not* say. It does not make any conceptual connection between truth and epistemological notions like justification or evidence. In this sense, the deflationary perspective retains the realist idea that truth is a *radically non-epistemic notion*.

Contrast this realist conception of truth with that implicit in reductionist theories like phenomenalism. Such theories, together with 'criterial' variants, are an articulation of a more general view of meaning: *verificationism*. According to verificationism, the meaning of a statement is constituted by its verification conditions: the facts or procedures that go towards confirming or disconfirming it. A proposition's being true is therefore logically connected with the fulfillment of those conditions. Verificationism goes with an *epistemic* conception of truth, in the sense that truth is defined (at least for non-basic propositions) in terms of epistemological concepts like verification or justification.

We have seen that verificationism is a non-starter. Individual statements do not have verification conditions they can call their own. They connect with experience only as part of some set of sentences with critical semantic mass. However, the idea that truth is some kind of epistemic notion is not tied to strict verificationism.

Let us step back and ask why we should understand truth in a realist rather than in some epistemic way. The answer is: because we want to distinguish between how things really are and how we (however justifiably) take them to be. After all, we are not omniscient. Even resting on evidence that is to all intents and purposes conclusive is not the same as being true, for we can never entirely exclude the possibility of our coming to see that evidence in a new light. However, there is a reply to this. The fact that we are fallible only shows that we should not identify truth with justification by current standards. Rather, truth consists in *ideal* verification, verification in the limit, verification at the end of inquiry, or something like that.[6]

This reply detaches the idea of understanding truth in an epistemic way from reductionist forms of verificationism, such as phenomenalism. A proponent of the 'ideal justification' conception of truth need not imagine that individual propositions have their own precisely demarcated verification conditions. But since he postulates a conceptual link between truth and verifiability, he does not treat truth as a radically non-epistemic notion.

Where verificationism is associated with foundationalism, the ideal justification theory appeals to coherence theorists. Foundationalists accept certain basic facts as directly known or 'given'. These given facts constitute the verification conditions for all non-basic statements or beliefs. To the coherence theorist, the doctrine of the given looks like an unpurged element of non-epistemic truth. The coherence theorist wants to unify his account of justification and truth for all types of belief: truth is final coherence—ideal justification—for all beliefs.[7] A coherence theory of justification combined with an ideal justification theory of truth treats justification and truth in a consistently epistemic way.

This line of thought has a certain charm. But how far do we understand the notion of 'ideal' justification? Coherence theorists explain it in terms of incorporation into an ideally coherent system of belief: one that is maximally comprehensive and integrated. I doubt that any clear ideas attach to this kind of talk. The same goes for references to the 'limit' or 'end' of inquiry. We have no clear conception of what it would be for inquiry to have a limit or end, thus no clear idea of what it would be for a system of belief to be maximally coherent. So far as I can see, the most sense we can make of 'ideal' justification is to understand it as involving procedures that take into account all relevant sources of error. This is as good as to say: the sort of justification we have when we are ideally placed for finding out the truth. If this is right, there is indeed a connection between truth and ideal justification but, from the standpoint of the epistemic theorist of truth, it goes the wrong way round. To the extent that we understand talk of ideal justification, it is because we have a prior understanding of truth.

Even setting this objection aside, it is doubtful whether the epistemic conception of truth really accomplishes its anti-sceptical goal. After all, we have no idea how close we are to making our belief-system ideally coherent. For all we know, our outlook at the end of inquiry might be quite different from our outlook today, so it is not clear that justification and truth have been connected by anything more than verbal sleight-of-hand: both may consist in 'coherence', but we are given no reason to suppose that coherence in the one case has much resemblance to coherence in the other.

Traditionally, coherence theorists have tended to think of inquiry in teleological terms, as heading towards a goal. This conception is implicit in the idea of the 'end' or 'limit' of inquiry. If we can make an assumption like this, perhaps we can do something to answer the sceptic. But of course, we can always answer the sceptic by making assumptions, including assumptions much simpler and more in tune with common sense than this one.

These are all serious concerns. But, as with our original objections to phenomenalism, they may not get at the deepest source of disquiet. The coherence theory of truth, in its own way, involves a retreat from common-sense realism. The association between the coherence theory of truth and Idealism—the metaphysical thesis that Thought and Reality are somehow one—is no accident. It arises from a problem we noted at the end of the previous chapter: that the coherence theory has difficulty allowing for any notion of genuinely external constraint. It insists that everything that is relevant to the epistemic status of a particular belief be swept up into our total belief-system.

The move from a coherence theory of justification to a coherence theory of truth depends on raising the spectre of radical and general scepticism. But this spectre, once raised, can be raised again. We can ask what makes even an ideally coherent system of belief *true of objective reality*. The traditional Idealist response is that 'reality' and 'the ideally coherent system of thought' are two ways of referring to the same thing. But what else is there is to say, once we have travelled this far down the coherentist road?

The more all-encompassing Idealism that grows out of the coherence theory prompts the same anxieties as the subjective idealism involved in phenomenalism, which reduces the world to a construction out of sense-experiences. Both approaches try to quiet sceptical doubts by retreating from common-sense realism. But common-sense realism is not easily cast aside. It is hard to shake the thought that most of what has happened in the universe happened before sentient beings came along and would have happened even if no such beings had ever existed. How can, then, the facts of the world be constituted by what anyone does or would have reason to think?

The advantage of adopting a deflationary view of the truth-predicate is that it allows us to sidestep problems like this. Deflationism captures everything worth capturing in the realist conception of truth. However, a deflationary view of truth is not an epistemological cure-all.

Scepticism and generality

Great philosophical battles have been fought over the Nature of Truth. The combatants have generally thought that the fate of human knowledge was at stake: that if we misunderstand truth, we will have no defence against radical scepticism. But I think that questions about the nature of truth have much less to do with epistemology than is commonly supposed.

As far as the Agrippan problem is concerned, it seems clear that no elaborate ideas about truth are presupposed. All the sceptic needs on this score is the minimally realist concession, granted even by deflationism, that our believing something to be true and its actually being true are not the same thing. Given this much, he can ask us to back up our belief, and we are off and running. But the concession in question involves no more than the generalizing use of truth-talk that deflationism highlights.

Cartesian scepticism may seem to be another matter, for this form of scepticism does seem to concern whether our experiences or beliefs correctly represent external reality. However, here too the heart of the problem lies with the unusual generality of the sceptic's questions. What the sceptic wants to know is how anything at all that we believe about the world amounts to knowledge: what justification we have to think that any of our beliefs about the world are true. Here, again, he is employing truth-talk in its generalizing capacity, to call in question the indefinitely many things we believe about the world around us, but cannot simply list.

To come to terms with scepticism, we must investigate the apparently innocent generality of the sceptic's questions. We shall make a start on this in the next chapter, though the argument will not be completed until Chapter 16.

Notes

1. Isaiah Berlin, 'Empirical Propositions and Hypothetical Statements', in Berlin (1979).
2. For a subtle elaboration of this theme, see Stroud (1984a), esp. chs. 4, 5.
3. For deflationary approaches to truth, see 'Facts and Propositions', in Ramsey (1990);

Quine (1990), ch. 5; and esp. Horwich (1998*b*). Blackburn and Simmons (1999) is an excellent anthology of papers about truth, many having to do with the pros and cons of deflationism.

4. Only more or less because, without some restrictions on admissible substitutions, a schema like '"p" is true if and only if p' will generate semantic paradoxes, such as the famous paradox of the liar. Much philosophical work on truth is devoted to explaining how the paradoxes can be avoided. For more on this (somewhat technical) topic, see Soames (1999).

5. This is emphasized by Brandom (1994), ch. 5.

6. This idea, which goes back to C. S. Pierce, has recently been defended by Putnam. See e.g. Putnam (1981), ch. 3.

7. Blanshard (1939), ch. 25. For more detailed criticism of the coherence theory of truth, and its relevance to scepticism, see Williams (1996*a*), chs. 6, 7.

13

Evidence and Entitlement

Diagnostic approaches to scepticism

Foundationalism and the coherence theory represent *direct* responses to scepticism. Taking the sceptic's arguments at face value, they attack one or more of his acknowledged premises. Diagnostic responses take a more roundabout approach.

We can make a rough-and-ready distinction between two diagnostic strategies. *Therapeutic* diagnosis treats sceptical problems as *pseudo-problems* generated by misuses or misunderstandings of language. On this approach, sceptical claims and arguments do not really make sense. The problem is, however, that we seem to understand such things well enough to appreciate how they generate a space of epistemological theories, structured by the possible forms of direct response. *Theoretical* diagnosis takes a different approach, questioning the naturalness or intuitiveness of the sceptic's arguments rather than their intelligibility. It aims at showing sceptical arguments to be much more complex and theory-laden than their proponents want to admit, deepening our understanding of such arguments by making available for critical scrutiny their *unacknowledged* theoretical preconceptions.[1]

I do not want to ride the distinction between therapeutic and theoretical diagnosis too hard. It may turn out that the sceptic's presuppositions extend into the theory of meaning. If they do, a theoretical diagnosis of the sceptic's presuppositions may encourage second thoughts about how well we understand everything he says. I introduce the distinction for two reasons. First, I want to head off a tendency to be too quick to accuse the sceptic of not making sense: for example by charging that his idea of a reality that transcends experience is obviously unintelligible. Second, I want to distance myself from the ideal of a *purely* therapeutic approach to philosophical problems. By this I mean the ideal of exposing philosophical problems as illusory while avoiding any theoretical commitments of one's own. We achieve a lot if we get the sceptic to share the burden of theory. We do not have to imagine that we ourselves escape it entirely.

A diagnostic approach is promising because of the conditions scepticism must meet to be a problem and not just a puzzle. First and foremost, scepticism must be intuitive, in the sense that it must exploit only our most everyday, lowest-common-denominator ideas about knowledge and justification. If sceptical arguments turn out to depend on contentious theoretical ideas, we can see scepticism as reflecting on those ideas, rather than on our everyday epistemic practices. Scepticism will prove to be rooted, not in the human condition, but in a particular genre of epistemological theorizing

Finally, a diagnostic approach is needed because sceptical arguments appear (or can be made to appear) intuitive. (That is one reason why they cannot simply be dismissed.) But perhaps appearances are misleading. The task of theoretical diagnosis is to show that this is so.

Let us now turn to scepticism itself, beginning with Agrippan scepticism.

Sceptical commitments

When I introduced the distinction between personal and evidential justification, I noted that many philosophers have been attracted to a strongly 'intellectualist' account of the relation between them, according to which personal justification is subject to what I called the *Prior Grounding Requirement*. My claim is that the Prior Grounding conception of justification must be presupposed by the Agrippan argument, *if it is to amount to an argument for radical and general scepticism*. In other words, scepticism is a serious problem only if it is *not* natural or intuitive.

To see why this is so, we need to look more closely at what the Prior Grounding conception of justification involves. I suggest that we analyse it into four sub-principles:

(PG1)   *No Free Lunch Principle.* Epistemic entitlement—personal justification—does not just accrue to us: it must be earned by epistemically responsible behaviour.

(PG2)   *Priority Principle.* It is never epistemically responsible to believe a proposition true when one's grounds for believing it true are less than adequate.

(PG3)   *Evidentialism.* Grounds are evidence: propositions that count in favour of the truth of the proposition believed.

(PG4)   *Possession Principle.* For a person's belief to be adequately grounded, it is not sufficient for there merely to be appropriate evidence for it. Rather, the believer himself or herself must possess (and make proper use of) evidence that makes the proposition believed (very) likely to be true.

These four principles accord well with the thought that knowledge requires both personal justification and adequate grounding, while also explaining why this distinction is not one of deep theoretical significance. (PG1) and (PG2) imply the uniform subordination of personal justification to grounding. By (PG2), believing on less than adequate grounds is always irresponsible and hence, by (PG1), never justified. Call this 'the Dependence Thesis'. (PG3) and

(PG4) add to this a strongly *internalist* account of what it is for someone's belief to be adequately grounded. On this view, a person's grounds must be evidence in the strong sense: further beliefs—or if not beliefs, some other personal cognitive state—in virtue of which he holds the belief in question and to which he has immediate cognitive access. A person's belief may have been formed by a method that is *in fact* reliable. It may even have been the result of a process that, in the circumstances, ensures that it is true. But this externalist form of grounding, where a person is not necessarily aware of the factors that make his belief truth-reliable, is just what (PG3) and (PG4) exclude. This exclusion is strongly motivated by the dependence thesis. Externalist 'grounding' is something that 'just happens'. It therefore fails to provide the kind of earned entitlement that epistemic justification requires. The Prior Grounding conception of justification involves ideas about the relation between justification, responsibility, and grounding that are made for each other.

At the heart of the Agrippan argument is the apparently fatal trilemma: any attempt to justify a belief must open a vicious regress, end with a brute assumption, or go in a circle. The sceptic concludes that no one is ever justified in believing one thing rather than another. Given the distinctions we have just drawn, we see that this conclusion concerns epistemic entitlement: personal justification. However, all the sceptic's argument shows is that there are limits to our capacity to *give reasons* or *cite evidence*. This is a point about grounding. To get from what he argues to what he concludes, the sceptic must take it for granted that no belief is responsibly held unless it rests on adequate and citable evidence. He needs the Prior Grounding Requirement. More precisely, he needs the Dependence Thesis (to link responsibility with grounding) and Strong Internalism (to identify grounding with the possession of evidence). Nothing less will do the job.

Another model

If this diagnosis is right, there are various ways to meet Agrippan scepticism, depending on which of the sceptic's presuppositions we decide to reject and how we reject them. Radical externalists reject them all. They have no interest in (PG1) and (PG2), since they deny that knowledge requires any kind of personal justification. This allows them to dispense with (PG3) and (PG4) as well since, detached from all questions of responsibility, grounding need have no links with the possession of citable evidence. However, since I have argued against radical externalism, this approach is not open to me. In my view, (PG1) to (PG4) are not wholly without point. But they are unacceptable as the sceptic interprets them.

We can preserve the link between knowledge and justification without accepting the Prior Grounding requirement. As we have noted, though so far without much elaboration, we can see justification as exhibiting what Robert Brandom calls a 'default and challenge structure'.[2] The difference between the 'Prior Grounding' and 'Default and Challenge' conceptions of justification is like that between legal systems that treat the accused as guilty unless proved innocent and those that do the opposite, granting presumptive innocence and throwing the burden of proof onto the accuser. Adopting the second model, epistemic entitlement is the default status of a person's beliefs and assertions. One is entitled to a belief or assertion (which, remember, is an implicit knowledge-claim, unless clearly qualified) in the absence of appropriate 'defeaters': that is, reasons to think that one is *not* so entitled.

Appropriate defeaters cite reasonable and relevant error-possibilities. There are two main types. Non-epistemic defeaters cite evidence that one's assertion is false: this evidence might be purely negative, or it might be positive evidence for the truth of some incompatible claim. Epistemic defeaters give grounds for suspecting that one's belief was acquired in an unreliable or irresponsible way. Here the objector concedes that his interlocutor's claim or belief might be true but denies that it is well grounded. The types are not exclusive. Sceptical scenarios are meant to work both ways.

There is something right about (PG1). The status of epistemic subject does not come with mere sentience: it has to be earned through training and education. But the sceptic (and the traditional epistemologist) give the No Free Lunch principle a much stronger reading: they take it to require that entitlement must be earned by taking *specific positive steps* in *each* situation in which entitlement is claimed. This is what allowing for default entitlements lets us deny. However, this is not to say that personal justification is completely independent of the ability to give grounds for what one believes, so there is some point to (PG2) as well. What we should reject is only the idea that a responsible believer's commitment to providing grounds is *unrestricted*. A claim to knowledge involves a commitment to respond to whatever appropriate challenges emerge, or to withdraw the claim should no effective defence be available. In claiming knowledge, I commit myself to my belief's *being* adequately grounded—formed by a reliable method—but not to my having *already established* its well-groundedness. This sort of defence is necessary only given an appropriate challenge: a positive reason to think that I reached my belief in some unreliable manner.

Notice that, on this view, the grounding required by knowledge can be understood, in appropriate cases, in the way that externalists recommend: I would only have to defend such externalist grounding if some appropriate doubt were raised. At the same time, if a belief of mine, no matter how responsibly held, were not well grounded, it would not amount to knowledge. Even though we do not have an unrestricted commitment to give grounds, our commitment to adequate grounding is always a potential entry point for criticism. The evidentialist conception of grounding, captured by (PG3) and (PG4), is the appropriate conception for the situation where, in order to maintain entitlement, I have to meet a challenge. Meeting challenges means citing evidence (to defeat defeaters). But being able to cite evidence is not the *sine qua non* of being justified.

It is easy to miss the fact that the practice of justifying is only activated by finding oneself in the context of a properly motivated challenge. Since we do not go around stating the obvious, we do not always have to wait for challenges to *emerge*. Interesting claims are typically *not* justified by default: that is why they are interesting. However, the fact that we enter claims in the face of standing objections, automatically triggering the Defence Commitment, should not mislead us into overlooking the connection between the existence of motivated challenges and the obligation to produce positive evidence. Overlooking this connection will lead us to transform the ever-present possibility of contextually appropriate demands for evidence into a unrestricted insistence on grounds, encouraging us to move from fallibilism to radical scepticism. We can and should resist the invitation.

Is scepticism intelligible?

Let us look more closely at how rejecting the Prior Grounding Requirement in favour of a default and challenge model of justification gets us out of Agrippan scepticism.

The Agrippan sceptic is committed to the Prior Grounding Requirement because he *must* assume that the question 'How do you know that?' or 'Why do you believe that?' can *always* reasonably be entered. Implicitly, therefore, he must deny that, to be reasonable, a challenge to a knowledge-claim itself needs to be motivated by reasons. His position is that, simply in virtue of entering a claim or holding a belief, anyone with pretensions to epistemic responsibility accepts an unrestricted commitment to demonstrate entitlement to opinion. Given the Prior Grounding Requirement, this position is entirely reasonable. If all responsible believing is believing-on-evidence, the sceptic is entitled to ask for the evidence to be produced. Absent this requirement, however, this question is not reasonable at all.

The crucial feature of the Default and Challenge conception is that it saddles challengers, as well as claimants, with justificational obligations. Assuming the Prior Grounding Requirement, a request to back up a belief or assertion needs no justification: in conceding an unrestricted commitment to produce grounds, the claimant grants the sceptic's entitlement to request them. The sceptic acquires the right to issue naked challenges.

If we reject the Prior Grounding Requirement, however, the sceptic loses this right. Entitlement to enter a challenge must itself be earned by finding specific reasons for questioning either the truth of the target belief or the claimant's entitlement to hold it, which means that naked challenges are out of order. The question 'How do you know?' or 'Mightn't you be making a mistake?' can always reasonably be met with 'What do you have in mind?' or 'What mistake do you think I might be making?' If no answer is forthcoming, no challenge has been entered and no response is required.

Rejecting the Prior Grounding Requirement thus defangs Agrippa's trilemma. There is no presumption that requests for further justification can be repeated indefinitely. At some point, they are brought to an end by default entitlements. Since these are genuine entitlements, and also subject to the Defence Commitment, they are not mere assumptions. But since they are *default* entitlements, they do not depend on any kind of citable evidence. In particular, they do not have to be self-evidencing or intrinsically credible. To be sure, default entitlement is always provisional. But this is fallibilism, not radical scepticism.

Summing up, the Prior Grounding Requirement generates a vicious regress of justification by enforcing a gross asymmetry in the justificational responsibilities of claimants and challengers. Because claimants are saddled with a standing obligation to cite evidence, challengers are accorded a standing license to request that it be cited. Since the entitlement to issue a challenge need not be earned, naked challenges are always in order. Thus, whatever a claimant offers to back up a claim, a new challenge is automatically authorized. Rejecting the Prior Grounding Requirement cancels the standing obligation to cite evidence, removes the license to issue naked challenges, and stops the regress in its tracks.

Blocking the regress this way raises deep questions about whether the sceptic can question the legitimacy of our beliefs in the general way he aspires to. On the Default and Challenge conception, which insists that claimants and challengers share justificational responsibilities, no move in the game of giving and asking for reasons is presuppositionless. Quite the reverse: all moves depend for their legitimacy—perhaps even for their full intelligibility—on commitments currently not under scrutiny, at least some of which have the status of default entitlements. This applies to challenges, as much as to claims. A motivated, thus concrete, challenge will presuppose a large background of default entitlements. All questioning, hence all positive justifying, takes place *in some definite justificational context*, constituted by a complex and often largely tacit array of current entitlements. In abstraction from all such contexts, epistemic questions simply get no purchase. It follows that although (perhaps) *any* belief may be challenged given appropriate stage-setting, there is no possibility of questioning the legitimacy of our beliefs in the *collective* way that the philosophical sceptic aspires to. On a Default and Challenge conception of justification, there is no room for either the sceptic's global doubts or the traditional epistemologist's global reassurances. Both foundationalism and the coherence theory, which try to provide such reassurance, are solutions in search of a problem. To reinstate the legitimacy of his highly generalized doubts, the sceptic will need some further theoretical resources.

I am greatly in sympathy with this line of thought. But we need to go carefully. What, exactly, have we accomplished? Have we sidelined the sceptic (and the traditional epistemologist) by delegitimating the idea of global justification? Or have we argued for the stronger conclusion that the sceptic's doubts *do not really make sense*?

Even the issue of delegitimation is not straightforward. In a sense, the Default and Challenge conception could be seen as responding to the demand for global reassurance, assuring us that beliefs not justified by evidence can nevertheless be justified by default. Of course, this is not at all what the sceptic and the traditional epistemologist have in mind. What they want is a kind of explicit general grounding, which the Default and Challenge conception expressly excludes. Nevertheless, the fact that the Default and Challenge conception can be seen as giving an account of how, in general, our beliefs might be justified shows that we should be hesitant to rule the sceptic's questions unintelligible merely on the basis of their unusual generality.

The issue of the intelligibility of scepticism requires careful handling. Sceptical reflections are inferentially articulated: for example, in the way they constrain what counts as a response to sceptical questioning. How, then, can the sceptic be talking utter nonsense? On the other hand, pushed far enough, theoretical diagnosis engenders second thoughts about whether the sceptic is altogether intelligible. A genuinely naked challenge—one that cannot be further explained—is no more a challenge than 'Because' is an explanation. If I want to make an objection, I must be able to say *what it is* that I am objecting to. If I can't, no intelligible objection has been made. When the sceptic asks 'Why do you say that?' and we reply 'What do you mean?', we are not just shifting the burden of proof: we are trying to understand what is being demanded of us.

Faced with these conflicting pressures, what should we say? Perhaps that making sense is not an all-or-nothing matter. In a general way, we can see what the sceptic is up to: he sees himself as entitled to issue naked challenges, because he has a conception of justification that underwrites their legitimacy. But this does not mean that such challenges are really fully intelligible. They have no content beyond that conferred by a highly abstract model of the structure of justification.

This is correct as far as it goes. But we can say more. Perhaps the sceptic's naked challenges are not quite as stripped down as they first seem. Perhaps his demand for a global legitimation of our beliefs involves further theoretical presuppositions. If so, our diagnosis is not yet complete. We shall return to this question in Chapter 16. For now, I want to turn to a different kind of objection: that we have not escaped from the sceptical trap but merely deferred the sceptic's triumph.

Meta-scepticism?

Agrippan scepticism is supposed to be intuitive: to depend only on ideas that are evidently implicit in our most ordinary understanding of practices of entering and evaluating claims to knowledge. The first task of theoretical diagnosis is to dispel the illusion of intuitiveness by making explicit the ideas that the sceptic takes for granted or passes off as mere common sense. Here we have made a beginning. If my argument is on anything like the right lines, Agrippan scepticism is not intuitive at all but rather depends on a complex theoretical account of the relations between epistemic entitlement, epistemic grounding, and the ability to cite evidence.

A sceptic can reply that this exercise in diagnosis doesn't get us anywhere. What we now have are two competing conceptions of knowledge— Prior Grounding and Default and Challenge—both with some plausibility. But unless we can show that one of them is correct, the sceptic simply triumphs at second order. If the default and challenge conception is the correct theorization of our ordinary practices of epistemic assessment, we have lots of justified beliefs. But if the Prior Grounding conception is the right way of seeing such things, we do not. If we cannot decide the issue, then, for all we know, radical scepticism is the right verdict on our pretensions to hold justified beliefs. This meta-sceptical conclusion is enough for any sceptic.

If scepticism really is to be a verdict on justification, as we ordinarily understand it, it is crucial that the sceptic not be imposing gratuitously severe epistemic standards. Even if they are not immediately intuitive, his standards must be reflectively recognizable as *implicit* in ordinary practices of epistemic assessment. So the question is: do we have any reason to suppose that the game of giving and asking for reasons, as ordinarily played, respects (or even aspires to respect) the demands of the Prior Grounding Requirement? More precisely, does the Prior Grounding conception fit ordinary practices of claiming, conceding, and denying justification better than does the default and challenge conception?

Before answering this question, let me say that even if the phenomenology of everyday justification were to seriously underdetermine the choice between the competing models of justification—in other words, if both models proved to fit everyday epistemic practices more or less equally well—it would still be theoretically reasonable to prefer the default and challenge account. By hypothesis, that model fits the agreed facts equally well and has the added merit of not generating gratuitous, sceptical paradoxes. It is therefore a better account of ordinary justification.

This point is worth expansion. The Prior Grounding conception both generates the threat of scepticism and constrains our responses to that threat: with the Prior Grounding Requirement in place, we are forced to choose between foundationalism and the coherence theory. If, as I have argued, neither option is satisfactory, the Prior Grounding Requirement leads to scepticism as the final verdict on our pretensions to hold justified beliefs. This means that the Prior Grounding conception of justification represents our ordinary practices of epistemic assessment as self-defeating. Although the whole point of such practices is to make invidious comparisons, there are no grounds for making them. A theory that represents working practices as unworkable is a bad theory.

On theoretical grounds, then, we would be entitled to prefer the default and challenge to the Prior Grounding conception of knowledge and justification, even if the two conceptions were equally faithful to the phenomenology of everyday epistemic practices. However, they are not.

Just as the Default and Challenge model requires, ordinary discussion of epistemic entitlement presupposes a sharing of justificatory responsibilities between claimants and challengers. The Prior Grounding Requirement places all justificatory burdens on claimants and none on challengers. It leaves no room for legitimate challenges to challenges. But such challenges to challenges are a pervasive feature of ordinary reason-giving.

Sceptical arguments, and the traditional epistemological theories to which they give rise, show an evidentialist bias that is far from obviously present in ordinary epistemic practices. It is certainly true that *to justify* a belief is typically to marshal evidence, offer one's credentials, explain away apparent counter-evidence, and so on. *Justifying*, in other words, just is giving grounds. But *being* justified is not always a matter of *having gone through* a prior process of justification.

Connected with this is that fact that ordinary practices of epistemic assessment reflect what Robert Brandom calls 'the social articulation of the space of reasons'.[3] Although knowledge cannot be detached in any general way from the ability to give reasons (when called for), nevertheless in special cases we can attribute knowledge to another person because *we* can defend his reliability, even if he cannot. This social distribution of reason-giving abilities allows us to inherit knowledge by deference to experts. In a complicated society, an enormous amount of knowledge is acquired this way. Here too, the Prior Grounding Requirement, which ties knowledge to an individual's ability to cite adequate evidence for what he believes, is seriously at variance with everyday practice.

These *prima facie* discrepancies are not absolutely decisive. That is, I am not claiming that the Prior Grounding conception of knowledge and justification cannot be squared with the phenomenology of everyday practices of epistemic assessment. Any theory can be squared with *prima facie* counter-evidence if we are willing to take on board enough *ad hoc* hypotheses. For example, while allowing that the Default and Challenge conception gives a good account of what we ordinarily *call* 'knowledge', the sceptic may claim that this so-called knowledge falls short of what we can reflectively see are our own standards. It is really something less than knowledge: knowledge for all practical purposes, say. However, if the only reason for accepting this claim is that doing so saves the Prior Grounding conception from refutation, we strengthen my earlier claim that the Default and Challenge conception is preferable on theoretical grounds. Since it fits more readily with obvious features of everyday practices of epistemic assessment, that conception does not have to be laden with *ad hoc* hypotheses to fill the gaps. It is therefore a better theory.

A defender of the Prior Grounding conception will reply that the advantages are not all on one side. His conception has virtues—and the Default and Challenge conception has corresponding vices—which have so far not been recognized.

When we first introduced Agrippa's trilemma, we agreed that the sceptic will not dispute the phenomenology of everyday justification. In particular, he will admit that ordinary cases of challenge and response will often come to what the interlocutors regard as a satisfactory resolution: typically, when the claimant is able to cite something that the challenger does not dispute. But the sceptic will claim that such justification is entirely dialectical; and we can all see on reflection that such purely dialectical justification is not sufficient for knowledge. Accordingly, if all the so-called 'Default and Challenge conception' amounts to is the claim that such dialectical justification is sufficient for knowledge, that conception is inadequate.

The answer to this is that the Default and Challenge conception is not committed to the view that dialectical justification is all the justification we need. One of the theoretical strengths of the Default and Challenge conception is that it can accommodate insights from epistemic externalism, thereby allowing for genuine external constraint. I shall develop this point further in Chapter 15. But for the present, there is no reason to suppose that our diagnostic strategy leads only to meta-scepticism.

The Problem of the Criterion

Some readers may feel that the argument of the preceding section is question-begging. I have claimed that the Default and Challenge conception of knowledge and justification meshes more smoothly with the phenomenology of everyday epistemic practices than does its competitor, the Prior Grounding conception. Further, I have claimed that the Default and Challenge conception is theoretically preferable, and would be even if both conceptions fitted the agreed facts equally well. But does all this show that the Default and Challenge conception is definitely correct? Or does my position amount to the claim that we are entitled to accept it because it copes with problems better than does its rival? I seem to be arguing that the Default and Challenge conception is default-and-challenge justified: acceptable according to its own standards. Why isn't this the Mode of Circularity?

This objection is an instance of a very ancient sceptical problem, the Problem of the Criterion. Get the anti-sceptic to articulate his own standard for knowledge or justification—his 'criterion'—and then argue that he cannot defend it in a non-question-begging way. Are we justified in adopting a Default and Challenge conception? If so, according to what standard of justification: the same standard or a different one? If we say 'different', not only are we threatened with a regress, we are admitting that the standard we want to defend is not ultimate. But if we say 'the same', we are begging the question. Since I have no wish to defend the Prior Grounding Requirement at any level, the charge of circularity is what I must address.

While the sceptic's argument sounds impressive, it invites diagnosis. The first point to notice is that there are two ways in which we might be interested in the 'correctness' of an abstract model of justification. One way, which has been our main concern up to this point, is descriptive or theoretical: is the model plausible as an explicit statement of the implicit normative structure of our ordinary practices of epistemic assessment? The other way is normative: is the Default and Challenge conception normatively correct? Is it the right way to think about knowledge and justification? Does it embody standards that ought to inform our practices, whether or not they do inform them, or that we are entitled to adopt, whether or not we have yet adopted them?

The distinction between the descriptive and the normative issue is not absolute. Bringing implicit structures to light may well involve an element of idealization, blurring the distinction between exposing our presuppositions and revising them. But distinctions can be useful without being knife-edged.

Taking the question of the 'correctness' of the Default and Challenge conception descriptively, there is a kind of circularity in defending it according to Default and Challenge standards. But the circularity is not vicious. We can responsibly accept this conception if we can meet the relevant challenges; but setting this as the standard we *must* meet does not guarantee that we *can* meet it. An epistemological theory can fail to be justifiably acceptable by standards that the theory itself sets. Self-vindication is not guaranteed in advance.

The same general answer applies, taking the question normatively. However, in this case matters are complicated by the issue of what considerations bear on the correctness of epistemic standards. Or is talk of correctness, in the sense of truth, out of place with respect to norms? For aren't norms like the rules of a game, mere arbitrary conventions?

The question of how to understand the correctness of epistemic norms is important. Indeed, it is the key to a deeper diagnosis of scepticism than we have achieved so far. I shall therefore explore it further in succeeding chapters. For now, however, I suggest that we look at the issue pragmatically. In saying this, I mean that we take into consideration the interests that are subserved by practices of epistemic assessment. (Recall from the Introduction my claim that there must be some *value* in knowledge, something that gives us an interest in having it.) Bringing in interests, we can see that likening epistemic standards to the rules of a game (the game of giving and asking for reasons) does not make them arbitrary. After all, the rules of football are not arbitrary. Rather, they are adapted to human physical capabilities, in the light of our interest in playing a game with a certain level of competitiveness. If the goals were forty feet wide, scoring would be too easy. If they were two feet wide, no one would ever score. Similarly with standards of justification: they can be evaluated in the light of our epistemic interests: avoiding errors, coming to believe significant truths, improving our theories, and so on.

Viewed in this pragmatic perspective, the Prior Grounding conception does particularly badly. No proposed normative structure for our epistemic practices is useful if it precludes making any distinction between justified and unjustified beliefs. Unless this distinction can be made, there are no such practices. The Prior Grounding Requirement, which makes scepticism unavoidable, is self-defeating in just this way. The Default and Challenge conception, which heads off scepticism, is normatively preferable.

Of course, this assumes that the default and challenge conception does not also self-destruct. To be sure that it is satisfactory, we need to develop it further. We also need to see how it helps us deal with Cartesian scepticism. In pursuing these projects, we will be led to deepen our diagnosis of both sceptical questioning and the traditional epistemological theorizing it inspires.

Notes

1. The distinction between theoretical diagnosis and direct refutation is not a sharp one. Inevitably, what the sceptic acknowledges and what he leaves unsaid depends on how sceptical arguments are formulated. In practice, however, the distinction is clear enough. This is because the need for sceptical arguments to appear to be natural or intuitive sets limits to what the sceptic can afford to acknowledge. The danger of over-explicitness is that his scepticism will modulate from philosophical scepticism to scepticism about certain philosophical theories of knowledge. He will not show, in an unqualified way, that knowledge is impossible but only that it is impossible given certain adventitious standards, dictated by controversial epistemological ideas.

2. Although the phrase is Brandom's, there are many prior articulations of this general conception. One of the most important is to be found in J. L. Austin's seminal essay 'Other Minds', in Austin (1961). I believe, however, that this conception of justification is very ancient, originating in Academic theories of 'sceptical assent', particularly Carneades' doctrine of the 'tested impression'. Since the ancient sceptics and their opponents contrast sceptical assent with knowledge, ancient attacks on the possibility of knowledge are not necessarily radical in my sense. However, it is notable that the Pyrrhonian sceptics attacked even 'sceptical' epistemologies like that of Carneades. Default and Challenge structures show up in non-epistemological accounting practices

too. Consider a different sense of 'responsibility': accountability for one's actions. Here, again, 'responsibility' is the default position: one is accountable unless in possession of an appropriate excuse. This view of responsibility is the one taken by Austin in his famous paper 'A Plea for Excuses', in Austin (1961). Austin's views on knowledge and freedom are importantly connected.

3. Brandom (1995).

14

Knowledge in Context

Contextualism

The Agrippan problem seems to force us to choose between two conceptions of knowledge: as having either a foundational structure or a coherence (mutual support) structure. Our critical examination of the Prior Grounding Requirement has thrown up a third possibility: that knowledge conforms to a Default and Challenge structure. In this model, questions of justification always arise in a definite justificational context, constituted by a complex and in general largely tacit background of entitlements, some of which will be default. Thus the Default and Challenge model leads to what I shall call (with some misgivings) a *contextualist* picture of justification.[1]

Because the contextualist picture shows affinities with both foundationalism and coherentism, it does not amount to a simple rejection of either of these traditional approaches. However, since it also differs sharply from both, it is best seen as *sui generis* and not as a variant of either traditional theory. But to make good on this claim, I need to clarify what I understand by a contextualist conception of knowledge and justification.

Aspects of context

The fundamental idea of contextualism is that standards for correctly attributing or claiming knowledge are not fixed but subject to circumstantial variation. We can classify the factors that influence the epistemic status of claims and challenges under five main headings.[2]

In the first place, justification is subject to *intelligibility or semantic constraints*. Wittgenstein remarks that, if you tried to doubt everything, you would not get as far as doubting anything. This is not a matter of practicality: one reason we have lots of default entitlements is that holding many true beliefs, or not being subject to certain kinds of error, is a condition of making sense, thus of being in a position to raise questions at all. Unless we routinely get lots of things right, it is not clear what we are talking or thinking *about*, if anything. Wittgenstein makes the point with characteristic flair: 'Suppose a man could not remember whether he had always had five fingers or two hands? Should we understand him? Could we be certain of understanding him?'[3] The answer is: no, we could not be certain. At some point, 'mistakes' shade off into unintelligibility. Someone who cannot do the simplest calculations, or perform the simplest counting operations, is not making arithmetical mistakes: he does not understand numbers. Of course, there is no sharp boundary here—that is why mistakes shade off into unintelligibility—but the fact remains that one cannot, in just any circumstances, be mistaken about anything whatsoever. A contextualist must therefore be careful about how he states his fallibilism. It is tempting to say that anything can be called in question, but not everything at once. But it is not true even that anything can be called in question in any situation. To be intelligible at all—and not just to be reasonable—questioning may need a *lot* of stage-setting. As we shall see, this is true of the sceptic's attempt to call in question our most ordinary and obvious judgements about the world around us.

Intelligibility constraints have to do with our being able to raise meaningful questions at all. But the exclusion of certain types of doubt can also arise from what is required to raise questions of some specific kind. I shall call these exclusions *methodological constraints*; and I shall call propositions that have to be exempted from doubt, if certain types of question are to be pursued, *methodological necessities.*

The boundary between intelligibility and methodological constraints is not a sharp one. Methodological constraints can be seen as intelligibility constraints specific to certain forms of investigation. We are thus led to our second—broadly methodological—type of factor influencing contextual constraints on justification. Methodological necessities are a source of default entitlements because they determine the *direction of inquiry*. For example, serious worries as to whether the Earth even existed five minutes ago, or whether every piece of documentary evidence is some kind of forgery, do not result in an especially scrupulous approach to historical investigation. Rather, they preclude any engagement in historical research. The need to recognize methodological limitations on doubt is not, as the sceptic has it, a reflection of our practical limitations but a fundamental fact about the *logic* of inquiry. Nor is it a matter of our applying more relaxed standards, lowering what Robert Fogelin calls the 'level of scrutiny' to which claims are subjected.[4] The direction of inquiry has to do, not with the level, but with the *angle* of scrutiny. There is no simple relation between level and angle. Within the practice of doing history, we can be more or less strict in our standards of evidence. But some questions have to be set aside for us to think historically at all.

While particularly clear with respect to the methodological necessities of organized forms of inquiry, such as historical research, the point that the direction of inquiry limits the range of the dubious is entirely general. What we *are* looking into is a function of what we are leaving alone. We can no more inquire into everything at once than we can travel simultaneously in all directions. This point applies as much to the most arcane theoretical inquiries as to practically oriented investigations. Indeed, to speak of it as a 'limitation' is misleading. The point of such constraints is to make focused questioning possible. Such constraints are agents of change, not bulwarks of dogmatism.[5]

Factors of the third type are *dialectical*. Given a certain direction of inquiry, various possible defeaters may or may not be in play. Sometimes, claims may face standing objections, in which case they will not enjoy default status. But default status can be lost as new problems arise, just as hitherto accepted justifications can be undermined by new evidence. The epistemic status of claims and beliefs changes with developments in the dialectical environment.

Factors of the fourth type are *economic*. A defeater does not come into play simply by virtue of being mentioned: there has to be some reason to think that it might obtain. How much reason we require fixes the severity of our epistemic standards or level of scrutiny. If we insist on ruling out even very remote error-possibilities, we are imposing severe standards for knowledge and justification. Costs and benefits—economic factors—figure in here. If it is important to reach some decision, and if the costs of error are fairly low, or if we gain a lot by being right and lose little by being wrong, it is reasonable to take a relaxed attitude to justificational standards. If the costs of error are high, more demanding standards may be in order. The opportunity costs of further inquiry can also be relevant. Of course, in referring to 'economic' factors I do not have in mind only monetary or material considerations. Anything we value is a benefit and anything we would rather avoid is a cost. I call these considerations 'economic' to stress the point that there is typically no purely epistemological answer to the question of what level of epistemic severity is contextually reasonable.

Methodological, dialectical, and economic factors concern primarily the epistemic responsibility dimension of justification. They reveal that the relationship between personal and evidential justification is multiply contextual. In the first place, with respect to maintaining epistemic responsibility, the *existence* of a properly motivated challenge determines whether evidential justification—in the strict sense of citable evidence—is required *at all* to secure personal justification. In the second place, contextual factors fix the adequacy conditions on evidential justification's securing personal justification. Most importantly, they determine what potential defeaters ought to be excluded. These will never amount to every logically possible way of going wrong, but will be restricted to a range of relevant alternatives.[6] However, there are two sources of irrelevance that must not be confused. An error-possibility may be beside the point—strictly irrelevant to the subject in hand—or, while not strictly irrelevant, it may be too remote a possibility to be worthy of serious consideration.

So much for personal justification. But for a person to have knowledge, his belief must be adequately grounded (whether or not he is aware of its grounds and can cite them as evidence). Here, contextual factors of a fifth type come into play. We can call these *situational* factors. Epistemic contexts are not exhausted by methodological and dialectical considerations: facts about the actual situations in which claims are entered or beliefs held are crucial too. This is because, in claiming knowledge, we commit ourselves to the objective well-groundedness of our beliefs. We are open to the existence of relevant defeaters that we have overlooked or not yet uncovered, even if blamelessly. Our commitment to groundedness is thus an important source of openness to self-correction.

Situational factors highlight the externalist element in contextualism. The 'adequate grounds' dimension of justification has a doubly 'external' character. Because there is default entitlement, a claimant need not always be aware of the grounds for his belief, in order to be epistemically responsible. But the adequacy of his grounds—whether he is aware of them or not—will depend in part on what real-world possibilities those grounds need to exclude. I say 'in part' because standards of adequacy are always standards that we fix in the light of our interests, epistemic and otherwise. Even when considering the objective adequacy of grounds for a belief, questions of epistemic responsibility can never be wholly forgotten.

An example

A simple example will illustrate how contextual constraints on justification operate. Seeing someone drive by in an old sports car, two people engage in the following exchange:

A: Isn't that old sports car an E-Type?
B: Yes, a rare early model.
A: What makes you say that: don't they all look pretty much the same?
B: Sure, but that one had external bonnet latches which you only get on the first five hundred cars.

Here A and B concede to each other various default entitlements—that an old car just passed by, and so on. Without such concessions, their conversation could not take the specific direction it does take (methodological factors). Indeed, if certain things (e.g. the capacity to tell a car from an elephant) could not be taken for granted, the speakers could not have any kind of intelligible exchange about the vehicle passing by (semantic factors). But B makes a claim implying special expertise. Although sometimes this alone may be enough to invite a challenge, here A has a specific reason for querying B's identification. He points out, correctly, that the various versions of this particular car are very similar. If, as A suspects, B's remark was prompted by a casual glance at the passing car, this is an epistemic defeater. Citing it challenges B to back up his claim, altering the dialectical context.

B's response is sufficient to meet A's challenge. Or rather, it is sufficient given the severity of epistemic standards appropriate to a casual conversation. For example, B has not ruled out the possibility that what seem to be external latches are non-functional, added to make a later car look like an early model. Normally he wouldn't be expected to. But if A were thinking of buying the car (an economic factor), this might be worth looking into.

Even if the evidence B cites is not defective this way, it still does not rule out every conceivable way in which his claim might have been false. For example, it does not exclude the possibility that what they have just seen is a *replica* of the model in question. But B has no obligation to exclude this possibility unless there is some reason to suspect that it might obtain. Of course, A could try to provide a reason (appropriate to the operative standard of justificational severity):

A: Maybe it's not the real thing. I read that some firm was making replicas of vintage Jaguars.

B: Not E-Types. There are so many survivors that a replica would cost more than an original.

Unless A can think of some way of challenging B's latest response, B maintains entitlement to his claim.

By showing that his original claim was not epistemically irresponsible, B secures personal justification. Still, we might wonder about his evidential justification. Evidence is supposed to be objectively adequate: to support a knowledge claim, it has to 'establish the truth' of what has been stated. Do B's grounds accomplish this, given that there are ways of going wrong that they do not exclude? After all, B's argument does not rule out the possibility that some wealthy enthusiast has had a replica built regardless of cost, perhaps with updated mechanical components to improve reliability.

It is in connection with the objective adequacy of grounds that situational factors come into play. We can think of these factors as determining a broader informational context or environment constituted by relevant facts, known or knowable, though not necessarily by or to the epistemic agents in question. To see what this comes to, suppose that, in fact, nobody does go in for building replica E-types, or for modifying later cars to look like early models: in this situation, B's grounds for identifying the car as an early model are objectively as well as dialectically adequate though, in a different situation, they would not have been.

There is considerable indeterminacy about the objective adequacy of grounds, resulting from the fluidity of contextual boundaries. Suppose that a few relevant replicas have been made. But all have been sold abroad, so that there aren't any where A and B live. Are B's grounds (the external locks) still objectively adequate? It depends how we draw the boundaries. How we do this always depends at least in part on considerations of epistemic responsibility.

Suppose that B had known that there were a few replicas in foreign hands: would he still have been responsible in making his claim? Surely he would: there is no reason to demand evidence that excludes such (literally) distant possibilities, even when their existence is acknowledged. However, the fact that standards of adequacy can never be fixed in total abstraction from questions of epistemic responsibility (and the interests that guide them) does not compromise the objective character of the grounding requirement. The fact that considerations of responsibility help set the standards for a belief's being adequately grounded does not guarantee us the ability to meet those standards. We can and do fail to satisfy standards that we set for ourselves.

Contextualism and foundationalism

To see how contextualism relates to foundationalism, we must recall that foundationalism comes in two forms. One is structural foundationalism:

> (STF) (i) There are basic beliefs, beliefs that are *in some sense* justifiably held without resting on further evidence. (ii) A belief is justified if and only if it is either itself basic or inferentially connected, in some appropriate way, to other justified beliefs.

The other is foundationalism proper, substantive foundationalism:

> (SUF) (i) and (ii) as above. (iii) There are certain kinds of beliefs (or other forms of awareness—e.g. experiences) that, by their very nature—that is, in virtue of their content—are fitted to play the role of terminating points for chains of justification. These beliefs (or other conscious states) are epistemologically basic because *intrinsically credible* or *self-evidencing*.

Contextualism is definitely *not* substantively foundationalist. Default justi- fication is not associated with any particular kinds of belief. Whether a belief enjoys this status depends on a large number of contextually variable factors: the current state of knowledge (including critical responses to received views), the particular inquiry in which we are engaged, and much else besides. Indeed, the very same belief can go from default to non-default justificational status. So, not only is there no need for the contextualist to postulate special 'epi- stemic kinds' of basic beliefs, it would go against the spirit of contextualism to do so.

While contextualism is definitely *not* substantively foundationalist, it looks *prima facie* like a form of structural foundationalism. Since our default entitlements do not depend on further evidence, don't they amount to a kind of heterogeneous and shifting foundation? If you like. The fact remains, how- ever, that contextualism differs sharply from traditional foundationalism, even when foundationalism is viewed as a largely structural doctrine. As we saw, foundationalism embodies an atomistic conception of justification:

intrinsic credibility ensures that each basic belief is justified all by itself, without regard to further beliefs, the context of inquiry, or our real world situation. The justificational relevance of basic to non-basic beliefs enjoys a similar independence of such contextual factors: justificational relations between beliefs depend on content (meaning) alone. Contextualism rejects both aspects of the foundationalist's epistemological atomism. In any context of justification, explicitly or tacitly, there will always be a large number of beliefs and commitments in play. As we shall see in the next chapter, some of these commitments can be epistemically relevant without playing a direct justifying role. For example, we may need to know certain things in order to be able to recognize what would or would not count as a reasonable challenge to a particular claim we have advanced. But this knowledge will not function as grounds for the claim in question. This means that, in a given context of justification, certain commitments function as fixed points without its being correct to see whatever judgement is the focus of interest as *resting* on them.

This point is worth elaborating. I have said that, in any context of justification, there will always be lots of further beliefs and commitments in play. Exactly what they are will depend on what is at issue. This does not exclude the possibility that certain propositions function as fixed points across a wide range of contexts. Indeed, for some propositions, there may be no contexts in which they are up for grabs: we simply have no idea what would count as a challenge to them. They will, as Wittgenstein puts it, 'lie apart from the route traveled by inquiry'.[7] Nevertheless, such fixed-point propositions need not be seen as foundations in anything like the traditional sense. As Wittgenstein explains:

I do not explicitly learn the propositions that stand fast for me. I can discover them subsequently like the axis around which a body rotates. This axis is not fixed in the sense that anything holds it fast, but the movement around it determines its immobility.

No one ever taught me that my hands don't disappear when I am not paying attention to them. Nor can I be said to presuppose the truth of this proposition in my assertions etc., (as if they rested on it) while it only gets its sense from the rest of our procedure of asserting.[8]

As this example suggests, ordinary practices of empirical inquiry and justification are not beset by sceptical doubts about the continuing existence of physical objects, such as my hands. But this is not just a matter of making an assumption. These bedrock certainties derive their content—their meaning— from the particular practices of inquiry and justification that hold them in place. To believe in an historical past, or an external world, just is to recognize certain types of error possibility, to demand certain kinds of evidence (in appropriate circumstances), and so on. Because such certainties are *semantically embedded* in our epistemic practices—thus unintelligible apart from them—it is a mistake to see those practices as justificationally dependent on the 'presuppositions' they embed. They are not assumptions because they are not, in the relevant sense, foundational at all.

These reflections point to a very deep difference between contextualism and traditional foundationalism. As I noted in Chapter 1, our epistemological tradition has tended to focus on propositional knowledge, drawing a sharp distinction between 'knowing that' and 'knowing how'. From a contextualist standpoint, it is wrong-headed either to insist on a sharp distinction or to treat knowing-that as theoretically fundamental. Certainly, we can investigate the contextual constraints and presuppositions governing particular kinds of inquiry: but it is doubtful in the extreme whether we can make them fully explicit in the sense of listing them exhaustively or reducing them to some simple set of rules. Relevant evidence, appropriate objections, and suitable replies are things we have to learn to recognize by projection from examples. No one who lacked this ability could make much of propositionally formulated rules or presuppositions. Possessing it is what we call having 'good judgement', though there is a (vague) limit to how bad a person's judgement can be without his lacking the capacity to judge at all. For a contextualist, there cannot be a sharp distinction between knowing-that and knowing-how because being able make judgements—the precondition of any knowing-that—involves know-how essentially. This is why propositional knowledge and certain kinds of know-how are acquired together. Propositional knowledge is not self-contained: not because it rests on some pre-propositional knowledge-by-acquaintance, but because it is embedded in the practical mastery of forms of discourse and inquiry.

Contextualism and the coherence theory

Contextualism and coherentism have certain affinities. Contextualism embodies a kind of local or modular holism. Thus, like the coherence theorist, the contextualist rejects the thought that particular beliefs have an intrinsic epistemic status and lacks an interest in sorting out our beliefs into *a priori* and *a posteriori*, necessary and contingent, or analytic and synthetic. It is not so much that these traditional distinctions are shown to be completely 'incoherent'. Rather, they begin to look like ways of talking we could usefully do without. From a contextualist standpoint, the empiricist account of *a priori* knowledge in terms of analytic or conceptual truth runs together a number of ideas that should be disaggregated: justification without empirical evidence, meaning-constitutivity, unrevisability, and truth in virtue of meaning alone. The methodological necessities that inform some particular kind of inquiry may be held as default entitlements and may fix what we mean by, say, 'historical evidence'. But this does not make them unrevisable: if the kind of investigation they sponsor runs into trouble, they may need to be changed. And if they do not have to be true, they do not have to be true by virtue of meaning.

Again, however, there are differences to balance the similarities. Principally, while anti-atomist, contextualism is not *radically* holistic. Although it insists that justification always presupposes a *critical epistemic mass* of contextually relevant beliefs, contextualism has no use for the coherence theorist's pseudo-totality: our 'system of beliefs' or 'total view'. It is not that we *cannot* think of the sum total of our commitments and methods of inquiry and argumentation as a system (unless doing so leads us to overestimate the extent to which the 'system' is systematic). The point is simply that radical holism gives a misleading picture of justification and inquiry. For the contextualist, all questions of justification arise against and depend for their full intelligibility on presuppositions that are (reasonably) not currently in question. Some will be standing commitments, held in place across a wide range of epistemic or investigative contexts, whereas others will be specifically relevant to the matter in hand. While in neither case will they be absolutely unquestionable, questioning them will shift the focus of inquiry in ways that take other commitments out of the line of fire. Furthermore, when we justify a claim by producing evidence, that evidence will always depend for its significance on a broader informational environment which is never fully surveyable. If these points are accepted, the idea of 'global' justification must be regarded as chimerical. Thus, by offering a principled rejection of the very idea of 'global' justification, the contextualist obviates the need for either criteria of global coherence or privileged access to the contents and structure of one's supposed total view. Contextualism therefore avoids the coherence theory's collapse into foundationalism.

The coherence theory builds in a sharp distinction between factual commitments and epistemic norms. Our factual commitments are expressed by the beliefs that make up our system or total view. Their epistemic status—how well justified they are—depends on how well the system they constitute satisfies certain general epistemic norms or standards: the criteria of coherence. In the contextualist picture, the norm/fact distinction is more methodological than ontological (to borrow a phrase from Brandom).[9] Exempting certain propositions from doubt fixes the direction of inquiry, making a particular context of inquiry or justification the context that it is. Such propositions thus play a normative role: not questioning them is part of the rules of the game. As Wittgenstein says, 'we use judgments as principles of judgment'.[10] Nevertheless, they may represent substantive factual commitments: situations may arise in which they can and should be subjected to scrutiny. They do not 'lie apart from the route traveled by inquiry' because of some special subject-matter but because of the functional role that we accord them in our investigative practices (and which with effort and imagination we might rescind).

From a contextualist point of view, both foundationalism and the coherence theory are overreactions. Seeing the need for fixed points to block the indefinite repetition of requests for evidence, the foundationalist postulates a stratum of intrinsically credible or self-justifying beliefs. The coherence theorist sees the problems that the demand for intrinsic credibility gives rise to. In particular, he notices that individual beliefs owe their justificational status and significance to relations with further beliefs. But he goes from this reasonable anti-atomism to radical holism, with its own serious difficulties. Contextualism, because it allows both fixed points and epistemic interdependence, has a good claim to incorporate the best features of its traditionalist rivals.

Contextualism and the sources of knowledge

From the outset, I have treated epistemological questions as normative. As Kant made clear to us, the philosophical question is not one of simple *fact* (Where do our beliefs come from?) but one of *right* (What entitles us to hold them?).[11] Historically, however, most philosophical discussions of knowledge have focused on identifying the sources of knowledge. The question has been 'Where does knowledge come from: Reason, the Senses, Revelation?' Indeed, it is because of this stress on sources that Kant is so insistent on distinguishing between *Quid facti?* (the question of fact) and *Quid juris?* (the question of right). He thinks that talk of sources of knowledge is apt to obscure the essentially normative character of epistemological questions. I agree. Such talk encourages us to think that asking 'Does knowledge comes from the senses?' is like asking 'Do diamonds come from South Africa?', whereas these questions are quite different in character.

Now, as I noted in Chapter 7, traditional talk of the sources of knowledge need not entail ignoring the normative dimension of epistemological assessment. This is because the faculties that are identified as the sources of knowledge (as opposed to opinion) are conceived in partially normative terms as recognizably reliable and therefore authoritative. Nevertheless, Kant has a point. Talk of the sources of knowledge is not harmless.

To begin to see why, we should take note of two further features of traditional 'sources' of knowledge. In the first place, they are generic: the sources of knowledge are 'the senses' or 'Reason'. Secondly, they are *ultimate*. Such authoritative faculties are sources of what Richard Rorty calls 'privileged representations', beliefs that are the basis for all further inference because they themselves possess a special credibility, derived from their pedigree. In identifying such beliefs, we reach rock bottom: questions of justification cannot be pressed any farther. The picture of knowledge as belief that derives from authoritative sources thus creates a strong prejudice in favour of substantive foundationalism. It also builds in a kind of meta-epistemological foundationalism. Once questions about justification are raised to the level of epistemological theory, citing a generic source, the pedigree that gives basic beliefs their special status, is the last word.

All this bears on questions raised in the previous chapter but not fully resolved there: whether the sceptic's apparently naked challenges are fully intelligible, and whether they are really naked. If I make a claim, implying that I know what I say to be true, the sceptic asks me how I know. Obviously, the sceptic's 'How do you know?' is asked, as Austin says, *pointedly*, the implication being that perhaps you *don't* know. His question is a challenge to me to defend my right to make or accept the claim I have made. Taking for granted the Prior Grounding Requirement on knowledge, the sceptic does not think that this challenge itself needs any licensing or even further explanation. Since I am the one laying claim to knowledge, I am the one who needs to provide grounds, which is as good as to say that naked challenges are entirely in order. By contrast, contextualism insists on further explanation. If a challenger implies that we might be making a mistake, we are entitled to ask how. If the challenger has nothing to say—if his challenge is genuinely naked—then no real challenge has been entered. We have no idea what sort of defence is being demanded of us.

Why doesn't the sceptic see this? And why doesn't he see the emptiness of his naked challenges as reflecting on the conception of justification that licenses them? I think we have the answer. The sceptic's challenge is not altogether naked. Rather, it is generic. The sceptic meets a claim, any claim, with a challenge. If we accept it, our immediate reaction will be to cite evidence specifically relevant to the claim under challenge. But the sceptic's willingness to renew his challenge at every stage indicates that this is not the sort of answer he is looking for. Indeed, my ability to give specific evidence is liable to run out fairly quickly. If you ask me how I know that the car that just went by is an early model E-Type, I can say that I recognized it by its external bonnet locks. But if you ask why I suppose it had bonnet locks, I am not sure what to say, other than that I had a good look at the car and could see them. This is the answer the sceptic wants. In giving it, I raise the debate to the epistemological level. As the sceptic interprets my reply, I commit myself to the authoritative character of a certain generic source of knowledge, in this instance observation or 'the senses'. The real, though typically unavowed, function of the sceptic's apparently naked challenges is to raise the level of the debate in just this way. From the word go, they are implicitly generic. As indefinitely renewable, the very first challenge, if simply accepted, is already a challenge to any and all specific responses it may give rise to. What makes this procedure reasonable—and intelligible, to the extent that it is intelligible—is the presupposition that there are and must be generic sources of knowledge, if there is to be such a thing as knowledge at all.

What we know of ancient scepticism comes mostly from the writings of Sextus Empiricus. In Sextus' writings, the Agrippan strategy is used almost exclusively in connection with the Problem of the Criterion: the problem of validating a proposed source of knowledge. If what I have been arguing is anything like correct, this is no accident. We ascend to the epistemological level to escape the sceptic's infinitely renewable challenges. But once we have agreed to trace knowledge to some ultimate, generic source, there really will seem to be no alternative to either refusing to defend it (thus making an ungrounded assumption) or appealing to that source itself (arguing in a circle). The Agrippan trilemma seems inescapable. However, from a contextualist standpoint, this entire way of thinking is deeply suspect. Many factors influence epistemic status; default credibility has no connection with one particular source or faculty; and since anything we presuppose is potentially criticizable, there is no point in thinking of any source of knowledge as ultimate. Given appropriate stage-setting, erstwhile default entitlements can be called in question. But this is just the open-endedness of inquiry, not a vicious regress of justification. The possibility of error does not imply the impossibility of knowledge.

Epistemological realism

The sceptic raises the Problem of the Criterion by getting his interlocutor to articulate some standard source of knowledge. He then argues that no such standard can be defended in a non-question-begging way. Applied to my diagnosis of scepticism, this problem can be used to suggest that neither the default and challenge conception, nor the contextualist picture of justification to which it leads, can be shown to be correct. Or at least, cannot be shown to be correct by any neutral standard. We may in some sense be entitled to adopt this picture, but we cannot know that it is true.

We are now in a position to see that this charge either ignores the normative character of justification, or treats it in an implausible way. To be sure, the Prior Grounding and Default and Challenge conceptions set different standards for epistemic responsibility, hence for epistemic entitlement; but it is a bad first move to ask, in a flat-footed way, which conception is true. This is to proceed as though there were some fact of the matter—some fact about what the correct standards of epistemic justification are, or ought to be— that holds quite independently of what we take them to be. This is not how things are. Norms, including epistemic norms, are *standards that we set*, not standards imposed on us by 'the nature of epistemic justification'. A belief is no more justified, wholly independently of human evaluative attitudes and practices, than a certain kind of tackle in football is a foul, wholly independently of our practices of judging certain types of tackle to be against the rules.

In saying that epistemic norms are standards we set, I am not supposing that we ever got together to set them. As I have already argued, the constraints that govern particular forms of inquiry exist, in the first instance, implicitly in practice rather than explicitly as precepts. But we can make them (partially) explicit should the need arise; and if it seems like a good idea, we can modify them.

The view I am recommending can be considered a pragmatic conception of norms. The alternative to pragmatism is *epistemological realism*. I briefly introduced the idea of epistemological realism back in Chapter 7, in connection with the distinction between structural and substantive foundationalism. To repeat, epistemological realism is not a metaphysical or ontological position within epistemology: the view that there is a real world out there, which we want to know about. It is a form of extreme realism about the objects of epistemological theory: the view that we have some fixed 'epistemic position' determined by facts about the nature of knowledge or the structure of justification. With the contextualist picture partially sketched in, we see how strong a theoretical commitment this is. We also see that epistemological realism is by no means forced on us by evident features of ordinary justification. It represents a definite choice of theoretical orientation and is, in that sense, optional.

By encouraging us to assimilate normative questions about epistemic standards to causal-factual questions about origins, traditional talk of the sources of knowledge tempts us into epistemological realism. If there are certain ultimate, generic sources of knowledge, which fix our 'epistemic situation', epistemically responsible believing must pay these sources due respect. If it turns out that our ultimate sources are not really up to the job, our epistemic situation is intrinsically defective and we cannot know anything. Or if we cannot show that they are up to the job, then for all we know, we know nothing. One way or another, the sceptic wins the day. By tacitly invoking epistemological realism, the sceptic implies that we are *stuck* with his conception of knowledge: that we cannot responsibly change it, unless we know (and can prove) that it is false. After all, the sceptic is merely opening our eyes to how things are. The right response is: so much the worse for epistemological realism.

This is not the end of the story. The contextualist/pragmatic outlook provokes anxieties of its own. If we set the standards, why can't we believe anything we like, so that objective knowledge is an illusion? Or allowing that, given a particular set of rules, there are correct and incorrect ways of proceeding, aren't different groups free to play by different sets? In other words, does contextualism imply relativism? And if standards can change, is there such a thing as progress?

We have already seen that, in the contextualist picture, inquiry and justification are constrained in several ways. But in allaying anxieties about objectivity, the most important constraint is that provided by observation. Accordingly, observational knowledge will be our next topic. Having developed contextualism further, and having applied its lessons to Cartesian scepticism, we will take up questions about relativism and progress.

Notes

1. My misgivings have to do with the fact that there are several epistemological views described by their advocates as 'contextualist'. See n. 2 below.
2. All contextualist epistemologies involve the basic idea that the standards for attributing knowledge, or justified belief, are in one way or another subject to contextual variation. However, contextualists differ over the sources and effects of this variability. For alternative contextualist epistemologies see Annis (1978), Cohen (1988), DeRose (1995), and Lewis, 'Elusive Knowledge', in Lewis (1999). I think that Fogelin (1994) is a kind of contextualist, though he repudiates the label. For a response to Fogelin that is also relevant to the views of Cohen and DeRose, see Williams (1999*b*).
3. Wittgenstein (1969), para. 157.
4. Fogelin (1994), ch. 5, p. 93f.
5. Similar remarks apply to the suggestion that, even if practically excusable, it is always *epistemically* irresponsible to believe anything on less than adequate evidence. Fogelin calls this view 'Cliffordism', after W. K. Clifford, and claims that traditional theories of knowledge and justification result from the attempt to live up to (unreasonable) Cliffordian standards. See Fogelin (1994), ch. 6. I have learned a great deal from Fogelin's insightful discussion of these matters.
6. The relevant alternative account of knowledge has its roots in Austin. It is further developed in a number of important papers by Fred Dretske. See Dretske (1972) and (1981).
7. Wittgenstein (1969), para. 88.
8. Ibid., paras 152–3.
9. Brandom uses this phrase in connection with Sellar's distinction between observational and theoretical terms. See Sellars (1997), 163. Sellars himself says that this distinction is methodological rather 'substantive' (ibid. 84). Brandom's reformulation is an illuminating gloss.
10. Wittgenstein (1969), para. 124.
11. Kant (1964), p. 120.

15

Seeing and Knowing

Observational constraint

Although foundationalism must be rejected, it can be misleading to say without qualification that knowledge has *no* foundations. As Sellars remarks, to put the point this way

is to suggest that [empirical knowledge] is really 'empirical knowledge so-called', and to put it in a box with rumours and hoaxes. There is clearly some point to the picture of human knowledge as resting on a level of propositions—observation reports—which do not rest on other propositions in the same way as other propositions rest on them.[1]

Foundationalism, especially in its empiricist form, is an attempt to respond to a legitimate demand: that our beliefs be responsive to observational evidence, which must in turn be intelligible as a reliable source of information about the world. Moreover, the requirement of observational constraint is not merely epistemological in a narrow sense. Unless we can see how our reason-giving practices hook up with the world, they are going to look like games played with meaningless counters.[2] Our problem has a semantic as well as an epistemic dimension.

How should we think about observational constraint? The need to see observation as a reliable source of information about our surroundings suggests that we must incorporate insights from externalist reliabilism. At the same time, pure reliabilism is not an option. If *de facto* reliability is to link up with reason-giving, we must make room for reliability-knowledge: knowledge of the extent to which we are reliable observers of the passing scene. But in allowing for reliability-knowledge, we must not relapse into the coherence theory. To find one's way through this maze is no simple matter.

Reasons and responses

The account of observational knowledge I shall present is due in all essentials to Sellars.[3] Following Sellars's lead, I shall begin by not worrying about 'inner' experiences. Instead, I shall discuss observational knowledge as if it were solely a matter of making and acquiring dispositions to make overt reports on various aspects of one's surroundings. But the fact that gives both empiricist foundationalism and Cartesian scepticism their deep appeal—that we get in touch with our surroundings by way of conscious experience—cannot be ignored. Eventually, we must allow for thoughts and sensations, in addition to overt reportings.

Sellars's fundamental insight can be summed up like this: observation reports are *non-inferential* because, as a result of training, they can be made on cue. In an appropriately trained observer, they are elicited—causally—by some aspect of the environment. In this way, they do not depend on inference from evidence. This is the reliabilist aspect of observational knowledge. But, as we noted in Chapter 2, pure reliabilism cannot capture conceptual content, which demands inferential embedding. Accordingly, observation reports *express knowledge* because (i) they function as reasons for further judgements, and (ii) they are subject to evaluation and may require defence. We must, when necessary, be able to justify our reports, even though our entitlement to make them does not depend on a prior justifying inference. Let me elaborate.

On Sellars's view, our capacity for being trained to report reliably on aspects of our surroundings—for example, for acquiring the disposition to respond to the presence of red objects with utterances of 'That is red'—is a necessary condition of observational knowledge. But it is not sufficient. To treat it as sufficient would be to revert to the 'thermometer view' of knowledge. The mercury-level in a thermometer responds reliably to changes in the ambient temperature but, lacking all conceptual abilities, the thermometer does not know how warm the room is. Conceptual thought is essentially embedded in complex practices of inference and argument. Our problem is to hold on to reliabilist insights while respecting the demands of conceptual content. Briefly: what is the role of reliable discriminative responses in what Sellars calls 'the game of giving and asking for reasons'?

A point that Sellars does not discuss is that we cannot take a naive attitude towards reliability. As we have seen, judgements of reliability are not straight-forward 'empirical descriptions' but have a definite normative component. Procedures are reliable only given a range of circumstances in which they are *supposed to operate*, which is something for us to determine in the light of our needs and interests. But even supposing that we have fixed the conditions on reliable reporting, we still cannot allow mere trained responses to express observational knowledge. Why? For the reason already given: mere responses do not express any propositional content at all. Although animals can be trained to respond differentially to environmental stimuli, this does not entitle us to see a pigeon pecking a red disc to get food as *saying that* there is a red disc present. Responses become reports in virtue of further things that we do with them: in particular, treating them as reasons for further judgements. This sort of thing comes with learning a language. Animals do not go in for it.

This is not all. Another reason why mere responses do not express knowledge concerns their epistemic status. To treat observation reports as providing reasons for further judgements is to accord them positive epistemic status,
not arbitrarily but reasonably. In one way, an observation report is reasonably
entered as a reason for further judgements because it is 'an instance of a
general mode of behaviour which, in a given linguistic community, it is reasonable to sanction and support'.[4] The reasonableness of such sanctioning
will reflect the community's experience with the sort of things that people can
be trained to report reliably on. In the context of such a reporting practice,
reports issuing from a properly trained reporter will enjoy default positive
justificational status. It will be reasonable to accept them unless there are
reasons for not so doing: for example, the reporter was not well placed to see
what he claims to have seen, the light was fading, or whatever.

If we are to be able to recognize occasions on which observation reports
must be defended or withdrawn, we need to know something about the conditions in which we are not so reliable. This point has an important consequence. To be capable of observational knowledge, it is not enough (as pure
reliabilists imagine) simply *to be* a reliable reporter on this and that: a person
must *know something about* how reliable he is. Again, this sort of reflective,
epistemic self-knowledge is available only to language-users. Animals and
small children do not have it. Accordingly, they are outside the game of giving
and asking for reasons.

An immediate consequence of this account of non-inferential knowledge is
that no one could have *only* basic observational knowledge. Thus, while a
source of non-inferential knowledge, observation is not the *foundation* of
knowledge in anything like the way that traditional foundationalists suppose.
Observation reports are not encapsulated. Rather, they are reports (and not
just responses) only because they are embedded in broader practices of
judgement and inference. It is worth underlining two aspects of this
embedding.

One aspect involves the 'same-level' linkage between observational and
non-observational uses of the same term and, via this linkage, to uses of other
terms. The inevitability of such connections becomes even clearer if—in the
spirit of the Sellarsian approach—we look beyond the reports that traditional
foundationalists have treated as paradigmatic: reports on 'sensible qualities'
like redness. We can all recognize cars. But to be able to report (with understanding) on the presence of cars—as opposed to being conditioned to utter
the vocable 'car' more or less reliably in the presence of a car—involves being
able to make inferences such as

> There's my car.
> So (if it's functioning, not out of petrol, etc.), we can drive to town.

But to have mastered such inferences is to know general facts about cars, which in turn involves knowing about engines, roads, driving, and much else besides.

The second aspect involves the 'trans-level' linkage of observation reports with the knowledge required for their epistemic assessment.[5] To be able to recognize the relevance of and respond appropriately to challenges to observation reports, I must know a good deal about my perceptual capabilities. It follows that I cannot come, by observation, to know anything, unless I already know lots of things. This consequence is fatal even to modest or 'two-level' versions of foundationalism. According to 'two-level' views, basic beliefs have an intrinsic initial credibility that can be reinforced (and perhaps occasionally degraded) by our subsequent development of a systematic, reflective view of our epistemic abilities. But if Sellars is right, there is no autonomous first level, however modestly conceived. We need reliability-knowledge to have any observational knowledge of particular facts.

This point should encourage second thoughts about Cartesian thought experiments, which are closely connected with the foundationalist conception of experience. Sceptical scenarios—Evil Deceivers and brains in vats—take it for granted that experiential knowledge constitutes just such an autonomous first level. Perhaps we do not understand such thought-experiments as clearly as we like to think.

Back to coherence?

The conclusion we have just reached may seem paradoxical. If acquiring new knowledge presupposes the possession of prior knowledge, how can the process of acquiring knowledge ever get started? Surely, some knowledge must be basic, if the process is to get off the ground. Call this 'the Genetic Argument'.

Far from providing a reason to adopt traditional foundationalism, the Genetic Argument takes that perspective for granted, simply assuming that learning requires isolated, first episodes of knowing: encapsulated knowledge. It doesn't. Observational knowing is complex practice that must be mastered as a whole. In this respect it is like a game: you don't really understand any rule of chess until you have learned them all (and quite a bit else besides). As Wittgenstein says: 'Light dawns gradually over the whole'.[6]

There is no mystery here. The idea that non-inferential knowing presupposes initiation into a complex system of inferential and evaluational practices does not imply that knowledge emerges out of thin air, or that by tugging on our own bootstraps we miraculously elevate ourselves to the level of knowing things. We are *trained* in epistemic practices by others who are *already* competent in them. Knowledge indeed emerges out of prior knowledge. However, this is not because all knowledge can be individually generated, but because the capacity for knowledge is a shared and socially transmitted accomplishment. The thought that all knowledge must in principle be capable of generation 'from within'—that the first-person perspective is the right one for epistemology—is an artefact of Cartesian scepticism, not a self-evidently correct condition on any theoretical approach to knowledge.[7]

The Genetic Argument is not the deep worry about Sellars's (or Wittgenstein's) view. The real question is this: if knowledgeable observation reports presuppose knowledge of our reliability as observers, doesn't this make them non-inferential only in a psychological sense? While 'non-inferential' in the sense of 'spontaneous', they depend justificationally on general beliefs that, in turn, depend justificationally on them. The problem is thus not to explain how a system is built up—to an extent, systems have to be mastered whole, like the rules of chess—but whether, in virtue of building in at least some degree of holism, Sellars's account of non-inferential knowledge collapses into the coherence theory. Notice, in this connection, that the Sellarsian account is the one I offered the coherence theorist as a way of meeting the isolation objection. In making the case that observational knowledge of particular matters of fact presupposes general reliability-knowledge, I have acknowledged the legitimacy of what I called the Rationalized Input Requirement. Why doesn't accepting this entail the collapse of the Sellarsian position into traditional coherentism, with an attendant loss of any genuinely external constraint on our beliefs? *

I am not sure that Sellars is always clear about how to cope with this problem. But we can certainly handle it. Traditional coherentism accepts the Prior Grounding Requirement and, as a result, is committed to a purely internalist conception of knowledge and justification. By contrast, on Sellars's view, reports entered by a properly trained observer enjoy default positive justificational status. To be in the game of observational reporting, we must know things about our observational capacities. But that knowledge does not provide evidential back-up. More importantly, in entering an observation report, we may often properly presuppose that conditions are sufficiently normal for our reporting dispositions to be reliable. Epistemic responsibility does not require that we first ascertain that conditions are normal. Such an inquiry is required only if reasons emerge for thinking that conditions may not be normal. Accordingly, two closely connected features save the Sellarsian account of non-inferential knowledge from collapsing into coherentism. One is that it embodies a Default and Challenge conception of justification; the other is that it involves an element of externalism. Indeed, it is able to involve an element of externalism because it embodies the default and challenge conception.

Recalling a point from the previous chapter, coherence theorists are right when they criticize traditional foundationalism for its extreme epistemic and semantic atomism. Applying this point to the matter in hand, observation reports are only reports because they are inferentially embedded in a larger system of beliefs and observational and inferential practices. They derive their semantic content from the way in which they are so embedded, as moves in a game owe their significance to their place in a system of permissible moves. Observation judgements, therefore, presuppose what I called a critical semantic mass of relevant background beliefs. But acknowledging this does not commit us to the traditional coherence theorist's radical holism: the idea that there are vital questions about justification at the level of 'total views'. On the contrary, the Default and Challenge conception entails that questions of justification always arise in a definite informational context, so that global doubts and global justifications are equally out of order.

Sellars connects his unwillingness to say flat out that empirical knowledge has no foundation with an important concession to empiricism. There is, he says, 'some point to the picture of human knowledge as resting on a level of propositions—observation reports—which do not rest on other propositions in the same way as other propositions rest on them'.[8] The key phrase here is 'in the same way'. Semantically, observation reports are embedded in a rich context of background knowledge, which includes not only a good deal of know-how but a considerable amount of explicit reliability-knowledge. However, this semantic embedding should not be equated with justificational dependence. I do not think that Sellars always makes it plain how the two sorts of dependence are to be separated. The key to separating them is to see empirical knowledge as conforming to a Default and Challenge structure.

Problems now arise from another direction. Given a Default and Challenge conception of justification, why do we need knowledge of our reliability at all? Granting that observation reports must be inferentially linked to further beliefs, why must explicit reliability-knowledge be included in the mix, if observation reports enjoy default credibility? Because without such knowledge we cannot recognize either properly motivated challenges to observation claims or appropriate defences of them. In this way, reliability-knowledge is conceptually presupposed by the game of giving observational evidence. But to repeat, this knowledge does not always play a justificatory role, since it is a rule of the game that observation reports do not normally need positive justification. For this reason, an observation report can presuppose reliability-knowledge and still be non-inferential in an epistemic and not merely a psychological sense. A report can be psychologically spontaneous, default credible (though defeasible), authoritative because an instance of a reliable reporting disposition, and fully justified when entered in conditions that are *in fact* standard. The externalist element in this account of non-inferential knowing, an element made acceptable by rejection of the Prior Grounding Requirement, is the critical factor here. The Sellarsian account of non-inferential knowledge embodies a key point from Chapter 13: that a person can *be* justified in what he accepts without having *gone through* a process of justification.

We can add a final point, again recalled from our discussion of the coherence theory. Because we cannot just ignore observations, in the interest of entrenched opinions, without doing violence to vital epistemic beliefs, our reliability beliefs give particular observations much greater epistemic weight than they would otherwise have. As an obstacle to dismissing inconvenient observations out of hand, our epistemic beliefs increase dramatically the inferential significance of local observational knowledge. In this way, reliability-knowledge plays a crucial role in the enterprise of inquiry.

Sellars sums things up this way: 'empirical knowledge, like its sophisticated extension, science, is rational, not because it has a *foundation*, but because it is a self-correcting enterprise which can put *any* claim in jeopardy though not *all* at once'.[9] This is contextualism, as I understand it: the view that all justification takes place in an informational and dialectical context. The coherentist idea of total justification plays no role in Sellars's thinking.

More on 'looks'

As we have seen, 'looks' or 'appears' talk does not iterate. Although things can appear to be other than as they really are, it makes no sense to suggest that they might appear to appear to be one way while actually appearing to be another. This point seems to speak strongly in favour of the foundationalist idea that experiential knowledge enjoys a special epistemic privilege. What should we say about this?

Sellars offers a way of understanding the failure of operators like 'looks' or 'appears' to iterate that makes no concessions to traditional foundationalism. The key idea is that reporting on how things look is a distinctively qualified or guarded way of reporting on how they are. When I make an unhesitating pronouncement, implicitly representing myself as a knower, I am claiming the right to use what I have just said in further inferences and authorizing you to do the same. When I report on how things look to me, I am reporting on how I am *inclined* to think things are but cancelling the claims that would normally be implied by an unqualified report.[10] Compare: 'That was a bad foul: he should get a yellow card' with 'That looked like a foul but let's wait for the replay'.

This account makes good sense of various features of ordinary 'looks' talk. Most obviously, it does not require any special 'phenomenal' or 'non-comparative' sense of observational predicates. 'Red' in 'looks red' means exactly what it means in 'is red'. The account also handles smoothly the distinction between 'qualitative' and 'existential' looking. Consider the following sentences:

1. There is oil on the road.
2. That liquid on the road looks like oil.
3. It looks as if there is oil on the road.

In making the first claim, I commit myself to the correctness of everything I assert. In making the second, I introduce an element of 'qualitative looking': I commit myself to there being liquid on the road, but withhold commitment as to its being oil. In the third example, the looking is 'existential': I am not committing to there being anything on the road (perhaps the road is just unusually shiny, so the appearance of oiliness is a trick of the light). The difference between qualitative and existential looking is simply a matter of the scope of the 'looks' operator, the scope determining which aspects of my claim I do and do not commit myself to.

On this account, 'looks' talk is not, as foundationalists suppose, an autonomous stratum of language, serving as the foundation for all objective claims. Rather, one could not master the use of 'looks' unless one were already able to make appropriate—thus justified—objective claims. Like our account of non-inferential knowledge, this way of thinking about the logic of 'looks' introduces a measure of holism into our conceptions of both meaning and knowledge. Making appropriate claims of one type is essentially connected with an ability to make appropriate claims of other types. But this qualified holism, while inimical to foundationalism, is not the radical holism of the traditional coherence theory. No use is made of the idea of a total view, which must be justified at a global level if anything we claim is to amount to knowledge.

Still, there is something incomplete about this account of 'looks' talk. The problem is that it is only an account of talk. What about looking itself? What about perceptual appearances? There seems to be something in common between cases of veridical perception ('There is a red triangle in front of me'), qualitative looking ('There is something in front of me that looks red and triangular'), and existential looking ('It looks as if there is something red and triangular in front of me'). What is this something? The answer seems to be that in all three cases we are in the same experiential state, which is why the three claims have a common propositional content (involving 'red' and 'tri-angular' and not, say, 'green' or 'square'). Here we finally make contact with experience as sentience, thus with 'experiences' as inner or private episodes. So far, we have discussed non-inferential knowledge in terms of the making of overt observation reports. Now we need to say something about inner experiences: thoughts and sensations.

Private lives

The idea of mental events as inner or private can be made to seem fraught with sceptical problems. If the thoughts and sensations of another person are utterly hidden from me, how can I know what they are like, or even that they exist at all? Perhaps I am the only person with an inner conscious life. This is the problem of solipsism or 'other minds'.

Since I have no direct access to the mental life of other people, it may seem that the best I can do is to base my beliefs about what others are thinking or feeling on some kind of inductive inference. I notice that when I am in pain, I produce certain characteristic behaviour: grimacing, wincing, and so on. So when I see you grimacing and wincing, I infer that you are experiencing sensations similar to those that produce these reactions in me. This is the 'argument from analogy'. How strong an argument it is has been disputed. I have only one case to go on, my own, and inductive arguments that generalize from one case are properly viewed with suspicion.

A radical response to the other minds problem is logical behaviourism. According to this view, psychological predicates do not describe hidden states or episodes, but rather have to do with overt behaviour. This approach is plausible for a wide range of long-term psychological traits. A vain person is one who is disposed to act in a certain characteristic ways: taking inordinate care over his appearance, seeking praise from others, and so on. To act out of vanity is to act out of such a settled disposition. No private feeling need be involved.

Logical behaviourism sidesteps the problem of other minds. Attributing mental states to other people seems to depend on a shaky argument from analogy only because we are tempted to suppose that such states are directly accessible only to the person whose states they are. If we give up the idea of irreducibly private experience, the problem disappears. But while this anti-sceptical strategy has its attractions, it seems to fly in the face of things we all know: that there are occurrent mental states as well as psychological-behavioural dispositions; that we do have sensations or experiences; that we have a special kind of direct access to them; and that they play an important part in our knowing what is going on in the world around us. We need to say more about 'experience' and its role in empirical knowledge.

Again, Sellars provides the essential ideas for answering such questions.[11] Scientific theories often introduce concepts of 'theoretical entities': objects that are not directly observable, but whose activities explain observable goings-on. Sellars suggests that we think of concepts relating to inner psychological states along just these lines: as theoretical concepts, relative to an observational vocabulary relating to behaviour. Of course, this suggestion will seem absurd if we are still tempted to assimilate sapience to sentience, thus to think of sensations as the objects of 'immediate' knowledge. But these are the very temptations we are trying to put behind us.

Sellars explains the introduction of theoretical entities in terms of 'model and commentary'. Theoretical entities are modelled on familiar entities, in the sense that the theory in which they figure treats them as interrelated in ways that mirror the interrelations of their familiar counterparts or models. But the analogy is never complete. To point out its limitations is the role of the commentary. Thus, the kinetic theory of gases treats molecules as being like minute billiard balls. They bounce around (model). But unlike billiard balls, they are not coloured and cannot be seen with the naked eye (commentary). We will see shortly how this conception of theoretical entities applies to mental events.

Now although theoretical entities are introduced as 'unobservables', they are not beyond the reach of observational evidence. On the contrary, because theories invoke them specifically to explain observable phenomena, it is built into such theories that certain observations are indicative of what the theoretical entities are up to. Theoretical discourse is always introduced with built-in links to observation. To this extent, such links belong to the 'logic' or 'meaning' of such discourse. That there must be such links is the truth grasped by philosophers who talk of 'logically adequate criteria'. However—to reiterate a point already made—criterial links like this, though built into certain meaning-constituting postulates of the theory, are neither analytically true nor unrevisable. Once a theory is up and running, we can modify our ideas about what counts as the best observational evidence for events at the theoretical level. If the theory ceases to pay its way, we can reject it altogether.

Finally and crucially, to speak of entities as 'theoretical' is not to imply that they do not 'really exist' or that talk about them is shorthand for talk about observations. Like that between norm and fact, the observable/theoretical distinction is methodological not ontological. Introducing theoretical entities by way of model and commentary ensures that the entities have properties and relations that cannot simply be read off the observational evidence that bears on them: properties and relations inherited from the model. If the theory works, this is reason to think that the world really does contain what the theory postulates. Indeed, we can come to think of 'theoretical' entities as more fundamental than the objects of common sense.

Turning now to the case of 'inner episodes', Sellars invites us to imagine a community—'our Rylean ancestors'—whose talk about mental states is limited to the sort of long-term dispositional states for which logical behaviourism seems plausible. Perhaps we also need to imagine them as more talkative than we are: they go in for a lot of reporting-out-loud, wanting-out-loud, hoping-out-loud, and so on. As a result, they get on fairly well, anticipating each other's behaviour and co-ordinating their activities. However, an outstanding theoretical genius among them conceives the idea that they would get along even better if they saw each other as going in for more 'speakings' than they give voice to. The model for such inaudible utterances—or, as they come to be called, 'thoughts'—is of course speaking-out-loud. The model stresses that these covert episodes stand in the same logical relations to each other and to overt utterances and actions as do overt utterances. They also show the same variety, including seeings, wonderings, hopings, wishings, wantings, plannings, and so on. But the commentary stresses that they are inaudible, even to the person whose thoughts they are. Thoughts are not to be assimilated to verbal imagery.

This conception of thoughts solves the sceptical problem of other minds. The inner episodes we call thoughts are 'hidden' only in the way that all theoretical entities are. They are not 'logically private', in the sense that no one has more than the shakiest of inductive grounds for attributing them to other people. On the contrary, criteria for their application are built into the theory (though, again, not in a way that makes them analytically true or unrevisable).[12] And the theory works so well that we can be confident that inner episodes really exist.

Have we gone too far in the opposite direction, losing sight of the special access that each of us seems to have to his own mental life? We would have, but for one last development. After becoming familiar with the 'theory' of thoughts, the Ryleans discover that thought-talk is capable of taking on a reporting role, along the lines sketched in our earlier account of non-inferential observation reports. This allows them to accord individuals a degree of epistemic privilege with respect to their own inner goings-on. We do well enough taking an individual's reports on his own thoughts at face-value to allow such reports default credibility. But this epistemic privilege is not absolute: we are sometimes confused or self-deceptive, and so not always the final authority on how we are thinking. My friends or my therapist may understand me better than I understand myself.

So much for thoughts. What about sensations? In our discussion of 'looks' talk, we left hanging the idea of 'something in common' between veridical perception and cases of qualitative or existential looking. Sensations are the something in common. They are introduced precisely to explain our tendencies to 'see' things that are not there. Cases of veridical and non-veridical perception can involve the same perceptual state, the same sensation. Thus it is part of the 'logic' of sensation-talk that a sensation of a red triangle is a state of a perceiving subject normally though not invariably brought about by the presence of a red and triangular object in the subject's field of vision. And as with talk about thoughts, talk about sensations or impressions proves capable of sustaining a reporting role.

The models for sensations are replicas: something like pictures. So the model for a sensation (or impression) or a red triangle is a red and triangular replica. What this means is that sensations are interrelated in ways that echo the interrelations of their models. For example, because no triangular object can be red and green all over, there cannot be a sensation of a red-and-green-all-over triangle. But while the theoretical entities introduced as 'sensations' or 'impressions' are modelled on objects (here comes the commentary), they are not themselves objects but *states* of the perceiving subject. They are modelled on pictures without being 'inner pictures', perceived by the 'eye of the mind'. If we think of them that way, we will fall right back into the

Cartesian picture of experience as a screen between ourselves and 'external' reality.

Because they are model-and-commentary theoretical entities, sensations do not have immediately obvious neurophysiological equivalents. If 'sensation of a red triangle' *meant no more than* 'state of a perceiving subject normally though not invariably brought about by the presence of a red and triangular object in the subject's field of vision', we might suppose that sensations were simply states of the brain-cum-visual-system. But sensation-talk has its own logic. It is an open question what neurophysiological states realize the psychological states that have the functional interrelations characteristic of sensations. Indeed, it an open question whether psychological states have *any* straightforward neurophysiological counterparts. (Functionally equivalent psychological states might have multiple physical realizations.)

It is important to see that the prime function of sensation-talk is explanatory. Sensations are causal intermediaries between events in the world and our seeing and reporting that things are thus and so. *They are not evidence for how things are.* It is true that we can have non-inferential knowledge of our sensations, just as we can have such knowledge of our thoughts; and it is true that we know that our impressions are normally reliable indicators of how things are in our surroundings. But our knowledge of how things are in our surroundings is not hostage to any such 'reliability inference'. Observational knowledge is causally mediated but epistemically direct: that is, non-inferential, in the sense explained earlier.

Does this mean that sensations and impressions are epistemically irrelevant? No, for reasons already given. To be capable of observational knowledge, we need to know a lot about our strengths and weaknesses as observers. The 'theory' of sensations extends and deepens this important aspect of our epistemic self-understanding.

Conclusion

In this chapter I have elaborated two distinctions. One is between conceptual embedding and justificational dependence. The other is between sensations as playing a causal-explanatory role in our understanding of observation and their being the foundations of knowledge. Making the first distinction, we get the epistemological benefits of direct realism without the foundationalist's commitment to encapsulated knowledge or encapsulated meanings. Making the second, we avoid the need to pretend that observational knowledge is 'direct' to the point of not being mediated in any sense at all by inner events. Knowledge is mediated by sensation. But sensations are not the foundations of knowledge. To suppose that they are is to assimilate sapience to sentience, empiricism's characteristic mistake.

Notes

1. Sellars (1997), 78.
2. McDowell (1994), ch. 1.
3. Sellars (1997), 73 ff.
4. Ibid. 74.
5. Sellars discusses 'trans-level' inference in his essay 'Phenomenalism', in Sellars (1963), 60–105. See esp. 87 f.
6. Wittgenstein (1969), para. 141.
7. For more detailed discussion of the Genetic Argument, see my (1999*a*), ch. 3.
8. Sellars (1997), 78.
9. Ibid.
10. Ibid. 32 ff.
11. Ibid. 85 ff.
12. 'Eliminative materialists' speculate that our advancing understanding of the brain indicates that this ought to happen with what they call 'folk-psychology': our common-sense way of talking about beliefs, desires, thoughts, and sensations. See Churchland (1981).

16

Scepticism and Epistemic Priority

Cartesian scepticism revisited

By allowing for non-inferential knowledge of the world around us, the Sellarsian account of observation bypasses Cartesian scepticism. However, those who have experienced Cartesian scepticism's power may well feel that the sceptic has been short-changed.

Most likely, the focus of such dissatisfaction will be the partially externalist character of the account of knowledge I am defending. Although it eschews pure reliabilism, my account is still developed within our common-sense and scientific picture of the world, and the sceptic wants to know why any of this lore amounts to knowledge. My argument seems to be: given that our beliefs about the world are more or less in good order, we can see how this is so. This strategy has definite whiff of circularity. I could go through all the arguments of the previous two chapters even if I were a victim of the Evil Deceiver, though my confidence in my conclusions would be completely misplaced. These lingering doubts show that we cannot just bypass the Cartesian problem about the external world. We must push our diagnostic inquiries farther.

We undercut Agrippan scepticism by rejecting the Prior Grounding Requirement in favour of a default and challenge conception of knowledge and justification. Unfortunately, by itself, this move seems to offer little diagnostic insight into Cartesian arguments. The Cartesian sceptic does not assume the right to enter naked challenges. Instead, he presents certain carefully chosen defeaters of ordinary knowledge-claims: sceptical hypotheses, like that of the brain in a vat. He doesn't say that we might be wrong somehow or other: he explains how we might be systematically deceived. Once entered, challenges based on these defeaters deprive ordinary knowledge-claims of default justificational status. The Cartesian sceptic doesn't assume that the claimant bears the burden of justification: he uses sceptical challenges to shift it.

Sceptical defeaters are special in two ways. First, it seems that they cannot be ruled out in any convincing way. In fact, they are *designed* to resist exclusion. Second, because they involve systematic deception, they call in question all our common-sense knowledge of the world. These features are connected.

If the deception is absolutely systematic, anything I cite to rule out a sceptical possibility might be part of the illusion. How do I know I am not dreaming right now? How do I know that my whole life isn't an elaborate dream? I can pinch myself, but maybe I am dreaming that too. For ordinary practical purposes, I properly ignore the sceptic's outlandish possibilities. But this does not affect his theoretical point. Our ordinary 'knowledge' isn't quite what we thought.[1]

When first encountered, the sceptic's arguments seem powerful and clear. But more closely investigated, they are both inconclusive and, in certain respects, deeply puzzling. Again, let us recall that sceptical arguments need to be intuitive. If they depend on contentious epistemological or metaphysical presuppositions, we are not obliged to deal with them exactly on their own terms.

Cartesian scepticism is no more intuitive than Agrippan. In particular, the contextualist view of knowledge strongly supports two diagnostic claims: that Cartesian scepticism presupposes substantive foundationalism, with the foundations of knowledge set at the level of experience; and that the sceptic's conception of experience incorporates the Myth of the Given.

To see this, the first question to ask is: in what sense is it impossible to 'rule out' sceptical possibilities? The most that the sceptic can show is that it is impossible to 'rule out' the hypothesis that I am a brain in a vat on the basis of experiential evidence alone, in the sceptic's restrictive understanding of 'experiential': that is, an understanding according to which experience tells us only how things appear, never how they are. If I know that I am sitting at desk in Evanston, I know that I am not a brain in a vat in the vicinity of Alpha Centauri.[2] My being in Evanston rules out my being anywhere near Alpha Centauri. Of course, if I initially know only that *it seems to me* that I am sitting at a desk, matters are less clear. But why assume that this is always my epistemic starting-point?

All this shows, someone may say, is that the foundationalist doctrine of the priority of experiential over worldly knowledge is sufficient for landing us in the Cartesian predicament. But what we need to show is that it is necessary.[3] Fair enough. But now the burden is on the sceptic to formulate an argument that does not depend on the doctrine. In my view, no such argument has ever been given.

Some arguments appear to give the sceptic what he wants, but only because they disguise their dependence on ideas about epistemic priority. As I noted in Chapter 6, some philosophers think that Cartesian arguments exemplify an 'Argument from Ignorance'. For example:

1. I don't know that I am not a brain in a vat.
2. If I don't know that I am not a brain in a vat, then I don't know that I have two hands.

So 3. I don't know that I have two hands.

Put this way, the argument does not have the structure of an explicit under-determination problem. But this feature of the argument only shifts our attention to its first premise. Why don't I know that I am not a brain in a vat? One possible answer is that knowing something is incompatible with there being even a possibility of error. Accordingly, to deprive us of knowledge, sceptical hypotheses need only to be bare logical possibilities. But as I have already argued, this answer is no good. It is not interesting to be told that knowledge is impossible, when knowing is held to some standard of absolute infallibility. This is just to remind us that we are fallible. To be a problem today, scepticism must be radical. It must be the claim that we are never so much as justified in believing one thing rather than another. The answer to the question—Why don't I know that I am not a brain in a vat?—must therefore be that I have no evidence that would decide the question. My experience is all the evidence I can possibly have; yet on the basis of experience alone, the sceptical hypothesis cannot be excluded. We are back to where we started.

Although in a way I am reiterating points made when I introduced Cartesian scepticism for the first time, the dialectical situation has evolved considerably since then. When I first introduced Cartesian scepticism, I with-held judgement on whether it is truly intuitive. Now that we have available a contextualist approach to justification, together with an alternative account of observational knowledge, matters stand differently. At this stage of the debate, the sceptic's assumptions about the relation between experience and know-ledge of the world cannot simply be conceded. Not merely does the sceptic assume the Prior Grounding Requirement, he insists on a very restrictive conception of our available evidence. From a contextualist standpoint, these views of the Cartesian sceptic are implausible and optional.

The contextualist alternative shows the sceptic's ideas, which he would like to pass off as mere common sense, to be heavily freighted with theory. My inability to rule out sceptical possibilities on the basis of purely experiential evidence affects my entitlement to believe that I am not a brain in a vat—and here I mean *epistemic* entitlement—only if that entitlement is hostage to a prior—and context-invariant—commitment to provide any and every belief about the world with an experiential grounding. If we accept, in some wholly general form, the doctrine of priority of experiential knowledge over know-ledge of the world, we are faced with the Cartesian problem. But the avail-ability of contextualism as a coherent alternative shows that this doctrine is not self-evidently true. It is a view for which we need an argument. If no good argument is forthcoming, we can set Cartesian scepticism aside.

The priority of experience

I am arguing that the sceptic's assumption that experiential knowledge is, in some wholly general way, epistemologically prior to knowledge of the world is a contentious and even implausible theoretical commitment. But some philosophers think that the priority of experiential knowledge is too obvious to need arguing, or much arguing anyway. Since the content of experiential knowledge, which concerns how things appear, is more modest than that of any putative knowledge of the world, it is intrinsically less open to doubt, hence (relatively) epistemologically more basic. Indeed, struck by the fact that talk of appearing to appear does not even seem to make sense, many philosophers have concluded that my knowledge of how things appear to me is not open to doubt at all: such knowledge is therefore absolutely basic.

A contextualist outlook leads us to question this whole way of thinking. A claim's being more modest does not make it automatically more certain. In the right situation, I can be unsure about how things appear to be. My tie looks wrong in this peculiar light: it looks blue; or maybe a bit greenish. It's hard to say. Nor does a claim's being less modest mean, in and of itself, that it needs evidential support (from more modest claims). There are many contexts in which claims about the world are barely dubitable and perhaps not dubitable at all. In cases like this, claims about the world would be no more certain, even if they could be experientially grounded. They are already as certain as things get to be.

Many philosophers have thought that the dependence of worldly knowledge on experiential knowledge follows from the fact that knowledge of the world 'depends on the senses'. But granting that there is some sort of dependence, why suppose that all 'the senses' ever really tell us is how things appear, never how they objectively are? The answer is: because there is a sceptical problem with respect to worldly knowledge that has no counterpart in the experiential case. However, we have found reason to think that the sceptical problem *presupposes* the general priority of experiential knowledge and is therefore no argument for it.[4]

Another argument is that the priority of experiential knowledge is established by the mere intelligibility of sceptical hypotheses. If my experience could be just what it is, even if the objective world were very different, I would retain my experiential knowledge even if I knew nothing about external reality. This means that experiential knowledge is more basic.[5]

This argument too is a failure. At most, it shows that experience is neutral with respect to the character of reality. It does not show—in fact it gives us reason to doubt—that knowledge of reality is always evidentially dependent on experience. The neutrality of experience cannot be equated with its priority.

There is a general moral here. There are no intuitive arguments for the doctrine of the priority of experience. Rather, that doctrine and the sceptical problem concerning our knowledge of the external world are comrades in arms. Neither is plausible without the other. Contextualism invites us to dispense with both.

Limits to understanding?

Another source of dissatisfaction with this diagnosis of Cartesian scepticism is the suspicion that it does not pay sufficient attention to the peculiar generality of the sceptic's question. Where my account of observation and experience is developed within our common-sense and scientific picture of the world, the sceptic challenges us to explain how, in the face of the possibility of systematic deception, we are entitled to see ourselves as knowing *anything whatsoever* about the external world, even that there is one. A theory of knowledge that presupposes knowledge of the world cannot be a satisfactory answer to this question. If, in some ordinary situation, we ask why a person is entitled to this or that particular belief about the world around him, then of course it will be appropriate to bring up further world-involving facts: that he was well placed to see what was happening, and so on. However, the sceptic invites us to step back from all such particular questions in order to reflect on our worldly knowledge as a whole. He imposes a *totality condition* on a properly philosophical understanding of our knowledge of the world.[6]

The sceptic means his totality condition to exclude theories that make use of worldly knowledge. If we accept this constraint, we will be compelled to retreat to a more primitive basis for our knowledge of the world; and what could this be if not experiential knowledge, however exactly such knowledge is understood? Thus the foundationalist commitment to the absolute priority of experiential knowledge over knowledge of the world is a by-product of an encounter with scepticism, not (as I have been claiming) a presupposition.[7]

This argument turns contextualism against itself. In the terminology of Chapter 14, the doctrine of the priority of experience is a methodological necessity of the project of understanding our knowledge of the world philo-sophically. To be sure, once we retreat to experiential knowledge as the only possible basis for knowledge of the world, the sceptic has powerful weapons to block any future advance.[8] If so, we cannot understand our knowledge of the world in the way that we would like to. We may indeed do what I have done: develop an account of knowledge and justification that pushes the sceptic's question to the sidelines. But can this procedure ever be fully satisfactory, as long as the sceptic's question looks like a good one?

I expect that some readers will think not. Things would be different if we had a way to argue decisively that the sceptic's question is not really intelli-gible. However, the sceptic's question does not seem to be defective in point of intelligibility. For example, we all seem to understand it well enough to appreciate why it is so difficult to answer. We seem to be left with a question that is both intelligible and unanswerable, a permanent gap in our understanding.[9]

Are we really in such dire straits? The sceptic argues that accepting the totality condition forces us to identify a more primitive stratum of knowledge to serve as the source of knowledge of the world. This is because, in the light of his totality condition, the question of our entitlement to claim knowledge of the world is simply begged if we answer it in ways that take knowledge of the world for granted. In other words, such a defence of our right to claim knowledge of the world is circular. However, the charge of circularity assumes that we are trying to prove that we have knowledge of the external world. My anti-sceptical strategy repudiates this assumption. It involves, first, tying sceptical doubts to questionable epistemological views and, second, presenting a way of thinking about knowledge and justification that makes the sceptic's questions look like bad questions to ask. Since it is not foreordained that such an alternative picture be available, there is nothing viciously circular about my approach. The only issue, then, is whether my diagnosis goes far enough, or whether it leaves the sceptic's question—How do we know anything whatsoever about the external world?—looking like a question that still deserves an answer.

While we should not be too ready to accuse the sceptic of speaking nonsense, we should not be too quick to concede that we understand him either. So let us look more closely at the generality of the sceptic's question. It is less innocent than it seems.

Epistemological realism again

Cartesian scepticism is not absolutely general. Rather, it encompasses a family of sceptical arguments, each member of which calls in question all knowledge belonging to some broad kind: knowledge of the external world, of other minds, of the past, and so on. But suppose, for the sake of argument, that we cannot legitimate, in a suitably general way, our claim to knowledge of some such kind: is this something to regret? We do not expect a general understanding of just any 'kind' of thing. There is no blanket explanation of how all the objects in my study got to be there. There is no science of things that have happened on a Wednesday. If a 'kind' is any definable totality, not all kinds demand or even allow theoretical understanding.[10]

Contrast the property of being in my study with that of being an acid. We think of acids as an important chemical kind. The reasons are not far to seek. First of all, the substances we call acids show striking commonalities in their behaviour (turning litmus paper blue, etc.). They are involved in observational laws, and not just a few either. Particular kinds of acid seem to allow for the discovery of many further regularities: how they interact with this or that alkali, how they respond to heating, and so on. Surely there is something about acids in general or this acid in particular that accounts for such facts. Accordingly, our confidence that the observational laws are genuine and significant—thus, that acids are a genuine kind—is reinforced by our discovering a significant underlying feature of acids (being a proton donor) that accounts for the regularities in question. Kinds like this are often called 'natural kinds'. By this more demanding standard, the objects in my study don't constitute a kind but are just an arbitrary and insignificant aggregate. They don't have any interesting observable properties in common and there is nothing to suggest that any important theoretical property binds them together either.

Summing up, we expect general intelligibility only with respect to kinds that have interesting, non-gerrymandered properties in common and which exhibit some kind of theoretical integrity. Noticing this, we can ask what binds together the 'kinds' of beliefs that interest the sceptic. Consider our 'beliefs about the external world': this 'kind' includes all of physics, all of history, all of biology, and so on indefinitely, not to mention every casual item of information about the world around us. On the face of things, there is no unity here, phenomenological or theoretical. Accordingly, there is no genuine totality, only a vague and arbitrary assemblage. The demand for a blanket explanation of 'how we come to know such things' is therefore misplaced. There is nothing to understand, hence nothing to regret not understanding.

As far as I can see, there is only one way to escape this conclusion: the sceptic's kinds are epistemological rather than topical. What makes beliefs about the external world a theoretically coherent kind is their common epistemological status. 'External' does not mean 'in the environment', for by the sceptic's standards even one's own body is an 'external' object. 'External' means, in an old fashioned phrase, 'without the mind'. Knowledge of the external world contrasts with knowledge of the internal world: that is, experiential knowledge. And the hallmark of knowledge of the internal world is its epistemic privilege.

This brings us back to foundationalism. The distinctive commitment of substantive foundationalism is that every belief has an *intrinsic* epistemological status. Beliefs of one kind can be treated as epistemologically prior to beliefs of some other kind because they *are* epistemologically prior; some beliefs play the role of basic beliefs because they *are* basic; others receive inferential justification because they *require* it; and all because of the kinds of belief they are, kinds being delineated by certain very abstract features of content. Our beliefs therefore fall into *natural epistemological kinds*, standing in natural relations of epistemological priority. I speak of natural epistemological kinds to stress the point that the foundationalist's epistemological hierarchy cuts across ordinary subject-matter divisions and operates independently of all contextual factors. It answers to what Descartes called 'the order of reasons': the fundamental, underlying, interest- and situation-independent structure of all empirical justification.[11]

Substantive foundationalism is an articulation of the outlook that I have called 'epistemological realism'. To repeat, this is not realism as a position within epistemology (the view that we have knowledge of a 'real' or objective world), but rather a form of naive realism with respect to the objects of epistemological theorizing. The name 'epistemological realism' first occurred to me by analogy with scientific realism. According to scientific realism, the various observable properties of natural substances like acids spring from their underlying atomic structure. Similarly for the foundationalist: behind the surface variety of epistemic procedures there lies a permanent epistemic structure. But as I have argued, we are under no obligation to be epistemological realists. We can be pragmatists with respect to epistemic norms, in which case we will not suppose that there is anything behind the visible features of everyday epistemic practices.

The Sellarsian account of non-inferential perceptual knowledge is relevant here. An important consequence of that account is that the distinction between the 'observable' and the 'inferential' or 'theoretical' is 'methodological not substantive'. Traditional empiricism imagines a fixed basic observational vocabulary pertaining to sensible colours, shapes, and so on, all other concepts belonging to a non-observational, hence theoretical, level of language. This fixed observational vocabulary reflects the basic range of sensible qualities with which we are capable of being 'acquainted'. But on the Sellarsian view, there is no fixed boundary between observational and theoretical, no permanent class of 'intrinsically observational' entities or properties. We can observe anything whose presence we can be trained to report reliably on. With suitable training and the right collateral knowledge, physicists can report on the presence of electrons in cloud chambers.

It is true that, on Sellars's view, the properties of sensations will be restricted. There are sensations of faint, thin, whitish streaks, but not sensations of electrons. However, the restrictions on the descriptive vocabulary of 'sensation theory' will be determined by the theory's explanatory requirements: particularly, its need to account for the kinds of perceptual illusions and errors we are subject to. But as we have seen, perceptual knowing can be causally mediated by our having sensations while remaining epistemically direct and *about objects in our surroundings*. It is possible to recognize an explanatory role for sensations—and even an epistemic role in the evaluation and criticism of observation reports—without supposing that the restricted vocabulary of sensation-talk entails a fixed vocabulary of observational knowledge.

What is finally important about contextualism, then, is that it makes visible and implausible the sceptic's epistemological realism. If all evidence is contextually relevant evidence, then, abstracting from contextual details, there is no fact of the matter as to what sort of evidence could or should be brought to bear on a given proposition. There is no immutable and universal order of reasons. There is no reason to think that the mere fact that a proposition is 'about the external world' establishes that it needs, or is even susceptible of, any particular kind of evidential support.

If this is right, substantive foundationalism is deeply implicated in Cartesian scepticism. Not only does foundationalism set the success-conditions for explaining how knowledge of the external world is possible, it is presupposed by the idea that there is such a 'kind' of knowledge to examine. Our beliefs about the world can only constitute an epistemic kind. But to suppose that there are such kinds is to suppose that there are immutable epistemological constraints underlying the shifting standards of everyday justification: for example, the universal dependence of beliefs about the world on experiential evidence. On this view, context-sensitivity does not go all the way down. Rather, there is an underlying structure of justificational relations that philosophical reflection exposes to view and which allows us to determine, in some fully general way, whether we are entitled to claim knowledge of the world. From the standpoint of contextualism, the sceptic's kinds do not exist. Our inability to explain, to the sceptic's satisfaction, how we have knowledge of the external world does not point to a gap in our understanding, because there is nothing to understand.[12]

Faced with this diagnosis, some philosophers will deny that the Cartesian sceptic needs to begin with such a general question. They will claim that the sceptic can reach his conclusion by examining a single carefully chosen case of knowledge. This case will be a 'best case': a case such that if knowledge fails here, it fails everywhere. So, for example, if I can't know that I am sitting at my desk right now (because, for all I know, I could be a brain in a vat) what can I know? Nothing.

This is a distinction without a difference. If my default entitlements include beliefs about the world, they rule out sceptical hypotheses. (I couldn't possibly be a brain in a vat somewhere near Alpha Centauri because I just got back from the office.) If I lack such default entitlements, ruling out sceptical scenarios may indeed be impossible. But then the argument assumes that, even in the best of cases, knowing about the world depends on experiential grounding, which is where we came in.

We can go further: the very idea of a 'best case', as the sceptic means to deploy it, is deeply problematic. In assuming that one can reveal a general problem for our knowledge of the external world by examining a single carefully chosen case, the sceptic assumes that such a case can be *exemplary* or *paradigmatic*, as a sample of sulphuric acid might serve as a paradigm case of sulphuric acid generally. But this is to assume, contrary to the spirit of contextualism, that 'knowledge of the external world' is a theoretically coherent kind of knowledge: the sort of thing that can be represented by a paradigm case. The sceptic assumes epistemological realism without even noticing that he does so.

'Knowledge of the external world' is like 'demonic possession': both concepts reflect false theories. There is no such thing as demonic possession; and in just the same way there is no such thing as knowledge of the external world.

Levels and angles

Sceptical hypotheses are often presented as remote possibilities that, while properly ignored in the context of ordinary, practical affairs, become relevant in the refined philosophical context of pure inquiry. In identifying defeaters that our evidence must eliminate if we are to claim knowledge, the more we prescind from practical considerations, the wider we cast our net. If we prescind from practical considerations altogether, the 'level of scrutiny' rises to the maximum. Here all defeaters, including sceptical hypotheses, must be ruled out if anything we believe is to count as knowledge. Since we cannot do this, nothing counts. The sceptic concludes that we never really have knowledge. At best, we have knowledge for some (or all) practical purposes.

Some philosophers suggest that we can avoid this conclusion by recognizing that standards for claiming and attributing knowledge vary with the range of defeaters. Although we may temporarily lose our knowledge when we project ourselves into the rarefied context of 'doing epistemology', we regain it as soon as we return to more ordinary pursuits.

This basic contextualist idea is one I endorse. However, the form of contextualism just described is too simple.[13] It ties scepticism to the imposition of high standards for knowing, and so does not deal with radical scepticism. To apply the contextualist move to Cartesian scepticism in its radical form, we must recall that contextual factors determine not only the *level* but also the *angle* of scrutiny: not just the severity of our standards but also the direction of inquiry.

The thought that I might be a brain in a vat defeats every claim to knowledge of the external world, if it defeats any. This is crucial. Sceptical defeaters are not just remote: they are generic.[14] To bring them into play is thus just another way of insinuating the totality condition on a properly philosophical understanding of our knowledge of the world. But in imposing this condition, the sceptic does not raise the standards: he changes the subject.

Here we need to recall a point from Chapter 14: that there is no simple relation between level and angle of scrutiny. In conducting an experimental test of a scientific theory, we can raise the level of scrutiny indefinitely: we can insist on taking measurements to a further decimal point and narrowing the limits of error; we can repeat the experiment under more stringently controlled conditions, and so on. But if we start worrying whether our whole apparatus is part of a brain-in-vat illusion, we don't raise the level of scrutiny within the context of the experiment: we stop doing physics altogether. The introduction of generic defeaters disrupts specific inquiries. Distinguishing severity of standards from direction of inquiry shows that there is no coherent idea of a universal, maximal level of scrutiny.

It might seem that this works to the sceptic's advantage. If the line between what is in question and what is not is fixed in part by the direction of inquiry, why can't the sceptic argue that the privileged status of experiential knowledge is fixed by *his* project of trying to understand our knowledge of the world *as a whole*? The answer is that calling in question the sceptic's epistemological realism blocks a crucial move. Let us agree that the sceptic's totality condition defines his notion of a 'properly philosophical' understanding of human knowledge. Given this understanding of 'philosophical', the sceptic discovers that we cannot justify any beliefs about the world, in the context of philosophical reflection. But he takes himself to have discovered, in the context of philosophical reflection, that such beliefs are never justified, in any context. This inference, which involves an illicit quantifier shift, is not justified by logic alone. To move to the unqualified sceptical conclusion, we must assume epistemological realism. We must suppose that philosophical reflection, as the sceptic understands it, is more than a particular way of thinking about knowledge, which might or might not lead to interesting results. We must take the context of philosophical reflection to be a uniquely privileged perspective that reveals the final, context-independent constraints on justification. If we reject epistemological realism, there are no such constraints for reflection to reveal and the sceptic's inference will not go through.

Breaking the deadlock (again)

Epistemological realism encourages scepticism; contextualism doesn't. But unless we can show that the contextualist picture is definitely correct, won't the sceptic triumph one level up? We have already addressed this question in connection with the Agrippan problem. Let me briefly recall what was said, adding a couple of wrinkles.

This objection supposes that the sceptic wins ties. So the first question to ask is whether we have a tie. The answer is that we do not. Far from shedding light on ordinary justification, epistemological theories that invite scepticism are hard to square with ordinary justificational practices. Their advocates invoke various *ad hoc* hypotheses to explain away the discrepancies: that everyday justification is only justification-for-practical-purposes or only 'local'. Contextualism lets us take the phenomenology of ordinary justification seriously. But even if, from an explanatory standpoint, we had a tie, why give the palm to the sceptic? If a picture of knowledge and justification leads to radical scepticism, thus erasing every important epistemological distinction, that itself is reason to replace it. Of course, no epistemological realist, for whom epistemic norms are determined by the epistemic facts, will see things in this light. But so much the worse for epistemological realism.

We can reinforce these considerations by recalling the requirement that scepticism be intuitive, in the sense that the sceptic's conclusions must not depend on optional theoretical assumptions. After all, with free rein to assume premises, one can argue for anything: this is not a surprise and not a problem. But given the intuitiveness requirement, we have done all we need to do if we sketch a picture of knowledge and justification that meshes smoothly with the obvious features of everyday justificational practices, without setting us on the road to scepticism. The very possibility of sketching such a picture reveals the sceptic's position as an artefact of theoretical preconceptions that we can reasonably dispense with.

We began with the objection that, whereas externalist epistemologies are developed from within our evolving views of the world and our place in it, the sceptic wants to pass judgement on all such views from a standpoint outside them. Unless we sign on to the metaphysics of epistemological realism, there is no such standpoint. The intuitiveness requirement commits the sceptic to arguing that our practices of epistemic assessment break down from within, not that they fail to measure up to some standard imposed from without. This means that if a coherent, non-sceptical epistemology can be developed from within our ongoing theories of the world, we have everything we need.

The intelligibility of sceptical hypotheses

So far, I have been allowing that sceptical hyptheses are intelligible. But though they seem to be so, how well do we really understand them? In the previous chapter, I hinted that we may not understand them as well as we are tempted to think, that we are perhaps subject to an illusion of understanding. To conclude my discussion of Cartesian scepticism, let me expand on the hint.

Contextualism allows for a qualified externalism in epistemology. Combined with an inferentialist view of meaning, this externalist element in epistemology leads to a partially externalist semantics. I can play the language-games I play, thus have the thoughts I have, only because I interact with objects in the world. An observation-term like 'red' means what it does in virtue of its functional role in the game of giving and asking for reasons. As we saw in the previous chapter, this role involves the ability to report reliably on the presence of red things. On this view, 'meaning' is not simply 'in the head'.[15]

Descartes, who introduces the problem of the external world, does not see things this way. This is because he does not see language as essential for thought. For Descartes, thought is a transaction with 'ideas', which are supposed to be intrinsically contentful. The question is not 'What gives our thoughts the contents they have?', but 'Given their contents, why suppose that any of them are true?' However, if we think of mastering a language as essential for thought itself, and if we link the meaningfulness of our linguistic performances with their being embedded in complex practices of reporting, inference, and action, things look very different. To suppose that everything we say and believe might be false makes no more sense than to suppose that no move in a game has ever been correctly made.[16]

If such an inferentialist and partially externalist approach to meaning is on anything like the right lines, there is something deeply misleading about Cartesian thought-experiments. Verificationists want to know what is supposed to be different in a world of demonic deception. But an equally interesting question is: what is supposed to be the same? The answer, of course, is experience. In this answer, experience is conceived as involving some kind of knowledge. Even as victims of the Evil Deceiver, we are supposed to know all about how things appear to us: they appear red, circular, sonorous, and so on. Thus these terms must be supposed to mean just what they always mean, even though in the Cartesian world of limitless deception nothing is red or circular or sonorous. On an inferentialist view of meaning, this cannot be.

The conception of 'experience' as what McDowell calls the highest common factor in veridical and non-veridical perception builds in what Sellars identifies as the Myth of the Given: the assimilation of sapience to sentience, of contentful thought to mere sensation.[17] This assimilation is what gives Cartesian thought-experiences their air of intelligibility. Even if we start to wonder whether our 'words' would retain their normal meanings under the conditions of some sceptical scenario, we find ourselves tempted to say 'Yes, but things would still look like *this*'. However, this is just the point at which we lose touch with meaning: the point at which, as Wittgenstein remarks, one would like to emit an inarticulate sound.[18]

I do not expect this argument to assuage all doubts. Some philosophers will be inclined to say that, if some kind of semantic externalism is correct, we are worse off than before. We started by wondering whether anything we believe is true. But if we cannot see our way around the sceptic's questions about knowledge of the external world, we find ourselves, given semantic externalism, wondering whether we even know what we mean. We swap a sceptical problem about knowledge for one about meaning. Of course, this is paradoxical. If we can't know what we mean, we can't even raise the sceptical problem about meaning. But so much the worse for a view that leads us to such an impasse.

Another reaction is to argue that, presented the right way, the brain-in-vat hypothesis is fully consistent with semantic externalism. We only need to imagine that we grow up in a normal world. At some point, we are kidnapped and hauled off to the Alpha Centauri system. It is strained (or is it?) to claim that, when we wake up, we have lost the ability to think or that our words have changed their meanings. So the question is still on the table: how do we know this hasn't happened to us?

For present purposes, I do not need to resolve these issues with complete finality. The very fact that we are led to them shows that we cannot take Cartesian scepticism to be the intuitive problem that it is often assumed to be. The problem is deeply embedded in obscure and controversial theoretical commitments, epistemological and semantic. If we can develop a conception of knowledge and justification (and a compatible conception of thought and meaning) that allows us to avoid sceptical entanglements, we are free to do so. Only the epistemological-realist assumption—that the Cartesian conception of the context-invariant priority of experience over knowledge of the world represents 'our epistemic situation'—underwrites the thought that the problem of the external world is unavoidable. We should dispense with this assumption. If that leads us to rethink the intelligibility of Cartesian thought-experiments, so be it. We have no obligation to cultivate paradox for its own sake.

Notes

1. Many philosophers, including of course Descartes himself, have connected scepticism with detachment from everyday practical concerns. See Clarke (1972); B. Williams (1978), ch. 1; McGinn (1989), ch. 1. Stanley Cavell (1979) stresses the importance of the sceptic's apparent mimicry of ordinary patterns of claim–challenge–response. Clarke, Cavell, and McGinn all offer diagnostic responses to scepticism that merit serious consideration. I discuss Cavell in my (1996a), ch. 4, and Clarke, McGinn, and Williams in ch. 5. Stroud gives a sceptic's response to Clarke and Cavell in his (1984), 'Coda'.

2. Some philosophers, notably Dretske, deny this. But Dretske's denial reflects his connecting the idea that justifying involves ruling out only certain relevant alternatives with the much more problematic thesis that knowledge is not 'closed under known logical implication'. Epistemic closure is the principle that, if I know that P, and know that P logically entails Q, then I know that Q. This thesis is said to be presupposed by standard sceptical arguments. So, for example, suppose I know that I am now sitting at a computer screen; I know also that, if I am sitting at such a screen, I am not a brain in a vat; but I do not know, and can never know, that I am not a brain in a vat: therefore, I do not know that I am sitting at a computer screen. According to Dretske, however, I do know that I am sitting at a computer screen, even though I do not know that I am not a brain in a vat. I know that I am sitting a screen because I can rule out various relevant alternatives: e.g. that I am writing this note on a pad of paper, or dictating it into a microphone. I don't have to exclude the possibility that my whole experience is a vat-delusion. This is a relevant alternative, not to my specific belief about what I am doing right now, but only to some much more general claim: for example, that my experience reveals an external world that is pretty much what I take it to be. I can know specific facts without knowing more general facts that they logically imply. The principle of closure is false. Certainly, this is a dramatic diagnosis of how sceptical arguments go astray. As my remarks in the main text will suggest, I think that the issue of closure is a red herring. Furthermore, contextualists are not committed to denying closure. Denial

results from thinking that the range of relevant alternatives to a given claim is deter-mined by the claim's propositional content alone, which no contextualist should sup-pose. Arguably, the basic idea is present in Austin's 'Other Minds' and Wittgenstein's *On Certainty*, but for detailed presentations see Dretske (1970); also Nozick (1981), ch. 3. For a critical evaluation of Dretske, Nozick, and others, see my (1996*a*), ch. 8.

3. For an objection along these lines, see Stroud (1984*b*).
4. A *locus classicus* for this 'argument from differential certainty' is Price (1932), ch. 1. I discuss Price in my (1999*a*), 43–6.
5. The best attempt to make an intuitive case for both Cartesian scepticism and the doctrine of the priority of experience is Stroud (1984*a*).
6. The view that their distinctive generality is the key to the sceptic's questions is very interestingly developed by Barry Stroud in 'Understanding Human Knowledge in General', in Clay and Lehrer (1989).
7. This formulation is due to Stroud (1984*a*), 550.
8. That scepticism is conditionally correct in this sense is the burden of Stroud (1984*a*).
9. Stroud, in Clay and Lehrer (1989).
10. The argument to follow is developed at much greater length in my (1996*a*), which is where I introduced the phrase 'epistemological realism'.
11. The idea of kinds of belief or claim with intrinsic epistemological status (i.e. as 'inferen-tial' or 'non-inferential') is criticized by Austin and also by Wittgenstein, though nei-ther employs my terminology of 'epistemological realism'. See Austin (1962), ch. 10 and Wittgenstein (1969).
12. For a critical response to the general line I take here, see Stroud (1996) and my reply in Williams (1996*b*).
13. The main advocate of this version of contextualism is Stewart Cohen: see Cohen (1988). For externalist variants, see DeRose (1995) and Lewis, 'Elusive Knowledge', in Lewis (1999). I discuss this version of contextualism, taking Lewis as my stalking-horse, in Williams (2001).
14. The way in which the sceptic turns our attention to generic defeaters and generic sources of knowledge by focusing on generic objects (the sort of things we just recog-nize, without a checklist of marks and features) is brilliantly analysed in Cavell (1979). See esp. ch. 3.
15. The phrase comes from Putnam's essay 'The Meaning of Meaning', in Putnam (1975).
16. Wittgenstein (1969), paras. 80–3. Also Davidson, 'The Very Idea of a Conceptual Scheme', in Davidson (1984).
17. McDowell, 'Criteria, Indefeasibility and Knowledge', in McDowell (1998), 369–94. See esp. 385 f.
18. Wittgenstein (1958), para. 261. I am indebted here to conversations with John McDowell and Robert Brandom.

17

Induction

Hume's problem

Like the problem of the external world, the problem of induction is modern. There may be a fragmentary anticipation of the problem in the writings of Sextus Empiricus, but it first clearly emerges in the writings of David Hume about a century after Descartes invented the external world problem.

We could not get by with only beliefs about particular matters of fact. We need to know how the world works generally. In taking any action at all, we rely on the world's following predictable routines. When I go to sit down, I expect my chair to support me. I do not worry that it might suddenly catch fire or vanish into thin air. Such things do not happen. This is common sense. But in Hume's eyes, advanced science represents only a precise and sophisticated extension of our capacity for generalization. What Hume wants to know is whether general beliefs, however indispensable, have any rational basis.[1]

Hume's starting-point is the claim that no general proposition about the world is necessarily true. That stones released near the surface of the Earth invariably travel downwards is a contingent fact that could conceivably have been otherwise. We could, without contradiction, describe a world that operated quite differently. This means that our knowledge of the world is never 'intuitive' or 'demonstrative'. Accordingly, it is never *a priori* but depends essentially on experience of how things actually are.

Hume thinks that everyone will admit the contingency of surprising scientific discoveries. Who would have thought that not even two teams of the strongest horses would be able to pull apart hemispheres enclosing a near vacuum? However, when we consider the simplest mechanical interactions— two colliding billiard balls, for example—we can be tempted to think that what happens 'stands to reason'. But this is an illusion. Intuitive obviousness is not rational necessity: it is just familiarity in disguise. Some facts are so simple and familiar that—in contrast to surprising discoveries—we cannot recall a particular occasion on which they first came to our notice. We are thus tempted to think, quite erroneously, that we never had to learn them at all. In this way, learning from experience is a self-concealing process. But to dispel the illusion, all it takes is a little imagination.

Hume's next step is to ask what kind of justifying inference is available to take us from the evidence we have to the conclusions we need. He focuses on the case of simple enumerative induction, in which we take observed correlations and extend them to new instances. If I have examined a lot of As and found that all of them are Bs, I will conclude that the next A I encounter will be a B (projective inference), or that all As (examined or unexamined) are Bs (generalizing inference). And the more cases I examine without meeting a counter-instance, the stronger my warrant for a projective or generalizing inference becomes. The sun has always risen; so the sun always rises.

Hume does not deny that we all do make such inferences. But are they justifiable? Inevitably, our hypotheses about the future are derived from what has happened up to now. According to Hume, there is no rational warrant for projecting past regularities into the future, or for generalizing to situations (past, present, or future) that we have not actually observed.

An inference is immediate if we can go straight from premise to conclusion without any further information or assumptions; and it is valid if it is contradictory to suppose that its premises are all true and its conclusion is false. Considered as immediate, the inference from

Premise: The sun has risen every day up to now.

to

Conclusion: Therefore the sun will rise tomorrow.

is invalid. It is entirely consistent to suppose that the premises of this argument are true and its conclusion is false. Perhaps some cosmic accident will intervene to block tomorrow's sunrise. Nothing in logic precludes this. Indeed, not only can such inferences go wrong, they often do. Every morning, when the turkey sees the farmer come into the yard, it gets a handful of food. So when it sees the farmer come into the yard on Christmas morning, it expects the usual breakfast. However, this time the farmer has something else in mind. (The example is Russell's.)

Perhaps the inference is not immediate: perhaps it depends on a suppressed premise. A natural suggestion is that we tacitly presuppose, in Hume's own words, 'that instances of which we have had no experience, must resemble those, of which we have had experience, and that the course of nature continues always uniformly the same'.[2] Nature, we assume, operates according to laws, regularities that do not suddenly break down. If this presupposition— call it the Uniformity Principle—is true, we can argue from observed regularities to future or otherwise distant cases.

Spelled out, then, inductive inferences go as follows:

Premise: The sun has risen every day up to now.
Premise: Nature operates uniformly.
Conclusion: Therefore the sun will rise tomorrow.

Of course, we have to take note of enough instances to be sure that we have a genuine regularity and not just a series of coincidences. But everyday inductive practice is sensitive to this requirement. A good inductive inference depends on many observations, not just one or two.

So far, so good. But how is the Uniformity Principle itself to be justified? Justifiable it must be: we cannot justify inductive conclusions by founding them on a mere assumption. This is where the problem arises. We are trying to justify predictive or generalizing inferences; and whatever its detailed formulation, the Uniformity Principle is itself a general statement that goes far beyond anything we have actually observed. This would not matter if the Principle were some kind of necessary truth, knowable *a priori*. But it doesn't seem to be like that. There seems to be no contradiction in imagining that Nature is fairly chaotic or that the laws of nature are subject to change over time, so that patterns we observe in the future deviate from those observed in the past. The Uniformity Principle must therefore be an empirical proposition, in need of justification on the basis of experience: that is, inductive justification. But if all inductive inference depends on presupposing the Uniformity Principle, we are arguing in a circle.

To make this clear, suppose (contrary to fact) that we have a *perfect* track record when it comes to making inductive projections. Whenever we have used observed correlations as a basis for predictions, our predictions have come out right. Still, the most this entitles us to claim is

> *Premise*:   Until now, Nature has operated uniformly.

What we need, however, is

> *Conclusion*:   Nature operates uniformly.

Just as in the case of the sun's rising tomorrow, our conclusion does not follow immediately from our premise. To bridge the gap, we need an extra premise, and this can only be the very Uniformity Principle we are trying to establish. Made explicit, our argument becomes:

> *Premise*:   Until now, Nature has operated uniformly.
> *Premise*:   Nature operates uniformly.
> *Conclusion*:   Nature operates uniformly.

This argument is valid, but only because circular. Hume concludes that there is no way to argue for the Uniformity Principle that does not take that principle for granted. The Uniformity Principle is thus both rationally indispensable and utterly beyond the scope of argumentative justification. This means that there is no way of mounting a rational defence of inductive inference.

According to Hume, the lesson to learn from this sceptical problem is that inductive inference is a not matter of 'reason' at all. Rather, it is a matter of habit or 'custom': conditioning, we might say today. For this reason, we need not worry that exposure to scepticism will disrupt our propensity to form inductive expectations. Since inductive inference is not based on 'reason', it is not vulnerable to sceptical attack on its supposedly rational basis. Our propensity to make inductive inferences does not depend on a prior conviction that Nature operates uniformly. Quite the reverse: belief in the Uniformity of Nature becomes stronger as a result of successful inductive practices. In Hume's view, scientists, who find regular mechanisms behind even apparently random events, are more attached to it than are peasants, who are content to think of the world as more or less uniform in its operations but far from completely predictable.

Hume calls his response a 'sceptical' solution. It is a solution because it shows that no practical conclusions follow from the sceptic's argument. The sceptic cannot recommend that we suspend our practices of inductive inference. To say that we ought to do something presupposes we can. But our propensity to form inductive expectations is 'hard-wired': it operates independently of conscious decision-making. It is sceptical because, from a purely theoretical standpoint, the sceptic is right. Inductive inference is beyond rational justification.

The course of nature

Although Hume is generally credited with discovering (or inventing) the problem of induction, his presentation of the problem differs from standard contemporary presentations in at least two ways, both having to do with his attitude to the Uniformity Principle.

Modern treatments of the problem of induction focus on the problem of explaining how a finite body of observational evidence can confirm an unrestrictedly general proposition.[3] By contrast, Hume tends to understand the problem in *temporal* terms. Hume thinks of inductive inference as primarily a device for anticipating *future* experience on the basis of *past* experience. He is more interested in prediction than in generalization: more interested in whether the sun will rise tomorrow than in whether the sun always rises.

Furthermore, his sceptical argument is directed towards the Uniformity Principle's epistemic status. Can it possibly be *justified*? A crucial move in Hume's argument is the claim that the Principle, because contingent, cannot be known *a priori*. This where Hume's tendency to conceive the problem of induction in temporal terms gives his approach a distinctive spin. His reason for thinking that the Uniformity Principle is contingent is that there is no contradiction in the thought that the course of Nature might change, so that regularities that held until today will cease to hold tomorrow.

The thought that the course of Nature might change is not the focal concern today. Rather, modern approaches to the problem centre on the ineliminable possibility that any finite body of empirical evidence, no matter how extensive, may prove to be restricted, slanted, or otherwise misleading. All swans in Britain are white: so if we take British swans to be representative of swans in general, we will conclude that all swans are white. But we will be wrong, since there are black swans in Australia. Newton's physics works very well at velocities that are low relative to the speed of light: so if we take objects travelling at such velocities to be representative of moving objects generally, we will conclude that the Universe is Newtonian. And again we will be wrong, since Newtonian physics breaks down at relativistic velocities. At the heart of the modern problem is the non-monotonicity of inductive reasoning: evidence that appears to strongly support a given conclusion can find its apparent evidential weight radically degraded by new information.

At an intuitive level, this is quite different from Hume's worry. Hume suggests that, from the standpoint of pure logic, laws that really have operated until now might cease to operate in the future. By contrast, if we say that the Universe was Newtonian until about 1905, suddenly became Einsteinian, and may be something else tomorrow, this is a only a picturesque way of talking about our *theories* of the Universe and our need to change them as their limitations become apparent. The Universe was never Newtonian. We only thought it was, given our limited knowledge.

There is a good reason for our seeing things this way. Einstein's theory explains why Newton's theory works as well as it does, thus why the evidence that appeared to support it is misleading. Journeying to the Antipodes does the same thing for the eighteenth-century Englishman's opinion that all swans are white. Swans in Britain are no more representative of swans generally than 'Newtonian' velocities are representative of velocities generally. Given such explanations, it is better to refer our disappointments to our limited knowledge than to changes in the course of Nature.

This does not mean that Hume's general strategy is inapplicable to the modern problem. Hume can argue that some kind of Uniformity Principle must be presupposed by any justification-conferring form of inductive evidence. Suppose we focus on the problem of misleading evidence. We want to know whether we can rationally assure ourselves that the evidence we have collected is representative of how things are generally. But in asking for this assurance, we are presupposing that Nature is sufficiently uniform across time and space for finite samples to be representative of events at large. And our history of inductive extrapolation, however successful, only provides a very limited sample of such inference, a sample that may be misleading. Circularity still threatens.

Nor is Hume wrong about the Uniformity Principle as he understands it. There is no contradiction in supposing that natural laws, even those belonging to fundamental physics, are subject to change. What we can say, however, is that even if Nature does operate according to stable laws, this will not help with the problem of misleading evidence, and so will not help with the problem of induction in its modern form. If evidence can always be misleading, both generalization and prediction are epistemologically hazardous.

Uniformity again

When Hume argues that immediate inductive inferences are not valid, he seems to mean that they are not deductively valid. The Uniformity Principle enters the discussion as a suppressed premise which, when made explicit, repairs this defect. Notably, Hume's objection to the Uniformity Principle is only that we are not epistemically entitled to it. He does not ask whether it is up to the job in the first place.

It isn't. To see why, consider a simple example of a failed inductive inference. Go back to the swans and, for the sake of argument, suppose that having white feathers is not part of the definition of being a swan. In this case, 'All swans are white' is a straightforward empirical proposition. Travelling the British Isles in the eighteenth century, Hume could easily have convinced himself of its truth by arguing:

Premise: All the swans I have observed up to now have been white.
Premise: Nature operates uniformly.
Conclusion: All swans are white.

As we have known since Cook's expedition found black-feathered swans, this conclusion is false. But an argument is deductively valid if it is impossible for all its premises to be true and its conclusion false. Since in the argument above the first premise is true and the conclusion is false, either its second premise (the Uniformity Principle) is true, in which case the argument is invalid, or the argument is valid and the Uniformity Principle is false!

I take it that the right choice is obvious. The argument is invalid. This is not a matter of detail. No version of the Principle could perform the task Hume assigns it. To say that Nature operates uniformly is to say merely that there are regularities in Nature: that is, some regularities or other. But this gives us no reason to think that we have caught on to them: no reason to think that the 'regularities' we have observed are other than coincidental. When our expectations are disappointed, the reason is not that Nature has suddenly proved to be irregular but that we can be led to false conclusions by misleading evidence. The Uniformity Principle is not just epistemically unavailable: it is epistemically impotent.

Now what I have been calling 'induction' Hume calls 'probable' reasoning. Although there are questions about what exactly Hume means by 'probable', which we need not go into, the mention of probability is still suggestive. The question to ask is whether the argument so far depends on expecting too much from the Uniformity Principle. Perhaps inductive arguments go as follows:

> *Premise*:   All As observed up to now have been B.
> *Premise*:   Nature is uniform.
> *Conclusion*: Probably, all As are B (or the next A observed will be B).

The conclusion of an inductive argument should not be that all swans are white or that the sun will rise tomorrow, but that such eventualities are highly probable.

Obviously, this reformulation does not respond to Hume's charge that the Uniformity Principle is epistemically unavailable. But it doesn't respond to the charge of impotence either. Even when, in attempting to confirm a generalization, we have made what we consider a lot of observations, we have sampled only a vanishingly small sample of that generalization's instances. Unless we are entitled to assume that our sample is representative, the objective probability that all As are B (or that the next A is B) could be effectively zero. The premises of even this weakened argument can be true while its conclusion is false. So the argument is not valid.

The sceptical problem is not getting any easier. Not only can't we argue for the Uniformity Principle in a non-question-begging way, we would be no better off even if we could.

Determinism and predictability

Hume's way of framing the problem of induction, in terms of the epistemic status of the Uniformity Principle, invites the thought that if we could find some way of giving the Principle an *a priori* rationale, we would be home and dry. Kant seems to have attempted something along these lines.

Kant is concerned with the principle that every event has a cause. This 'causal maxim' is a close relative of the Uniformity Principle, if we think, as Hume and Kant both do, that an event's being caused entails its falling under a law. However, whereas Hume thinks that belief in the causal maxim is the *result* of extensive experience with successful inductive inference—and is thus confined to sophisticated inquirers—Kant spends considerable ingenuity arguing that the maxim is in a certain special sense *a priori*; and he seems to think that, in so doing, he is addressing 'Hume's problem' of providing inductive inference with a rational basis. But if we understand the Principle's role in grounding induction as Hume does—as plugging the gap in a deductively invalid argument—Kant's strategy is no help.

I am not sure what connection Kant saw between the causal maxim and the problem of induction. Perhaps we can understand the maxim's role less ambitiously. For Kant, the causal maxim implies determinism: everything that happens does so in accordance with natural law; nothing in the Universe is a matter of chance. But a deterministic Universe, we might suppose, is in principle predictable. So even if our predictions are sometimes frustrated, it is reasonable to try again. In a causally ordered world, it is reasonable to be guided by observed regularities, even if some of them turn out to be misleading.[4] However, there is no clear connection between determinism and predictability. A device may be deterministic but so complex as to be in practice unpredictable. A roulette wheel is such a device (unless the croupier has his foot on the brake). We have also come recently to understand how deterministic systems can be unpredictable in virtue of being 'chaotic' (in the sense of chaos theory). Chaotic systems are extremely sensitive to small variations in some of their parameters. In such systems, practically undetectable events may spiral into vast and unforeseeable consequences. (For the want of a nail, the shoe was lost, etc., etc.) It is not always clear what it means to say that the behaviour of such systems is even 'in principle' predictable.

All these thoughts point in the same direction: the Uniformity Principle is not the key to inductive scepticism.

The 'new riddle'

The discussion in the previous section may suggest that, *pace* Hume, we are inclined to treat the Uniformity Principle, or something very like it, as *a priori*. When our expectations are disappointed, we blame ourselves rather than Nature. However, there need be no interesting metaphysical commitment here. If the Uniformity Principle is *a priori*—a fairly large 'if'—it is because it is vacuous. We want to claim that events we have not sampled resemble those we have. But of course they do *in some way or other*. They could hardly fail to.

This point is dramatically illustrated by Nelson Goodman's 'new riddle of induction'.[5] Letting 't' stand for some future point in time, Goodman defines a predicate 'grue' to mean 'either examined before t and green, or else blue'. He then points out that the evidence we accept as confirming 'All emeralds are green' is equally compatible with 'All emeralds are grue'. Here the problem is not so much that the green emeralds we have observed so far are a misleading sample, but that there is no logically mandated answer to the question as to what class they are a representative sample of.

Why do we take our evidence to confirm the first proposition—that emeralds are green—but not the second, that they are grue? In Goodman's terms, why do we treat 'green' but not 'grue' as a 'projectible' predicate? According to Goodman, there is no deep logical or metaphysical reason. Because 'green' has figured in many useful past projections, it is an 'entrenched' predicate. 'Grue', by contrast, hasn't and isn't. End of story and all very Humean. There have been attempts to improve on Goodman's response. Without getting involved in the details of the debate, let me just say that the results have not been encouraging.

The point I want to make here is simply this: that even if all the emeralds in the world turned blue, we would not have to say that the course of Nature had changed. We could say that emeralds are and always have been grue. If this seems unthinkable, consider the case (invented by Peter Heath) of two very small insects whose life involves walking up a green-blue candy-striped may-pole. They are arguing about whether the surface of their world is green or grue. The insect defending the common-sense position that it is green is in for a shock. With a somewhat more complicated definition of 'grue', involving periodic flipping, their world is uniformly grue. Whether the future is 'like' the past depends on the similarities we are willing to countenance. Out of all the similarities we can think up, we countenance those we have found useful to mark. But this gives us no lien on the future. Categories can always be revised or replaced.

I said that Hume's problem seems different from the modern problem at an 'intuitive' level. On further reflection, it is not easy to say what is involved in a change in the course of Nature. We can always keep Nature 'uniform' if we recognize no restrictions on the categories in terms of which Nature may permissibly be described: this is why the Principle is epistemically impotent. Admittedly, disjunctive predicates like 'grue' strike us as highly unnatural. But if Goodman is right—and no one has argued convincingly that he isn't— naturalness or intuitiveness is more a matter of familiarity than of logic or metaphysics.

It may seem that this discussion ignores an important aspect of the Uni-formity Principle. The Principle need not be the banal claim that, given an unlimited licence to manufacture descriptive terms, the future can always be made out to be 'like' the past, but that Nature operates according to uniform *laws*. However, if Goodman is right, there is less to this distinction than meets the eye.

Natural laws support subjunctive conditionals. Contrast the two general statements: that blue litmus paper dipped in acid turns red; and that all the coins in my pocket are pound coins. Although I did not dip this piece of litmus paper in acid, if I *had* done so, it *would have* turned red. But it is not true that if the penny on my desk were (or had been) in my pocket, it would have been a pound. But how do we determine which generalizations are genuinely lawlike? It seems, by seeing whether they involve projectible predi-cates. We have lots of predictive-explanatory uses for concepts like 'litmus', 'acid', and 'red', but none for 'coin in my pocket'. Accordingly, we treat true generalizations involving the last as accidental. If this is right, 'lawlikeness' is not an 'intrinsic' or 'logical' feature of certain statements, a feature that could ground or justify their inferential or explanatory role. Rather, it reflects the history of the concepts they involve: specifically, those concepts' having played such roles in the past. Here again Goodman is close to Hume, who also argues that we identify laws by reference to our inferential habits. But if Hume and

Goodman are right, we cannot appeal to the notion of law to ground those habits. Not to the satisfaction of a determined sceptic, anyway.

Notes

1. Hume (1978), 1.3.6. See also Hume, *Enquiry Concerning Human Understanding*, in Hume (1975).
2. Hume (1978), 89.
3. Skyrms (1975) offers a useful introduction to contemporary theories of inductive inference.
4. See the 'Second Analogy' in Kant (1964). Kant thinks that the causal maxim—which he takes to imply strict determinism—is a necessary presupposition of scientific inquiry. The quest for scientific understanding just is the quest for deterministic laws. We are no longer so sure about this. In quantum physics, the fundamental laws are statistical, not deterministic.
5. Goodman (1955), ch. 1.

18

Projection and Conjecture

Induction as a Cartesian problem

The problem of induction is broadly Cartesian in the sense that it is an underdetermination problem. Like any other Cartesian conundrum, the problem derives its force from an *a priori* partition of our beliefs: those about the past and those about the future, or those about the observed and those about the unobserved, or those about particular and those about general matters of fact.

With such a partition in place, there is no arguing for the Uniformity Principle: it is just one more general commitment, as much in need of justification as any other. And even if we could provide it with some kind of *a priori* justification, it would be too abstract to underwrite any particular inference. However, for a contextualist, there is no more reason to accept Hume's partition than there is to accept the partition between experience and knowledge of the external world.

For a contextualist, particular contexts of inquiry are always characterized by a range of justified background presuppositions (some default justified) concerning matters of general as well as particular fact. Even when not explicitly held, a rich range of such presuppositions will be implicit in our regarding some predicates as projectible and others not. Accordingly, we do not need a general recipe for going from the past to the future, the observed to the unobserved, or the particular to the general, unguided by general factual considerations. In insinuating that we do, the problem of induction buys into the entire apparatus of foundationalism and epistemological realism.

'Deductivism'

We can confirm this diagnosis of the problem by looking briefly at some typical direct responses to it, all of which reflect the standard dilemma of foundationalism versus the coherence theory.

One line that has been taken against Hume is that Hume's argument rests on a prejudice in favour of 'deductivism'. When Hume argues that inductive inferences are not immediate, but presuppose some kind of Uniformity

Principle, all he has shown is that they are not deductively valid: that is, that the conclusions of such arguments can be false even though their premises are true. But the fact that such arguments are deductively invalid does not mean that they are not sometimes inductively strong. All that Hume has really shown is that induction is not deduction. This would underwrite a sceptical conclusion only if we took logical implication to be the sole warrant-conferring relation between premises and conclusion, which we have been given no reason to do.

An argument along these lines used to be popular with so-called 'ordinary language' philosophers. Thus P. F. Strawson argued that it was analytic—true in virtue of the meanings of our words—both that it is reasonable to proportion one's degree of confidence in a statement to the strength of the evidence in its favour, and that the evidence in favour of generalizations is strong in proportion to 'the number of instances and the variety of circumstances in which they have been found'.[1] Accordingly, with respect to projective or generalizing inferences, following normal inductive practices is part of what 'being reasonable' *means*. The sceptical 'problem' of induction mounts a challenge to the reasonableness of our ordinary procedures only by distorting our ordinary conception of what reasonableness consists in.

If we take Hume's problem at face value, this response fails to speak to it. The question is not whether following inductive methods is in some sense 'reasonable', but whether following such methods yields conclusions that are objectively likely to be true, or objectively more likely to be true than conclusions reached by different methods: wild guessing, for example. And the sceptical problem arises because there does not seem to be any non-question-begging way of arguing that they are. This problem arises, in turn, because (as Hume points out and as Strawson himself concedes) it appears to be a contingent matter that our usual inductive methods will continue to work as well in the future as they have in the past. If this is contingent, it cannot be analytic.

To respond to the sceptical problem, a rejection of 'deductivism' must amount to the claim that there is a non-contingent, hence *a priori*, relation of 'making probable', holding between the premises and conclusion of a good inductive argument. According to this way of thinking, the proper form of an inductive argument is:

Premise:	All As observed so far have been B.
(Makes [more] probable)	_____
Conclusion:	All As are B.

For philosophers who follow this line, Hume's mistaken deductivism consists in his failure to recognize that there can be inference-grounding *logical* relations weaker than entailment but stronger than irrelevance. Hume does not realize that there are relations of 'logical' probability.[2]

Clearly, this is a close relative of the 'criterial' view of evidence, according to which it is analytic that certain statements are good though not conclusive evidence for the truth of others. The trouble with this idea, as Hume's own argument implies, is that there is no good reason to suppose that such criterial relations exist. Abstracting from everything we know about how the world works, anything could be correlated with anything else. Indeed, the world could be entirely random. Is it really *a priori* true that, if something has happened a lot, it is likely to happen again? Many people think that, at least in some circumstances, the opposite is true: the slugger who has struck out every time at bat is 'due' for a home run (the 'gambler's fallacy'). The world may not work this way. But that it doesn't is hardly a matter of meaning or pure logic.

A more technical version of the same basic strategy, closely associated with the leading Logical Positivist, Rudolf Carnap, consists in an attempt to develop formal systems of 'inductive logic', based on 'confirmation-functions' that determine the degree to which a given body of evidence-statements supports a given conclusion.[3] One problem with this approach is that any number of such functions can be defined, and it is an empirical matter as to which, if any, would lead to reliable predictions in the actual world. More than that, however, one of the lessons to be learned from Goodman's new riddle of induction is that 'inductive logic' has no hope of being formal in the way of deductive logic. Consider a simple deductive argument.

> All huskies are friendly.
> Nikki is a husky.
> So: Nikki is friendly.

The validity of this argument depends completely on its abstract logical structure. It is an instance of a general pattern:

> All Fs are Gs.
> a is an F.
> So: a is a G.

No matter what particular terms we insert into this structure, the argument is valid. But induction doesn't work like this. There is no *formal* difference between strong inductive arguments involving 'emeralds' and 'green' and crazy arguments involving 'emeralds' and 'grue'. Predicates like 'grue' aren't suitable for use in projective inferences. But this is a matter of content, not form.

Some philosophers would say that there is a *hidden* formal difference. Since 'grue' means 'either examined before time t and green or examined after time t and blue', 'grue' is disjunctive in a way that 'green' is not. However, the distinction between disjunctive and non-disjunctive predicates seems to be language-relative. Given a predicate 'bleen' which applies to blue objects examined before t and green objects examined afterwards, 'green' can be defined as 'grue and observed prior to t or bleen and observed subsequently'. Anyway, what makes a normal predicate like 'red' non-disjunctive, even in a language without grue-like terms? After all, 'red' can be taken to mean 'either crimson, or scarlet or . . .'.

In considering proposals for an inductive logic, it is important not to confuse induction with statistical inference. In statistical inference we infer certain facts about a large population—say, the average height of New Yorkers—from measurements made on a sample. Given certain assumptions about both the target population and the sample—for example, that heights are 'normally' distributed (the [in]famous bell curve) and that the sample is random—we can calculate the probability of the sample-derived value's falling within a given range about the true mean. The empirical assumptions involved in particular applications of statistical methods are strong. Since they reflect assumptions about both the target population and our sample, they are much stronger than a generalized uniformity principle, which says only that Nature is regular in some way or other. This does not prevent their enjoying default positive status, though of course they are open to revision if they lead to problematic results. In general, such presuppositions are apt to be highly defeasible ('lies, damned lies, and statistics'). Still, in its mathematical aspect statistical reasoning is entirely deductive and owes nothing to the sort of 'inductive logic' proposed by Carnap. Statistical inference is not 'probabilistic reasoning' but 'reasoning about empirical probabilities'.

The question to ask is not whether the idea of a purely *a priori* basis for inductive argumentation can be convincingly worked out but why anyone would want such a basis in the first place. The answer lies in the Cartesian structure of the sceptical problem of induction, and in the attempt to give that problem a straight foundationalist solution. As with any Cartesian problem, once the sceptic's partition of our beliefs into privileged and problematic classes is accepted, nothing less than some form of *a priori* evidential connection will allow us to make warranted inferences from members of the one class to members of the other. To postulate an empirical connection will appear to beg the question against the sceptic. To question the foundationalist presuppositions of Cartesian sceptical problems is the correct way out of this dilemma.

Holism again

The postulation of relations of logical probability reflects a foundationalist approach to the problem of induction. Not surprisingly, there is a coherentist response too. As we have seen, a coherence theorist is likely to harbour his own suspicions of 'deductivism'. According to Harman, the view that the only admissible form of inference is deductive must be wrong because, if inference involves reasoned change of belief, there is simply no such thing as deductive inference.[4] The rules of deduction are rules of entailment, not rules of inference. They tell us what follows from what, not what to believe on the basis of what. We may believe that P, and come to realize that P entails Q; but Q may be so implausible that we ought to rethink our commitment to P rather than accept Q as an ineluctable consequence of a prior belief. According to Harman, all inference is 'inductive' in that it is a matter of revising our total view so as to make it less *ad hoc*, more plausible, more coherent. All inference is 'inference to the best explanation'.[5] Such holistic reasoning is a matter of judgement rather than the rigid application of formal rules. There is no such thing as deductive inference and no such thing as inductive logic.

I have already criticized the coherence theory in this radically holistic form and will not repeat myself. But I do want to say something more about logic and inference.

First of all, contrary to what Harman implies, there is no strict opposition between coherentism and acceptance of the idea of inductive logic. Granted, a coherence theorist cannot treat the rules of inductive logic as rules of inference, in Harman's sense of 'inference'. But this does not prevent his adding relations of inductive confirmation to the stock of *logical* relations between beliefs on which global coherence supervenes. Not that I think there are such relations. My point is only that the coherence theory alone does not compel us to reject them.

Secondly, I do not want to deny that we sometimes reason in something like the holistic way Harman describes. What I do want to claim, however, is that such reasoning never takes place in a vacuum but always in a context (informational, disciplinary, dialectical, and situational) where not everything is up for grabs. The sort of reasoning coherence theorists describe is locally rather than globally holistic.

The idea of inference to the best explanation is important. Not all inductive inference takes the form of extrapolation from observed correlations. There is also 'abductive' inference, where we accept a hypothesis because it best explains a certain range of data. However, inference of this kind should not be seen through the lens of radical holism. Explanations are inferred as explanations of specifically relevant data, relevance being fixed by our interests and collateral knowledge. As we have seen, it makes no sense to think of our 'total view' as one big explanation. At that level of abstraction, explanatory relations disappear. Furthermore, the 'best' explanation is the best out of the available alternatives, not the best possible. Indeed, it is often hard enough to find any explanation for a given range of facts.

Statistical inference, and the knowledge it underwrites, can be involved in inference to the best explanation. I may decide (correctly) that the roulette wheel is fixed because that is the best statistical explanation of why the house has been winning so often: that is, so much more often than would be likely if the wheel were fair. (Note that this explanation need not show that the precise sequence of numbers that I observed was likely to come up. Even with systematic cheating, lots or other sequences could easily have been generated. But if my explanation is correct, all of them would have been favourable to the house.) However, this statistical explanation will be the best explanation only given certain presuppositions. If further extensive investigation fails to uncover any evidence of irregularities, I may have to conclude that the house has simply been exceptionally lucky.

It seems to me that this contextualist outlook is reinforced by Goodman's arguments. Goodman at first seems to suggest a different view. To undermine the idea that there is a sceptical problem of induction, Goodman invites us to ask how we would justify *deduction*, a question that Hume notably fails to pose. According to Goodman, we formulate rules of deductive logic by taking our cue from intuitively valid deductive inferences. Given an illuminating set of rules, we may in turn be led to modify some of our intuitive judgements of validity. We shuttle back and forth, modifying rules in the light of particular judgements and particular judgements in the light of rules, until we reach a satisfying balance: reflective equilibrium. But although this looks at first like a straightforward coherentist response to the sceptical problem, in the light of Goodman's new riddle it takes on a different appearance. As we saw, a consequence of Goodman's argument is that inductive 'logic' can never be purely formal. Goodman's own solution to how to exclude predicates like 'grue' depends on appealing to a predicate's past history in matters of inductive inference. So with respect to canons of inductive methods, reaching reflective equilibrium is not a matter of matching purely formal rules to particular applications. Rather, the quest for such equilibrium is constrained by prior views about how the world can usefully be described: in effect, by general views about the way the world works.

If we abandon radical holism, there is no reason to deny that there is such a thing as deductive inference. Such inference takes place in contexts in which certain commitments are so firmly set that we may justifiably add their perceived consequences to our stock of beliefs. Of course, we will endorse such an inference only if these consequences do not bring to light unnoticed difficulties. But often they don't. And when they don't, there is no reason not to say that we have reasoned deductively.

By the same token, we do not have to suppose that the sort of projective inference targeted by Hume is implicitly holistic, in any interesting way. Rather, we should see it as a simple form of inference—in effect, a crude form of 'sampling' inference—acceptable in fairly routine matters where our general views of the world, justifiably held fast in context, allow us to single out predicates for projection. True, such reasoning is always non-monotonic, in that new information can radically degrade the evidential significance of what previously seemed strong evidence. In particular, we may acquire reason to think that the cases we have observed are not a representative sample of the class of cases we are interested in. However, this is just the inevitable defeasibility of any form of inference that depends on background empirical presuppositions. Recognizing such defeasibility is no concession to radical scepticism.

Conjectural knowledge

On the picture I am sketching, there are various forms of 'inductive'—that is, non-demonstrative—inference, acceptable in appropriate contexts. However, Karl Popper has famously argued that there is no need to respond to Hume's problem, since neither science nor rational thinking generally has any connection with inductive procedures.[6]

Popper's epistemology takes off from the simple observation that unrestrictedly general statements of the form 'All Fs are Gs' are asymmetrical with respect to verification and falsification. No finite number of observations can ever conclusively verify—or, according to Popper, even significantly confirm—a generalization ranging over a potentially infinite number of instances. All observed Fs may have been Gs, even though the overwhelming majority of actual Fs are not Gs at all. However, if we encounter even one F that is not a G, the claim that *all* Fs are Gs is conclusively refuted.

On the basis of this simple observation, Popper builds an elaborate epistemological structure. According to Popper, the aim of scientific testing is not to establish the definite truth of our theories but to eliminate errors. We do not test scientific theories in order to confirm them but to try to refute them: to see where they go wrong, as all do eventually, in order to replace them with better theories. Science does not proceed by induction from observations but by 'conjecture and refutation', trial and error.

In Popper's view, theories (albeit sometimes inchoate or implicit) are always prior to observations. Only in the context of some general conceptions can we have any ideas about *what* to observe. An instruction to go out and 'observe Nature' is vacuous. The masses of unrelated facts collected in Francis Bacon's 'natural histories', conceived by Bacon as necessary preparations for 'true induction', are worse than useless.

Aligning Popper's views with more conventional epistemological stances is not altogether straightforward. My original classification of epistemological problems explains why. Popper is much more interested in methodological and demarcational questions than he is in 'refuting the sceptic'. His aim is not so much to reply to scepticism in a conventional way as to alter our sense of what epistemology ought to be about.

Popper values falsifiability because he takes it to be the hallmark of science. A theory is scientific only if it is possible to say what would count *against* it. In Popper's eyes, some of the most influential theories of our time are not scientific at all. When the patient of a Freudian analyst accepts the analyst's account of the unconscious meaning of his (the patient's) actions, the hypothesis is confirmed. But if the patient denies the hypothesis, he is exhibiting resistance, which is also strong evidence that the hypothesis is on the right lines. For such theories, confirmations are everywhere. This is a vice, not a virtue.[7]

What is wrong with theories designed to resist refutation? The answer is that to resist refutation is to resist improvement, hindering the growth of knowledge. Accordingly, falsification is the key to the problem of method as well as that of demarcation. This is useful advice. It is all too easy to find evidence that fits in with views we are attached to, overlooking the equally or even more abundant evidence that creates difficulties for them. However, this advice is less original that Popper likes to think. It can be found in Bacon, Popper's paradigmatic naive inductivist. (The history of epistemology would have been very different if Bacon's philosophical ideas had eclipsed those of Descartes, rather than the other way around.) Moreover, Popper tends to misunderstand the character of his own best ideas. What he presents as desirable characteristics of theories—openness to counter-evidence, and so on—are better seen as desirable attitudes on the part of theorists. Any theory can be insulated from falsification by the incorporation of *ad hoc* hypotheses. Such insulation can even be reasonable: for example, to protect promising new ideas from premature demise. Equally, any theory—even Freudian psychology or Marxian historical sociology—can be cast in a way that makes it vulnerable to criticism. Theories become permanently irrefutable only when dogmatic theorists choose to make them so.

Still, in several ways Popper's ideas represent a significant advance over empiricist foundationalism. There is much in Popper that a contextualist ought to welcome. But although Popper can be seen as trying to reorient epistemology towards demarcational and methodological questions and away from an overriding concern with scepticism, his own emancipation from standard forms of sceptical argumentation is far from complete.

The first thing to notice is that falsification is nowhere near as simple as Popper's early views imply (and as Popper himself came to recognize). We don't automatically abandon a successful theory because one result runs counter to our expectations. Nor should we: after all, observations can themselves be misleading. As coherence theorists emphasize, theories are never tested alone but always in a context of collateral commitments—about our situation, our experimental apparatus, and much else besides—so a recalcitrant result may reflect an error in our background presuppositions rather than in the theory under test. Of course, sometimes we are entitled to reject the theory and do so. But never in an informational vacuum. Moreover, it is not clear that the idea of falsification is detachable from our entertaining inductive expectations. After all, we expect refuted theories to *stay refuted*. We don't say, 'Oh well, our theory did badly today but it will do fine tomorrow'.

In taking Hume's inductive scepticism at face value, and thus completely dismissing the idea of justification, Popper in effect contrasts a rigidly foundationalist conception of justification with a contextualized notion of falsification. However, once the move to contextualism is made, there is no need to dismiss justification.

Popper's problems stem from his failure to make crucial distinctions. He does not distinguish the two aspects of justification: entitlement and grounding. He therefore fails to see that the Prior Grounding conception of justification is not the only possible conception. In fact, he swallows it hook, line, and sinker. As a result, he does not see that his 'conjecture and refutation' model of inquiry can be recast as a model of justification—the Default and Challenge model—in which certain unchallenged beliefs represent default entitlements. Nor does he distinguish between radical and non-radical scepticism. Accordingly, he endorses radically sceptical views like Hume's, when his real interest is only in fallibilism.

We can keep the fallibilism and drop the scepticism.

Notes

1. Strawson (1952), 256.
2. Keynes (1921).
3. Carnap (1961).
4. Harman (1986), chs. 1–2, App. A.
5. Harman (1973), ch. 10.
6. Popper (1972), ch. 1, is a good statement of Popper's views.
7. Popper (1963), ch. 1, sec. 2.

19

Relativism

Relativism and scepticism

Relativism is much in the air. Various intellectual movements, such as 'post-modernism' and 'social constructivism', are associated by their critics (and sometimes their proponents) with a relativistic outlook, though how far and in what sense the programmes and positions that go under these labels are relativistic is not always clear.[1]

Relativism takes two main forms, subjective and cultural. The subjectivist says that nothing is justified *simpliciter*: things are only justified-for-me. The cultural relativist is less individualistic: he thinks that beliefs are justified for particular 'cultures'. Cultural relativism sometimes leads to the embrace of a 'standpoint epistemology', according to which ethnic, class, gender, or other 'cultural' differences are associated with distinct 'ways of knowing'. But in general, relativism, whether subjective or cultural, can encompass not only substantive beliefs about the world but criteria of justification, methods of investigation and inference, styles of explanation or understanding, and so on. There is no common ground, substantive or methodological, on which argument between those who see the world from different standpoints can proceed. Clashes between them are thus power struggles, 'objectivity' being no more than the dominant world-view's preferred self-description.

I have stated relativism as a thesis about justification. But relativism can also be presented as a doctrine about truth: that nothing is true *simpliciter* but only true-for-me or for some culture. However, I doubt that there is a deep difference here. Relativists reject the idea of objective truth because they have grave doubts about the existence of neutral methods or criteria for establishing the truth. Relativists are suspicious of objective truth because they are suspicious of objective justification, not the other way around. An 'objective truth' that was beyond any human being's capacity for knowledge would be no threat to relativism.

No one needs to be told that human beliefs vary widely across time and space; that differences of opinion can extend to fundamental methodological ideas; and that when they do, disputes can be difficult, or even practically impossible, to resolve. However, relativism is a philosophical doctrine that goes far beyond such obvious facts. The relativist does not hold merely that differences of outlook are often so profound that disputes involving them can be intractable, but rather that there are principled, across-the-board objections to such ideas as objective truth or objective justification. In this respect, the relativist is like the philosophical sceptic. The sceptic does not hold merely that we know a lot less than we like to think, but that knowledge is impossible.

Many philosophers distinguish between scepticism and relativism on the grounds that, whereas the sceptic denies the possibility of knowledge, the relativist holds that knowledge, in its properly relativized form, is not just possible but actual. We might even think of relativism as a defence against scepticism. The thought would be that scepticism results from a hankering after an impossible form of objectivity. Give this up and the sceptic has nothing to say to us.

While this is a fair point, we must not press it too hard. The fact is that, pre-theoretically, we are inclined to accept the possibility of objective justification and objective truth. Of course, we may not take this attitude towards all areas of inquiry, in which case we commit ourselves to significant demarcational views, worthy of further exploration. But the relativist rejects the idea of objectivity completely. In this respect, relativism is close to scepticism.

We should not place too much faith in prepositions. The relativist allows me to speak of things being justified (or true) *for* me or for my culture. How does this differ from their being justified (or true) *according to me*, hence perhaps not really justified at all? Isn't the point of justification—for example, the collection and weighing of evidence—to help us *resolve* differences, not to enshrine them? Like idealism, relativism is a reaction to scepticism that is difficult to distinguish from scepticism itself.

Limits to relativism

So far I have treated relativism as a doctrine about justification or truth. But there is also conceptual relativism, the doctrine that different cultures 'carve up the world' in different ways: that is, think in terms of fundamentally different categories or 'conceptual schemes'. According to conceptual relativists, 'reality itself is relative to a scheme: what counts as real in one system may not in another'.[2] Since everyone must think in terms of some conceptual scheme—there is no neutral standpoint from which rival schemes can be compared—different schemes are 'incommensurable'.

Conceptual relativism is a dramatic doctrine, but as Davidson has famously (or notoriously) argued, not one that it is easy to make clear sense of. What do different conceptual schemes 'carve up' differently. The standard answer is 'the world' or 'experience'. But what is 'the world' here? If 'the world' is something beyond all description, an ineffable thing-in-itself, no real answer to the question has been given. On the other hand, if it is the familiar world of trees and rocks, it is the world as we already know how to describe it; and while different people may have strikingly different views about how this familiar world operates, any sense of pervasive conceptual disparity has evaporated. Parallel remarks apply to 'experience'. Indeed, the notion of experience operative here is the one we already rejected: experience as a kind of 'non-propositional' knowledge. In other words, the Myth of the Given.

Different conceptual schemes are presumably embodied in different languages. Where languages express different concepts, there must be problems of translation. So perhaps the best way to make sense of conceptual relativism is in terms of the impossibility of translating one language into another. It is a commonplace that some languages have words with no precise equivalent in others: there is no English word for *Schadenfreude*. Perhaps, then, we want to say that English lacks the concept although, since even in English the meaning of *Schadenfreude* can be explained in a more roundabout way, perhaps we don't. Either way, such failures of easy translatability are far too localized to encourage talk of different conceptual schemes. For that, we need languages that are globally non-intertranslatable.

On the suggestion we are exploring, beings with a conceptual scheme different from our own would have to speak a language that we could not translate. So our question becomes: can we make sense of the idea of a language that is (in principle) untranslatable? It is not clear how. What would justify us thinking of an untranslatable 'language' as a language? What would distinguish the 'words' of such a 'language' from mere noise?

If, like Descartes, we held that thought is prior to language, we might see no problem here. But if we think of language as the vehicle of thought, and if we think of the meaning of linguistic utterances as immanent in patterns of use, we cannot be so cavalier.

First of all, if we think of meaning as immanent in use, we cannot attribute massive illogicality (or wildly different logicality) to other speakers.[3] This is not a matter of being indulgent: a large measure of consistency is necessary if we are to find patterns, or uses, at all. But where we cannot find patterns, we cannot find meanings; and where we cannot find meanings, we cannot find language. Thus, we can find language only where we can find a common sense of the logical.

The second point is that language needs to be tied to the world. As we saw in Chapter 15, the tie is effected by observation-sentences, keyed by training to circumstances that come and go. But this means that we can find meaning, hence, language, only where we can find reactions to worldly conditions that we ourselves can recognize. This means that finding language requires more than finding a common sense of the logical: it involves finding lots of common beliefs too. Davidson calls the need to find massive agreement, wherever we can find language at all, the 'Principle of Charity'. But as I have stressed, being 'charitable' is not a matter of being indulgent. The meaningful is the interpretable; and in the methodology of interpretation, charity is not an option. (These points recapitulate our earlier discussion of intelligibility constraints on demands for justification.)

Supposing that this argument is broadly correct, how far does it get us? Not very far. As Davidson himself emphasizes, his aim is not to eliminate disagreement but to delineate the conditions that make meaningful disagreement possible. This being so, it seems to me that the global conceptual relativism Davidson argues against is something of a red herring. The kind of variability in belief that draws people to relativism exists within the bounds of Davidsonian possibility. The animist thinks that trees are the homes of spirits; the scientifically minded person does not. In order to disagree about trees in this way, there is a lot the parties have to agree about. But their world-views remain deeply at odds, even though they agree at the level of 'That's a tree'. For all that the argument from charity shows, when it comes to disputes like that between an animist and a physicalist, relativism could be the right view.

We should also remind ourselves that not all disagreement is contradiction. Sometimes whole ways of talking go by the board. The profoundest form of atheism is not the one that involves strenuously denying the existence of God but the one that lets theistic ways of talking fall into desuetude. Or to take a case central to the concerns of this book, consider certain traditional distinctions: the analytic versus the synthetic, the *a priori* versus the *a posteriori*, and the necessary versus the contingent. For foundationalists, it is vitally important to understand how the distinctions line up and what beliefs fall into what categories. But from the standpoint of the fallibilist, contextualist, and inquiry-centred epistemology I have been defending, the usefulness of such ways of thinking is much less obvious. So when a thoroughgoing fallibilist expresses doubts about *a priori* knowledge or necessary truth, he is not claiming, in a straightforward spirit of contradiction, that everything is *a posteriori* or that everything is contingent. He is questioning the theoretical utility of these traditional classifications.[4]

Roots of relativism

I said that, for all that the argument from charity shows, relativism could be the right epistemological outlook. But how can a relativist claim to be right? It is often suggested that he cannot, since, like scepticism, relativism is self-defeating. When the relativist claims that nothing is 'absolutely' true (or justified), he doesn't intend his conclusion to be taken as merely true (or justified) for him. If he did, I could dismiss his conclusion by saying that relativism isn't true for me. If arguments for relativism are meant to make a general epistemological point, they must invoke the very notion of truth (or justification) they reject. However, like its counterpart in the case of scepticism, this argument suffers from being too purely dialectical. As in the case of scepticism, the problem is not simply to silence an awkward opponent but reach a deeper understanding of how relativistic arguments work.

One of the founding distinctions of Western philosophy is that between what the Greeks called *physis*, nature, and *nomos*, custom or convention. While far from unproblematic, the observation that leads to this distinction is simple and (at first sight, anyway) compelling. Some of what we believe seems to be true in virtue of facts that hold independently of human wish and will. Stones fall to earth always and everywhere, whether we like it or not. Such facts belong to nature. But other beliefs, particularly those having to do with values or right conduct, seem to vary widely from place to place and time to time. They reflect the custom or conventions of particular groups of people. As human creations, customs and conventions do not belong to nature. Of course, if we never venture far from home, we may not realize this. That certain actions are wrong may seem as 'natural' as the fact that stones fall to earth. But the Greeks were traders and travellers. It was soon brought home to them that some things are accepted everywhere, others not.

There is no doubt that this perception tends to raise the spectre of cultural relativism: *autres pays, autres moeurs*. However, the mere fact of variation does not imply the impossibility of invidious comparison. The roots of relativism lie not in empirical data but in certain epistemological and metaphysical preconceptions. In the remainder of this chapter, I want to look at relativism primarily from an epistemological angle, leaving more metaphysical considerations for the next.

Epistemologically, the first and most important root of relativism is the idea that all justification takes place in a 'framework' of 'ultimate' commitments. What makes commitments 'ultimate'? The answer is that commitments that make justification possible must of necessity themselves be beyond rational assessment. In other words, what makes commitments 'ultimate' is the (alleged) impossibility of defending them in any non-circular way. But this makes it clear that relativism is not at bottom an empirical thesis at all. Relativism springs from Agrippan scepticism and the traditional conceptions of knowledge with which it is associated. In effect, the relativist accepts the foundationalist picture of the structure of knowledge while denying that there are any (or enough) foundational elements that are universally valid. The Agrippan argument thus functions in a double role: first to enforce the idea of ultimate commitments as necessary for knowledge and then to deprive those commitments of any objective significance. Relativism, we might say, is pluralistic foundationalism.

In connecting relativism with foundationalism, I do not mean to suggest that the coherence theory is wholly innocent. As we saw, the distinction between coherentism and foundationalism is far from clear-cut. The coherence theorist's radical holism pressures him to assign to his criteria of coherence a foundational role, an idea easily adapted to 'standpoint' epistemology.

Instead of modelling itself on the atomistic foundationalism of traditional empiricism, standpoint epistemology can postulate systematic methodological orientations that colour all input and determine its relevance. In this way, variant 'total systems' become incommensurable.

I said that relativism, however much it has been associated with cultural anthropology, results more from epistemological preconceptions than from anthropological data. But I would go farther. I think that the 'data' easily become shaped by the preconceptions. Writers on exotic cultures can be tempted to present them as embodying hermetically sealed total views, able to accommodate any objections, with no loose ends and no invitations to criticism or further inquiry. Such bodies of belief may also be represented as shared by all members of the culture in question. The aliens are taken to accept the local tenets down to the last detail, as if critically or sceptically minded individuals are unknown in foreign parts. Views like this smack more of *a priori* epistemological ideals than of empirical findings.[5]

Contextualism, which is hostile to both foundationalist and coherentist pictures of justification, discourages the reification of all-encompassing 'frameworks' or 'standpoints'. For the contextualist, such ways of thinking are all too reminiscent of epistemological realism with its talk of 'our epistemic position'. Pluralizing such talk effects no improvement. No one occupies a single framework or standpoint: there are as many 'frameworks' or 'standpoints' as there are contexts of inquiry. None amounts to a hermetically sealed 'total view'; none rests on 'ultimate' commitments, beyond rational criticism. Furthermore, because contextualism has no use for the radically holistic idea of a total view, it is not under pressure to be dismissive of the idea of external constraint. Contextualism is thus an antidote to relativism.

Contextualism takes fallibilism seriously. Justification, in matters where serious issues of justification arise, is always provisional, never watertight. And it often involves less-than-algorithmic procedures, such as inference to the best explanation. This brings me to the second epistemological preconception underlying relativism: the lingering influence of the demonstrative conception of knowledge and the 'quest for certainty'. Despairing of universal, objective certainty, the relativist settles for personal or group certainty. Perhaps, in the end, the two roots of relativism are really one: the relativist, like the sceptic, is a disappointed foundationalist.

A thoroughgoing fallibilism, hence a contextualist epistemology, is once more the proper antidote. Apparently intractable disagreement no more implies dogmatic relativism than our vast contingent ignorance implies radical scepticism. Just as contingent ignorance invites further inquiry, intractable disputes invite a search for common ground. We might not be able to find it, just as we cannot always fill gaps in our knowledge. But then again we might. Or we might be led to some different views altogether. Whether we succeed or fail depends on ingenuity and luck. We cannot predict the future of inquiry. Success is not guaranteed, but neither is failure.

Contextualism and relativism

Some philosophers will find implausible the claim that contextualism is the cure for relativism. They think that contextualism itself is a form of relativism.

It is not hard to see why. It is tempting to think of the presuppositions that are held in place by the direction of inquiry and other contextual factors as constituting a kind of 'framework' within which justificational questions can be raised and answered. I think that this way of talking is best avoided. It is almost bound to lead to contextualism's being confused with the relativist thesis that all justification is 'framework-relative', in a way that places frameworks themselves beyond justification or criticism. For example, Fogelin represents the contextualist as claiming:

(FR)   S is justified in believing that p if p is justified within the framework in which S is operating.

However, as Fogelin points out, there are at least three ways of resisting the move from a claim to be justified 'within a framework' to a claim to be justified *simpliciter*:

(a)   I may reject S's justificatory framework. (S may be using astrological tables.)
(b)   I may accept S's justificatory framework, but think S has not used it correctly.
(c)   I may grant that S has been epistemically responsible, but think his grounds have been defeated.

Fogelin rejects contextualism because he takes it to exclude critical reactions like these.[6] This is a mistake: a contextualist can and should accept the potential legitimacy of all three critical moves.

A contextualist view of knowledge and justification does not commit one to holding that a reference to context is part of the *content* of a knowledge-claim. We must recall the *sotto voce* proviso. A knowledge-claim commits one to holding that all significant potential defeaters—possibilities which, if realized, would make one's belief either false or inadequately grounded—have been eliminated: the contextual element comes in to fix what defeaters should be counted significant. But presuppositions as to what is significant are themselves open to criticism, which can be informationally or economically triggered.

More precisely, a contextualist will hold:

(C1)   All justification takes place in a context of presuppositions (e.g. relating to which potential defeaters need to be excluded) and other circumstances which are not currently under scrutiny.

(C2)   These presuppositions and circumstances can themselves be articulated and challenged, but only by a recontextualization of the original justificatory procedure, a recontextualization that will involve presuppositions of its own.

(C3)   Recontextualization can go on indefinitely. But this is the open-endedness of inquiry, not a vicious regress of justification.

Bringing to light questionable background commitments is an important strategy for raising motivated challenges to accepted claims. This is a crucial element in contextualist epistemology, not a criticism of it.

I said that talk of 'frameworks' is harmless provided that we do not take it too seriously. But such talk is best avoided. Almost inevitably, it encourages us to think of contexts of justification as insulated from external criticism, a view that contextualism is simply not committed to. Intelligibility constraints guarantee the existence of a wide range of cross-contextual commitments and entitlements. Furthermore, observational evidence operates cross-contextually. Of course, such evidence is not mechanically determinative of what we ought to think, for it is always potentially subject to considerations of relevance and reliability. But it is always there and is not simply to be dismissed.

Another unfortunate feature of framework talk is that it invites us to think in terms of an overly sharp distinction between norms and facts. We may be tempted to conceive different 'ways of knowing' as constituted by divergent epistemic norms which, since they govern the conduct of inquiry, cannot themselves be the objects of critical examination. This temptation should be resisted. A proposition that serves as a 'methodological necessity' has a special normative status within a particular type of inquiry, in the sense that exempting it from doubt is a precondition of engaging in inquiry of that type. A methodological necessity thus owes its normative status to its functional role in a particular investigative practice. But the norm/fact distinction is here methodological rather than ontological. Viewed from another angle—that is, recontextualized—a methodological necessity can appear as a substantial empirical commitment, open to scrutiny and revision.

The new angle of scrutiny can be provided by theoretical advances outside the 'framework' in question. Fogelin's example of astrology is a good one. What killed astrology was not detailed empirical problems within the 'framework' of astrological inquiry (though there were always lots of failed predictions) but a new conception of the physical universe, a conception that made the astrologer's geocentric world of stellar and planetary influences incredible. The astrological 'framework' was never in principle insulated from such external undermining.

Framework talk encourages relativism by leading us to think of contexts of inquiry as more rigid than they are. Contextualists had best not go in for it.

Reason and tradition

It might be argued that my argument is question-begging in a different way. It is conducted entirely within a broadly critical-rationalist perspective on belief. However, rationalism itself is a specific cultural tradition: the 'Western' tradition. In fact, rationalism is just another faith: faith in reason.

Baldly stated, this claim misses something very significant, which is that a broadly rationalist outlook is reflexive, so that adopting it is not a matter of uncritical commitment, still less uncritical commitment to our favourite ideas about rationality. Once we embark on the path of critical inquiry, epistemological goals, norms, and procedures themselves become potential objects of critical scrutiny. We can ask what we are pursuing in our quest for knowledge (the analytic problem), whether the quest has its limits (the problem of demarcation), how to go about it (the problem of method), whether the quest is fundamentally flawed or self-defeating (the problem of scepticism), and even whether the whole thing is really worth the candle (the problem of value). Epistemology is a third-order tradition of inquiry created by the capacity of a broadly rationalist outlook to reflect critically on its own presuppositions. The fact that norms, including epistemic norms, are instituted by attitudes does not exempt them from criticism.

If 'traditionalism' entails blind adherence to inherited views, a fallibilist epistemology is obviously anti-traditionalist. But in another way, contextualism is anything but hostile to tradition. All inquiry takes place in a rich informational context. Such contexts are never the creation of a sole inquirer: they are the legacy of past co-operation. Tradition—the inheriting of results and methods—is the prerequisite of investigation, thus of self-correction.

This obvious feature of inquiry has been obscured by modern epistemology's radical individualism. This individualism is different from classical epistemic individualism, which is a reflection of the moral-practical significance classically accorded to knowledge. Modern epistemic individualism results from modern epistemology's subjectivism, which is the legacy of Cartesian scepticism. Taken at face value, Cartesian scepticism forces the individual inquirer to suspend belief in the objective world and everything in it. It forces the individual to rely entirely on his or her own resources. This result was welcomed by Descartes, who dreamed of personally reconstructing science on a secure foundation. But it is a wholly unrealistic hope. Because contextualism grows out of a theoretical diagnosis of scepticism, it allows us to take the social-historical character of knowledge seriously. This is one of contextualism's virtues.

We are now in a position to see why the contextualist will not be moved by the claim that his broadly critical-rationalist outlook is an unjustified presupposition. The objection is self-defeating: anyone who can even raise it is already a fellow rationalist. This looks like the 'relativism is self-defeating' argument earlier criticized for being too dialectical. But it isn't. Or rather, this sort of objection takes on a different character when conjoined with an independently defended contextualist epistemology. For a contextualist, questions of justification only arise in contexts of motivated challenges. For views to which there are no serious alternatives, such questions do not arise. This is our situation with respect to a broadly rationalist outlook. Being who we are and knowing what we know, blind traditionalism is no longer a live option. Once released, the rationalist genie cannot be put back in the bottle. Our problem is to say what knowledge and rationality amount to in the situation we are actually in, not to defend them against imaginary alternatives.

Notes

1. For a sympathetic but critical account of social constructivism, see Hacking (1999).
2. Davidson (1984), 183.
3. Quine (1960), 58 f. criticizes the notion of a 'prelogical mentality'.
4. The defence of Rationalism in BonJour (1998) seems to me to be vitiated by a failure to consider this possibility.
5. Reasons for being suspicious of 'descriptive cultural relativism' can be found in Moody-Adams (1997), chs. 1–2.
6. Fogelin (1994), 95–8.

20

Objectivity and Progress

Nature and convention

In the previous chapter we investigated the epistemological roots of relativism. Now we turn to more metaphysical considerations.

The distinction between nature and convention does more than record the facts of variability in belief: it suggests an explanation. In the case of matters belonging to nature, the universality of belief is explained by the existence of 'hard facts': facts that obtain independently of what we think or believe. Such facts are found, not made. In the case of matters that are customary or 'conventional', our judgements and responses are not answerable to any such external standard. Our standards of morality, say, are made, not found. There is no question of one group's being right and another's being wrong, the argument continues, for there is nothing to be (objectively) right or wrong about. This is another route to a position that might be thought of as relativistic. The thought is not so much that truth is relative as that, in some areas of discourse, the notion of truth gets no real purchase, so that any view is as good as any other. Plato's opponents, the Sophists, seem to have adopted a kind of relativism on something like these grounds: they offered to teach the art of speaking well as a neutral skill, adaptable to the values and customs of whatever city the pupil found himself in. Plato, by contrast, thought that even in matters of value, there are ultimate universal and objective truths that, with sufficient diligence, we might hope to discover.

One of the fundamental tasks of philosophy has always been to determine what belongs to nature. This is another way of understanding the task of metaphysics, as the investigation of what is ultimately real. A certain conception of nature as what is there *anyway*, independently of human perception, custom, or artifice, gives content to this metaphysical concern. However, philosophers who have taken up this task—with the possible exception of certain Idealists—have tended to assume that *something* belongs to nature, so that there are significant demarcational lines to be drawn. In particular, philosophers in the analytic tradition, whatever their views of moral or aesthetic judgement, have tended to view science 'realistically'. The goal of science, which it sometimes reaches, is to discover facts that belong to nature. This is what makes science objective and capable of progress.

Whereas philosophy of science used to concern itself with highly abstract questions about explanation and confirmation, many contemporary students of science take an interest in the historical and sociological details of scientific research. The main impetus for this historical and sociological turn, at least for philosophers of science, comes from Thomas Kuhn's theory of 'scientific revolutions'. Kuhn's writings have probably had more impact—especially outside professional philosophical circles—than any other writings concerned with broadly epistemological issues. But Kuhn's views seem scandalous to many philosophers, and one of the main reasons is that they appear to challenge the realistic perspective. On a certain reading, which his rhetoric does a lot to encourage, Kuhn's social-historical account of scientific change implies that 'scientific facts' are just claims that (reputable) scientists endorse. The 'facts' are, so to say, made in the laboratory. To use a phrase that is popular today: scientific facts (or 'facts') are socially constructed.[1] For realists, to take such a position is to give up on the notion of fact altogether.

Has Kuhn really given us reason to think that scientific facts are made rather than found? This is an important issue for me, since Kuhn's picture of science has a definite contextualist slant. Discussing Kuhn's ideas will be a way of further clarifying what a contextualist ought to say about notions like truth and progress.

The two-phase model

Kuhn's views develop out of sharp criticisms of what was, when he wrote, the standard empiricist account of science. Standard empiricism embodies substantive foundationalism. It postulates a fixed 'observation language' capable, in principle, of capturing any empirical finding, and connected to theoretical statements by an inductive logic (or rules of confirmation). Kuhn finds this picture to be wildly at variance with the actual practice of science. Scientific observations never take the form of the foundationalist's reports on simple sensory occurrences, but are 'theory laden'. The telescopic observations used by Galileo to confute the Aristotelians are bound up with complex assumptions having to do with optics: this penetration of observation by theory is typical. Also, theories play a role in determining what observations are relevant to their confirmation. It used to be thought important to explain the number of the planets, but after Newton no one thought this any more. Newton's theory was so successful that facts it couldn't explain became not worth explaining. But this decision on the part of the scientific community was not, in any simple way, mandated by Nature.

Kuhn also objects to Popper's idea that science aims constantly at refuting theories. Such a policy would be destructive of science. Even the most successful theories are 'born refuted', in that there are typically many phenomena that, it seems, the theories ought to be able to explain but can't. Some phenomena may even amount to Popperian refutations. However, researchers treat them as 'anomalies' rather than counter-examples. The existence of anomalies is not a signal to reject a theory but a challenge to develop it further. In any case, testing a theory is by no means as simple as Popper's writings sometimes suggest. As science becomes more sophisticated, devising ways to subject theories to experimental test is itself a challenging undertaking. Refutation is never routine.

These reflections lead Kuhn to a two-phase model of scientific change. A striking achievement like Newton's mechanics constitutes a 'paradigm' around which future research crystallizes. This crystallization gives rise to 'normal science'. In normal-scientific research, the fundamental assumptions, theoretical and methodological, implicit in the paradigm—what Kuhn later calls a 'disciplinary matrix'—are simply not in question. The challenge for normal science is to further refine the theory, to take care of apparent anomalies, and to extend its application to new phenomena. Normal science's characteristic activity is not debate about fundamentals but 'puzzle solving'. However, for even the most successful theory, a time comes when anomalies begin to accumulate at a rate that taxes the ingenuity of even the theory's most devoted adherents. At this point, investigators begin to look for alternatives. Science now enters a revolutionary phase, in which there are no rules to guide research. If a new theoretical paradigm emerges, the grounds for preferring it will not be straightforwardly observational but will also involve broad holistic considerations of economy and elegance. Once the new theory is in place, erstwhile anomalies come to be seen as refutations. A scientific revolution has taken place and a new period of normal science begins.

Kuhn has a pronounced tendency to emphasize the non-rational elements in scientific change. For example, he notes that older scientists who have given their lives to a certain type of research may be unwilling to abandon it. The triumph of a new paradigm may therefore depend as much on this generation's dying off as it does on decisive confirmation or refutation, as more traditional philosophies of science understand such things.

This aspect of Kuhn's work has done a great deal to encourage the so-called 'strong programme' in the sociology of knowledge.[2] According to this conception of science, scientific change is to be *completely* accounted for in terms of social factors: generational shifts, the politics of the laboratory, influences from the surrounding culture and society, and so on. This is an odd view. Sociology is supposed to show that physics is just a social construction, as if the social 'sciences' were in better shape than physics.

In fact, nothing in Kuhn's account of science, as presented so far, mandates such extreme reactions. Indeed, Kuhn's views are much closer to Popper's than they first seem. What obscures the similarity is that, whereas Popper remains mired in the methodological individualism of traditional epistemology, Kuhn is interested in scientific research as a socially institutionalized endeavour. Popper presents his falsificationist methodology as rules for how the individual scientist should conduct his investigations. Kuhn points out that this couldn't work. The normal-scientific testing of an advanced theory is a difficult business. Working out how to do it demands intense efforts from committed adherents, who will not regard the first disappointing result as a signal to go back to the drawing-board.

In revolutionary times, the situation is more fluid. But though anomalies are now potential counter-examples, there is no algorithm to tell us when to abandon the received view, or exactly how to trade off theoretical elegance against empirical precision. Sometimes it may be best if competing theories exist in tandem for a while, so long as all attract a critical mass of competent investigators (which means that there can't be too many options in play). Only this way can one theory eventually acquire decisive advantages over its rivals.

What all this shows is that it makes sense for the institution of science to tolerate investigators displaying a range of 'epistemic styles' and theoretical preferences: for example, some more empirically oriented, others inclined to place more weight on general theoretical considerations. Over time and transpersonally, science may still function as something like a Popperian conjecture-and-refutation machine, though it will do so only if individual practitioners do not adopt a Popperian methodology. On Kuhn's model, science works because, as an institution, it has managed to strike a delicate balance between freedom and constraint, and because its procedures, however theoretically mediated, involve interactions with nature that we do not fully control. Normal-scientific research is what throws up the anomalies that eventually provoke theoretical advance.

We should remember, too, that abandoning foundationalism allows us to see the observational/theoretical distinction as methodological, not ontological. With advancing techniques of experimentation, theoretical entities cross the line into the domain of the observable.

I do not mean that there is nothing to be learned from sociological analyses of science. However, we should follow Ian Hacking and distinguish between analyses that are *refuting* and those that are not. With regard to particular bodies of theory, we may well come to think that genuine empirical constraint is wholly lacking, so that the apparent credibility of such theories is completely accounted for in ideological, political, or other non-epistemic terms. By contrast, in other instances we may find that theories, though equally subject to such social-historical influences, pay their way, so that their credibility is not exhaustively accounted for in non-epistemic terms. In my view, refuting analyses are available in connection with much of the theorizing that makes up the 'human sciences'. In abnormal psychology, for example, theories seem all too easily blown by the winds of fashion, changing with changes in what is thought to be 'normal' behaviour. But how we sort things out in particular cases is an empirical matter. Recognizing 'external' influences on scientific theorizing and non-rational factors in scientists' decision-making does not commit one to dogmatic, across-the-board relativism or social constructivism.

Different worlds

Given the way Kuhn's work has been received, surely I must be leaving something out. I am. What has made Kuhn an icon for sceptics and relativists (although Kuhn always repudiated the relativist label) is not his socialized Popperianism but his provocative remarks about how scientists on opposite sides of a revolutionary change live in 'different worlds', so that their theoretical views are 'incommensurable'.[3]

We should not read too much into this talk. Kuhn's scientists are not living in 'different worlds' in any sense of that phrase that conflicts with Davidson's strictures on global conceptual relativism. Galileo and his Aristotelian rivals could agree on lots of mundane facts: they disagreed about what 'world system' best accommodated them. Furthermore, their disagreement extended into fundamental methodological issues: the questions a physical theory ought to answer, the importance (and appropriateness in physical matters) of mathematically precise laws, and the sorts of observation that could be trusted. Even so, their dispute—however wide-ranging and fundamental—lies in the region of intelligible disagreement that Davidson's argument leaves open.[4]

That said, there is something fishy about Kuhn's talk of meaning-shifts. In one way, it involves taking talk of meaning too seriously, and in another, not seriously enough.

The doctrine of incommensurability is underwritten by the view that the meaning of a term is entirely a function of the theory in which it occurs. Newton and Einstein both use the word 'mass'; but since their laws of motion are different—indeed, since Einstein recognizes two quantities, rest mass and relativistic mass, where Newton recognizes only one—they are not talking about the same thing. Or as Feyerabend (another devotee of incommensurability) explains, the replacement of old principles by new entails 'the elimination of the old meanings'.[5] This is an overreaction. Because Newtonian mechanics is approximately correct for bodies moving slowly relative to the speed of light, there are various ways of relating Newton's theoretical vocabulary to Einstein's. We might take Newton to be talking mostly about rest mass but believing falsely that it is the only sort of mass there is. Or we could take him to be referring indifferently to rest and relativistic mass, not realizing that any such distinction could be made. Provided we understand how the theories as a whole are related—particularly, the way in which one can be seen as approximately true of a restricted range of phenomena—it doesn't much matter. For such questions of interpretation, there is no definitely right way of proceeding. It depends on what similarities and differences we are interested in highlighting, which is a pedagogical matter, of no great theoretical import. This is the way in which Kuhn makes too much of the idea of meaning.

In another way, however, he doesn't look at the idea of meaning hard enough. Kuhn sees that a term's 'meaning' is partly determined by its inferential position in a wider range of assertional commitments. He also takes on board Sellars's point that the distinction between the 'observational' and the 'theoretical' is methodological rather than ontological. However, by stating this point in terms of the penetration of 'observation' by 'theory', he slides towards the view that nothing is really observational, or that observation exerts no independent check on our theoretical commitments. But no such conclusions follow from the epistemological and semantic views that Kuhn shares with Sellars. Observation reports are still causally tied to circumstances, and thus constitute a body of evidence whose contents we do not fully control. This much independence of observation from theory is not only consistent with but required by Kuhn's socialized Popperianism.

Not so sceptical

Kuhn's tendency to overstate his 'sceptical' conclusions is connected with a tendency, shared with Popper, not to distinguish between radical and non-radical scepticism. It is one thing to say that, when theoretical choices have to be made, there is no algorithm that singles out a uniquely right answer; it is something else again to say that it never matters what choice we make, or that any choice is always as good as any other. The locally holistic character of theoretical inference does not support any such radical conclusion. An amusing example due to Thomas Nagel makes the point. Suppose I adopt the theory that eating lots of ice cream is the way to lose weight. It is true that in testing my theory by stepping on the bathroom scales I am taking for granted a lot of extra theoretical ideas, for example, the principles of mechanics that determine how the readings on the scales correspond to different weights. But it would be lunacy for me to conclude, in the face of the constantly rising numbers I encounter, that my diet must be affecting the laws of mechanics. One reason for this is that I have to take those same laws for granted in many other inquiries. Since they are effectively held fast, my weird dietary ideas are what have to go. It is not contextualism but an ill-thought-out form of radical holism that encourages relativism and irrationalism. It does so by encouraging us to see empirical inference as a largely unconstrained choice between competing 'total views' in which anything and everything is up for grabs. Something like this form of holism may lie behind Kuhn's talk of 'different worlds'.

The effects of failing to mark the radical/non-radical distinction can be compounded by playing back and forth between the considerations available to guide inference during the initial phases of a scientific revolution and those available when an alternative theory has emerged as a mature alternative to a received view. It may be that, in the early days, choices can only be made flying by the seat of one's pants. But they can become practically unavoidable as further evidence accumulates (though to accumulate that evidence, some investigators may have to make a seat-of-the-pants commitment).

I think that these failures—making too much of meaning and failing to mark the distinction between radical and non-radical scepticism—afflict Kuhn's critics too. For example, according to Hilary Putnam, we need to block a disastrous meta-induction, encouraged by the Kuhnian model of progress through revolutions. Past revolutionary changes in science suggest that 'all the theoretical entities postulated by one generation invariably "don't exist" from the standpoint of later science'. There is thus a serious chance that electrons will go the way of phlogiston. Indeed, the conclusion to be drawn seems to be that 'no theoretical term ever refers'.[6] In theoretical science, we have no reason to suppose that we are ever talking about anything.

Putnam's hope is (or was) that the theory of reference—the theory of the word—object relation—is our best hope for responding to this sceptical view of theoretical discourse. But why suppose that a theory in the philosophy of language either could or should block this argument? (Hasn't the electron of the 1920s already gone the way of phlogiston?) How are we to rule out the possibility of drastic theoretical change at some point in the future? Putnam wants something that is neither possible nor desirable: he wants philosophy to underwrite the truth of our current theories.

Putnam's problem looks dramatic at first sight but proves less than compelling on closer examination. Like Kuhn's reflections on incommensurability, it takes questions about meaning, or reference, too seriously. We aren't by any means compelled to suppose that the terms belonging to rejected theories 'don't refer', so that the objects postulated by the theories don't exist. We could say that, because atoms as we conceive them are very different from the 'atoms' conceived by Dalton, Dalton was never referring to anything. But we can just as well say that, while Dalton was talking about atoms alright, he had lots of false beliefs about them: for example, he didn't realize that they were composed of particles even more elementary. Again, the difference is more rhetorical than epistemologically significant.

Putnam sees a serious issue here because he sees far too close an analogy between the possibility of saying that even currently favoured theoretical entities 'may not exist' and radical, general scepticism. That he fails to make the radical–non-radical distinction is evident from his noting that his disastrous meta-induction is a form of the old sceptical argument from error, an argument which, we have noted repeatedly, enforces only fallibilism and not radical scepticism. That our current theories *may* be false is compatible with our having powerful reasons for holding them true. That he assimilates his problem about theoretical entities to general scepticism is apparent from his remark that an argument for the view that our words really do refer to things will turn on 'the success of science, or, in an earlier day, the success of common sense material object theory'.[7] However, there is no reason to worry that the terms of 'common sense material object theory' don't refer or that most of our everyday beliefs about such things might be false. Those beliefs are covered by the argument from charity. By contrast, beliefs about theoretical entities belong to the area of possible significant disagreement that the argument from charity opens up. In that area, we don't want philosophical guarantees.

I am not questioning the success of science. Indeed, I am happy to agree that the rhetoric of 'scientific revolution' is overblown. The phrase inevitably calls to mind the dramatic intellectual developments surrounding the overthrow of the medieval world-picture and the emergence of modern mathematical physics. But Kuhnian revolutions are typically much more local and small-scale affairs. The fact is that modern science is remarkably stable. It is not remade every time some theory or other is replaced. At the same time, we should accept the stable yet progressive character of science for what it is: an empirical fact. We should not try to provide it with any kind of metaphysical underpinning.

A new paradigm

Although Kuhn's incautious talk about meaning is one of the reasons why his work has been taken to encourage irrationalism and 'mob rule', it is not the only reason why some philosophers find his work hard to assimilate. In a way, Kuhn's work exemplifies what it describes. It represents a new paradigm: a way of thinking about epistemological questions—especially methodological and demarcational questions—that does not put scepticism first. Kuhn is careless about his sceptical-sounding remarks because he is not interested in the sort of scepticism that has dominated mainstream epistemology: scepticism that is both radical and general.

Although Kuhn's ideas are often seen as promulgating relativism and irrationalism, Kuhn is better viewed as exploring the social and institutional dimensions of rational inquiry: an exploration with clear normative implications for the conduct of successful research. What prevents our seeing Kuhn as making a normatively significant contribution to epistemological self-understanding—to our seeing him as a methodologist and not as either a 'mere' historian/sociologist of science or epistemological nihilist—is our Cartesian blindfold, which make us think that all rationality is individual rationality, hence all method 'rules for the direction of the mind'.

Now we have seen that, while the dominant tendency in epistemological theorizing, ancient and modern, is individualist, individualism can take radically different forms. Ancient individualism reflects the ideal of self-control: of a life lived according to self-conscious knowledge of nature, human and non-human. By contrast, post-Cartesian epistemology is individualist because subjectivist. The sceptical problem of our knowledge of the external world apparently forces us to seek the foundations of knowledge within: in the contents of our minds, conceived as an inner arena of irreducibly private happenings. Breaking with individualism of both sorts, we can see knowledge for what it is (and always has been): a socially shared and transmitted achievement, where entitlements are passed on by testimony and where not everyone needs or can reasonably aspire to know everything there is to know. We can even see knowledge as a social construction, provided we detach this conception from the sceptical thought that there is no such thing as worldly constraint, and that knowledge is therefore just what some group or other says it is.

The source of modern individualism is methodological scepticism in its Cartesian variant. Kuhn is not an individualist because he is not wedded to methodological scepticism of any kind. He is thus not wedded to something I shall discuss further in the Conclusion: the idea that all epistemology worthy of the name is epistemology-as-first-philosophy. I noted in Chapter 18 that something like this could be said of Popper too. However, Kuhn makes a much cleaner break with scepticism than does Popper. Being free of sceptical entanglements, Kuhn is able to move methodological questions, such as 'How and why does science progress?', to centre stage. Moreover, he is able to answer such questions by developing ideas that are rooted, not in *a priori* reflections on the possibility of knowledge, but in views about the specific history and institutional structure of modern science.

Kuhn was anticipated in his social and non-sceptical approach to methodological questions by Francis Bacon. Again, epistemological theorizing might have taken a very different form if Bacon, rather than Descartes, had captured Europe's philosophical imagination.

Truth as goal

Kuhn has attracted a lot of fire for denying that science is making progress towards the truth. To many philosophers, this seems like irrationalism of the worst kind. I disagree. I have suggested that truth can be understood in a 'deflationary' way and that, so understood, truth is not an epistemologically interesting notion. Of course, we want our beliefs to be true, in the sense that we will modify or reject them if we find reason to think that they are in error. But the process of evaluation is guided by epistemic factors, observational and theoretical. Truth is not a goal or norm that guides, even in the most theoretical matters. 'Hold true beliefs' is as useful a piece of advice as 'To win, score more goals than the other side'. Quite, but how? Lacking a hot line to Nature's mysteries, we choose theories for their epistemic virtues. We want theories to fit well with the relevant empirical data, theories that 'work'. Finding theories that work is a way of finding theories that are (as far as we can tell) true, not the other way around.

'Working' involves more than accounting for well-known data. We want theories to make novel predictions and to sponsor new and interesting lines of inquiry. Good research programmes keep inquiry moving: they are 'progressive'. When they get to the point of being able to accommodate, *via* modification, new (and initially inconvenient) findings, while no longer suggesting new investigations to pursue, they are 'degenerating' and it is time to consider something new.[8] So long as a research programme is in a progressive phase, whether the latest theory it has produced is strictly true is not all that important.

I would go farther. Although we do not want to hold false views, truth alone is not a goal at all. There are countless matters that we will never look into, countless truths that we will never know, because they are of no conceivable interest or importance. We want interesting truths: truths that bear on matters we have some reason, practical or theoretical, to care about.

So far, I have been talking about truth with a little 't': the sort of truth that can be explained in a deflationary way. But I think that when Kuhn talks about truth he has something grander in mind. He is thinking of truth with a capital 'T': the truth embodied in an ideally completed theory that gets everything right, leaving no stone unturned and no anomaly unexplained, so that the prospect of further revolutionary developments can be discounted. I think Kuhn is right to be suspicious of this idea. We no more need—and no more understand—the idea of Truth in science than we need or understand the idea of utopia in politics. We measure progress more by where we have been than where we are going: by the ways in which current theories improve over their predecessors, not their distance from the end of inquiry. This scepticism about Truth as the Goal of Inquiry should not be seen as an invitation to either relativism or irrationalism but simply as a salutary reminder that we can always turn out to know less than we think.

The idea of (significant) truth as a goal has its clearest application to matters of practical concern, where the facts at issue are close to the observational level. (Not that they have to be observed, but that they could be.) These are the sorts of facts at issue in courts of law, for example: we want to know whether the accused was where he says he was when the crime was committed. But as the goal of theoretical inquiry, truth is uninteresting and Truth is implausible (if even fully intelligible).

What goes for truth goes for knowledge. Our concept of knowledge involves the idea of conclusive reasons, and this idea is most at home in relatively commonsensical matters. In more theoretical pursuits, theory choice can involve reasons that, while not negligible, are visibly less than conclusive, even when 'conclusiveness' is understood in a contextualized and non-demonstrative fashion.

I think that the temptation to think of truth (or knowledge) as the (dominant, if not sole) goal of inquiry has the same roots as infallibilist intuitions about knowledge: the classical or demonstrative conception of knowing. This conception is deeply bound up with the ancient, contemplative ideal of knowledge. It expresses the urge to settle things once and for all, to bring inquiry to an end. A fallibilist can have no sympathy with this ideal.

Notes

1. The original statement of Kuhn's position can be found in Kuhn (1962), perhaps the most widely read epistemological work of the post-war period. Today there is almost no limit to the range of facts that someone or other has claimed to be a social construct. Hacking (1981) contains a useful set of papers reacting to Kuhn's ideas about normal versus revolutionary science.
2. 'Strong programme': see e.g. Bloor (1976).
3. Kuhn (1962), ch. 12; 'different worlds', 150.
4. Though Davidson sees himself as criticizing Kuhn. I think he is mistaken.
5. Feyerabend (1981), 83.
6. Putnam (1978), 22–5.
7. Ibid. 19.
8. Imre Lakatos, 'The Methodology of Scientific Research Programmes', in Lakatos and Musgrave (1970).

Conclusion

Epistemology After Scepticism?

The end of epistemology?

Not so long ago, it was thought to be obvious that there was a philosophical *theory* of knowledge because there was a philosophical *problem* of knowledge. This problem was scepticism. Today, however, many philosophers doubt that 'refuting the sceptic' is a worthwhile undertaking. For such philosophers, what becomes of epistemology?

According to Quine, epistemology should be 'naturalized'. This means that traditional *a priori* epistemology needs to give way to some properly scientific discipline: empirical psychology or 'cognitive science'. On this view, questions about what human beings know and how they come to know them can still be pursued, but in a natural-scientific spirit. By contrast, Richard Rorty argues that the theory of knowledge needs less to be reformed than avoided altogether. Where Quine is a naturalist, Rorty is an obituarist, announcing the death of epistemology.[1] But although Rorty's view may sound more radical, naturalists and obituarists have a lot in common. Neither party thinks that 'philosophical' epistemology has much of a future.

The death of epistemology has serious implications for philosophy generally. I suggested in the Introduction that philosophy, at least as we understand it in the West, is a theoretical tradition that takes epistemological problems to be among its essential concerns. Both Quine and Rorty tend to assume this understanding of philosophy. As a result, they take the end of traditional epistemology to signal the end of philosophy itself as a distinctive form of inquiry.[2]

This issue is important for me. The epistemological views developed in this book have definite affinities with pragmatism, the philosophical tradition with which both Quine and Rorty identify themselves. I need to explain why a broadly pragmatic outlook does not commit me to being either a naturalist or an obituarist.

Epistemology as 'first philosophy'

Rorty argues that epistemology is a modern subject. It originates in the seventeenth century, especially with Descartes, and assumes something like its final form in the writings of Kant. On first hearing, such a suggestion sounds absurd. Philosophical discussions of human knowledge are as old as philosophy itself. On the other hand, the word 'epistemology', like the phrase 'theory of knowledge', appears to be a nineteenth-century invention. Could it be that—appearances to the contrary—the subject itself is a recent invention?

Not surprisingly, the answer to this question depends on what we understand by epistemology. Philosophers who think of epistemology as a relatively recent invention have in mind a highly specific conception of the subject, one rooted in Descartes's idea that epistemology should play the role of 'first philosophy': the division of philosophy on which all other philosophy and indeed all other knowledge depends. Quine too, though uninterested in the antiquity of epistemology, thinks that philosophical epistemology pretends to the role of first philosophy, judging science from some point outside science itself. This conception of epistemology imposes three methodological requirements:

Unity: All fundamental epistemological questions should be addressed by a single, unified theory of knowledge.

Autonomy: Epistemological questions must be settled independently of all particular metaphysical (or scientific) commitments.

A Priori *Status*: As autonomous, epistemology must be wholly *a priori*.

Of course, merely laying down such general desiderata is insufficient to characterize a distinctive form of theoretical inquiry, for the desiderata themselves give no clue to how a form of inquiry satisfying them might proceed. This gap is filled by methodological scepticism. Methodological scepticism is a device for identifying the foundations of knowledge. These come in two flavours:

Epistemic Foundations: types of claim or belief that are 'epistemologically basic', hence capable of standing to 'inferential' claims as evidence to conclusion. Accepting foundations in this sense also requires identifying types of warrant-conferring inference to take us from basic to non-basic knowledge.

Metaphysical Foundations: principles constituting the framework within which all detailed empirical inquiry is conducted. Where the quest for epistemic foundations aims to identify the *types* of claim or belief that are intrinsically credible, the quest for metaphysical foundations aims at uncovering *specific propositions* which function as the 'presuppositions' of whatever else we might come to know. For example, Descartes presents his confrontation with scepticism as leading him to the discovery that extension is the essence of matter and thinking the essence of mind. In a similar vein, Kant argues that causal determinism is presupposed by any claim to knowledge of an objective world.

By determining the foundations of knowledge, in either or both of the senses given above, epistemology determines the *a priori* framework within which all knowledge-seeking takes place. Forms of discourse that cannot be fitted into this Procrustean bed are not genuinely cognitive: they cannot be understood to aim at truth or knowledge, strictly so-called. 'Refuting the sceptic' thus becomes the key to demarcational and methodological issues.

I began this book by suggesting that we think of 'epistemology' in a rather different way: as a tradition of theorizing that addresses fundamental epistemological *questions*. Thought of like this, epistemology is anything but recent. Of course, this is because my account of epistemology is, in certain respects, highly elastic. It says nothing about the relative importance of the questions that guide epistemological inquiry, nothing about the methods by which such inquiry is to be conducted, nothing about whether all epistemological questions should be answerable by a single, tightly integrated body of theory, nothing about the relation of epistemological reflection to other 'first-order' pursuits, nothing about the epistemic status of epistemology itself, and nothing about the place of epistemology in philosophy generally. But I think of this elasticity as a virtue. Understanding epistemology in terms of certain guiding problems allows us to see changes within an intelligibly continuous tradition of philosophical inquiry. It leaves open the possibility that putting scepticism first, or understanding it as the key to all further problems, is only one approach to epistemological theorizing, not constitutive of epistemology in the broader sense of 'normatively significant philosophical reflection on issues concerning human knowledge'. So, for example, by my standards Kuhn can be read as making important contributions to such philosophical reflection, though in a notably post-sceptical way.

In this connection, it is worth noting that Descartes's methodological use of scepticism has never been a model followed by all philosophers with developed epistemological views. Consider Plato and Locke, one ancient philosopher and one modern, both of whom address all the epistemological problems on my list. Thus:

The Analytic Problem. According to Plato, knowledge is distinguished from opinion, even true opinion, by being infallible. Locke, too, with some qualifications, accepts a demonstrative conception of knowledge.

The Problem of Demarcation. Partly because of his acceptance of the Heraclitean doctrine of flux, Plato restricts knowledge to Forms: ideal abstract objects. The things in the material world that we call 'triangular' are at best unstable and imperfect approximations to the ideal geometrical objects studied by the mathematician, which are known through reason rather than the senses. Thus our 'knowledge' of the material world is really opinion. Locke's metaphysical starting-point—the corpuscular-mechanical view of nature—is of course quite different; but he too is pessimistic about our prospects for attaining genuinely scientific knowledge of material things. Such knowledge would require determining 'real essences'—the distinctive corpuscular microstructures of various natural kinds of stuff. Locke's views about the nature of our 'ideas' make him dubious about our capacity for making such determinations.

The Problem of Method. For Plato, the proper method for seeking knowledge is not observation but demonstrative proof, or perhaps some other form of *a priori* reasoning. (Plato thinks that even mathematical 'knowledge' is only second-best.) Ideally, Locke agrees. But he thinks that, in scientific matters, we will have to content ourselves with an experimental approach. Experiment will acquaint us with what properties in fact go together in various natural kinds ('substances'), though it will not yield understanding of why, say, gold is both yellow and soluble in *aqua regia*. Only knowledge of real essence, which we don't have and are unlikely to get, would provide that. We must be empiricists *faute de mieux*.

The Problem of Scepticism. For Plato, knowledge is possible but, since there is no knowledge of the material world, it will be less extensive than we like to think. Locke has similar doubts. There is some demonstrative knowledge: of the existence of God, for example. For the rest, experience will yield as much certainty as our condition needs, though not knowledge in the full sense. What we can neither demonstrate nor experience, we must leave to faith.

The point to notice about Plato and Locke is that, in their approach to epistemological questions, scepticism comes last. While the views of both philosophers display a notably sceptical strain, the scepticism is entirely consequential, growing out of independently established results regarding demarcation. Neither philosopher even pretends to be a *methodological* sceptic.[3] In consequence, neither gives epistemology a privileged place within philosophy at large. Rather, for both, metaphysical and epistemological concerns exert reciprocal influence.

Epistemological reflection does not stand or fall with the idea of epistemology as first philosophy. But how do the views defended in this book bear on the list of questions with which I began? That is the next question. Having dealt with it, we can return to the issues of naturalism and the death of epistemology.

The analysis of knowledge

The analytic problem challenges us to state explicitly what knowledge is: how it is distinguished from ignorance, error, and lucky guessing. Ideally, we would like to be able to state necessary and sufficient conditions for the truth of 'S knows that p'.

I have expressed doubts about whether we should expect to come up with very precise necessary and sufficient conditions for knowing. But subject to that qualification, I defend the standard analysis, which links knowledge with justification. This puts me in opposition to many contemporary philosophers, who are attracted by purely reliabilist, purely externalist, and thus radically non-justificational accounts of knowledge.

Much more is involved in this dispute than a clash of 'intuitions'. For one thing, the link between knowledge and justification is mandated by more than narrowly epistemological considerations. Claims with propositional content—the sort of content that involves the use of concepts—are essentially embedded in practices of asking for and providing reasons. The possession of propositional knowledge, while often importantly dependent on tacit know-how, is thus essentially involved with practices of justifying what one says.

To make this view acceptable, and to take account of externalist insights, we have to detach the idea that knowledge is essentially connected with justification, not only from the classical demonstrative ideal and its infallibilist descendants, but from all conceptions of justification that insist on respecting the Prior Grounding Requirement. Effecting this detachment leads us to see justification as exhibiting a Default and Challenge structure, where constraints on the reasonableness of challenges and the appropriateness of justifications are contextually variable along several dimensions.

Purely reliabilist accounts of knowledge are attractive to many philosophers because they seem to advance the project of naturalizing epistemology. But in my view, epistemological concepts are irreducibly normative: justification involves entitlement, responsibility, and adequate grounding. Standards of responsibility and adequacy are not fixed by nature: they are fixed by us in the light of our interests, projects, and assessment of our situation. Even judgements of reliability reflect tacit presuppositions of this sort and are thus covertly normative. If naturalizing epistemology means eliminating the normative element from epistemic concepts, or reducing that element to non-normative vocabulary, then epistemology cannot be naturalized.

Demarcation

The *problem of demarcation* divides into two sub-problems. The *external* problem is: given some account of what knowledge is, can we determine in a principled way what sorts of thing we might reasonably expect to know about? The *internal* problem is: are there important boundaries *within* the province of knowledge, for example, between knowledge that is *a posteriori* or empirical and knowledge that is *a priori* or non-empirical?

Contextualism certainly precludes drawing demarcational distinctions in ways that depend on identifying foundations for knowledge. But whether it is hostile to demarcational projects as such is much less clear. It may well be open to a contextualist to think that some forms of inquiry are more 'factual' or 'objective' than others.

In the previous chapter, I discussed the claim that scientific facts are made rather than found. In one way, this claim is a truism. Theories are made up, tested, and accepted or rejected by human investigators. But, I argued, this does not mean that there is no element of external constraint. The moral is that the 'made/found' distinction, in its traditional sharp form, is just not that useful. However, even if nothing is simply found, it does not follow that, with respect to objectivity, all areas of discourse are on a par.

Consider the distinction between the so-called 'primary' and 'secondary' qualities. Primary qualities are those qualities that objects possess in virtue of their physical constitution. Secondary qualities, today often called 'response-dependent', are those that are in some way bound up with our human perceptual constitution. Most philosophers today hold that colours fall into the secondary or response-dependent category. From a physical standpoint, an object's colour has to do with its capacity to selectively absorb and reflect light of different wavelengths. We humans happen to be sensitive to such differences. But given a different perceptual system, we should have seen the world in monochrome, even though the physical 'colour-properties' of objects remained unchanged. Indeed, neurological damage can destroy the capacity to see the world in colour; and of course less extreme forms of colour-blindness—such as the inability to tell green from red—are not uncommon.

The idea of response-dependence interacts with the idea of objective fact as what is there *anyway*. There are many facts that we think would have obtained even if human beings had never evolved. But are response-dependent features of things objective in this way? Perhaps not. Certainly, this seems the natural reply with properties that are even more 'response-dependent' than colour: for example, that of being funny. Would things have been amusing even if beings that *find* them amusing had never appeared? Aren't they amusing only in so far as they are amusing *to* some beings or other? (So, we might expect the Martians to share our mathematics and physics, but maybe not our sense of humour.)

The issue of response-dependence should remind us of the demarcational strategy that I illustrated in Chapter 10 with the 'explanationist' case against recognizing 'moral facts'. This strategy, as we saw, is open to philosophers who adopt a broadly coherentist view of justification. I say 'broadly' because this strategy, while consistent with radical holism, is not tied to it. The argument exploits the fact that, while our best explanations for why we hold beliefs about the physical world appeal essentially to physical facts, the same is not true of our moral beliefs. Whether or not we are attracted to 'unmasking' explanations, which trace moral beliefs to low motives, we do not need response-independent moral facts to explain moral beliefs: moral responses are quite sufficient.

Now, even supposing that there is a genuine metaphysical distinction here, it is not obvious, given a contextualist view of justification, that it has any particular epistemological significance. The contextualist's fallibilist attitude applies across the board. Values, as much as facts, are open to correction and in much the same way. A medieval sense of humour can be as crude and incredible as medieval physics. Moral judgements are not beyond criticism simply in virtue of being normative.

My purpose here is not to resolve any of these issues but simply to note that the arguments that they turn on have nothing to do with methodological scepticism. Rather, they arise out of explanatory asymmetries that are part of our current intellectual situation. Accordingly, a contextualist cannot dismiss them out of hand. Contextualism with respect to justification does not settle every philosophical question.[4]

Turning to the internal problem, the contextualist epistemology I have defended is inhospitable to many traditional distinctions, such as that between *a priori* and *a posteriori* knowledge. It does not encourage drawing those sorts of abstract internal boundaries. But contextualism is not committed to denying the existence of all significant epistemological boundaries. We have seen the rise of entirely new sciences: evolutionary biology and, more controversially, experimental psychology and various social sciences. These new undertakings raise questions about whether models of explanation and confirmation developed with the physical sciences primarily in mind are really adequate to (what purport to be) new types of scientific knowledge. Interesting demarcational and methodological issues arise: should we liberalize our ideas about explanation and confirmation, or is the proper conclusion that some new claims to knowledge are less than 'scientific' (or not really knowledge)?

The so-called human sciences are especially problematic because they give rise to 'looping effects'.[5] Quarks do not get up to whatever they get up to because they have overheard physicists talking about how quarks are supposed to behave. But the case is quite otherwise with respect to theories in psychology and sociology. Human beings are self-conscious. Accordingly, when psychological and sociological categories make their way into the general culture, people may modify their behaviour so as to conform to them. Young people may learn from the newspapers what it is to be a 'juvenile delinquent' and act accordingly. Psychological and sociological theories interact with their subjects in ways that physical theories do not. This seems like a difference with profound methodological consequences.

Again, my intention is not explore this issue for its own sake but to make a point about epistemology. If the human sciences differ from the natural sciences, it is in virtue of the peculiarities of their subject-matter. For a contextualist, significant methodological and demarcational issues may arise; but if they do, it will be for detailed and subject-specific reasons. They will not arise as consequences of a general picture of knowledge.

Method

The *problem of method* also subdivides. The problem of *unity* poses the question: Is there just one way of acquiring knowledge, or are there several, depending on the sort of knowledge in question? The *ameliorative* problem asks: Can we improve our ways of seeking knowledge? The problem of *reason* or *rationality* is to determine whether there are methods of inquiry, or of fixing belief, that are distinctively rational.

Inevitably, our discussion of the problem of demarcation has already touched on methodological issues, particularly on the problems of unity and amelioration. In general, the same moral applies: how much unity our methods of inquiry display and how those methods are to be improved are retail questions, not susceptible of wholesale answers derived from our general conception of knowledge and justification. One reason why methodological issues are retail rather than wholesale is that, from a contextual standpoint, there is no sharp distinction between method and content. Particular forms of investigation are structured by methodological necessities, propositions whose exemption from doubt fixes the direction of inquiry. But, viewed from another angle, such propositions can often be seen to embody substantive empirical commitments. In consequence, the idea that one can learn the methods of science or history without learning any science or any history is an illusion.

As for the problem of reason, the contextualist picture of knowledge embodies a strongly fallibilist conception of rationality. This conception has some affinities with Popper's critical rationalism but has no trace of Popper's animus against the concept of justification. Taking fallibilism seriously heads off the charge that contextualism encourages strongly anti-rationalist positions such as relativism. The boot is on the other foot. Sceptics and relativists are disappointed foundationalists, of one sort or another.

Scepticism

Most of the views just sketched were elaborated in the course of a detailed consideration of scepticism. Does this make me a methodological sceptic? We need to distinguish two forms of methodological scepticism. *Strong* methodological scepticism, the kind practised by Descartes, assumes that scepticism admits of a direct answer, an answer on the sceptic's own terms. *Broad* methodological scepticism hopes to learn important lessons about knowledge by discovering how sceptical arguments go wrong, if indeed they do, but understands 'going wrong' more flexibly. Sceptical arguments can go wrong without being susceptible to direct refutation. We may learn most from scepticism by approaching it in a more roundabout, diagnostic way. This is what I have tried to do.

Taking this approach, I first argued that Agrippan scepticism is rooted in the Prior Grounding Requirement. Turning to Cartesian scepticism, I identified a further sceptical commitment to what I called 'epistemological realism'. For an epistemological realist, fundamental constraints on justification are 'just there', written into 'the human condition' or 'our epistemic situation', independently of what we think about them. Epistemological realism is false: epistemic norms are created in the course of inquiry and are thus ours to change and improve. But taking fallibilism seriously, and allowing for observational and intelligibility constraints on practices of assertion, immunizes this view against any threat of arbitrariness with respect to justificational standards.

Value

In one way, the question of the value of knowledge is moot. Knowledge is justified true belief, and both justification and truth are deeply connected with meaning. Since to be a thinker at all is to be in the game of giving and asking for reasons, there is no question of getting by with true beliefs, avoiding all involvement with justification. Nor is there any question of our holding mostly false beliefs. Getting lots of things right is a precondition of mastering concepts, thus of having beliefs at all. If this is right, thinkers are inevitably knowers.

Some philosophers think that truth itself is the supreme epistemic value: Truth is the Goal of Inquiry. I find this slogan misleading. It is all too reminiscent of 'truth with a capital "T"', the ideally complete theory of everything. This is an idea we are better off without. But what about the more modest goal of believing truths rather than falsehoods? Of course, if we are conducting an investigation, we want to get things right. But this does not mean that, in and of itself, believing truths is ever a goal. What we want are truths that are significant. Their significance may be purely theoretical: we want to resolve a problem or explain some phenomenon, whether or not this will have any practical payoff. But having purely theoretical interests does not amount to having an interest in truth as such.

Should we therefore explain the value of truth instrumentally? Some philosophers take this line, arguing that we are more likely to fulfil our goals if the beliefs we hold are true than if they are false. No doubt this is true on the whole, although in the right circumstances particular false beliefs can be very helpful. (My mistaken belief about its departure time makes me miss the flight that crashes.) But even though holding true beliefs is generally useful, the deepest reason for our commitment to true beliefs is the connection (via the notion of meaning) between truth and belief itself. Only if we are already believers can questions about the instrumental value of particular beliefs arise at all.

An instrumental conception of truth is closely associated with pragmatism. Truth is, in William James's phrase, what is 'good in the way of belief': true beliefs are beliefs that 'work'. Pragmatists of this stripe go beyond an instrumental conception of the value of truth, which assumes that truth has a nature intelligible independently of truth's instrumental value. True beliefs just are those that are, in some way or other, instrumentally valuable.

Most modern philosophers sympathetic to the pragmatist outlook think that the instrumentalist account of truth is unnecessarily revisionist. They tend to favour a deflationary account of truth. This is a sound instinct. What pragmatists like James want to get away from is the idea that truth is a goal or guide to inquiry. For James, the interesting questions are not about the nature of truth but about how we go about determining (when disputes arise) what is true. In this sense, far from being hostile to the idea of epistemology, pragmatism stands for the priority of epistemology over metaphysics, though it detaches this priority from the quest for foundations. A deflationary approach to truth, according to which truth doesn't have much of a 'nature', fits well with this outlook while avoiding revisionism with respect to the ordinary use of 'true'.

Rorty is fond of contrasting the view that the goal of inquiry is to represent reality correctly with the view that what we are or should be after is beliefs that help us 'cope'. Another virtue of a deflationary approach to truth is that it avoids this spurious dilemma. But the notion of 'working' or 'coping' itself needs to be viewed with suspicion. As a goal, 'coping' is as idle and empty as believing truly. 'Working' is a concrete goal if we understand it Bacon's way as the 'relief of man's estate': the increase of human material welfare through the development and deployment of technology. But pragmatists recognize that this sense is too restrictive: our goals are not exclusively practical in the Baconian sense. Theories also 'work' when they help resolve purely theoretical problems. This means that there is no concrete account of 'working' available to us. Theories work when they help us to cope with some problem that interests us; and what counts as coping depends on the problem.

We see from all this that there are two senses in which knowledge-seeking can be called a 'practical' matter. One is that knowledge-seeking is always embedded in socially transmitted practices of inquiry: practices constituted by an array of (often largely tacit) background beliefs, methodological constraints, techniques of investigation, and relevant know-how. The other is the Baconian view that knowledge-seeking is always answerable to some set of independently specifiable practical goals, such as the advancement of material welfare. On the view I have defended in this book, it is only in the first sense that knowledge is essentially a 'practical' affair.

Naturalism and normativity

The question of the death of epistemology is not merely verbal. Quine and Rorty do not just reject the idea of epistemology-as-first-philosophy: they reject the idea of any epistemological theorizing that is normatively significant. Thus Quine proposes that philosophical epistemology give way to some straightforwardly empirical successor discipline: empirical psychology or 'cognitive science'. Rorty diverges from Quine in part because he is inclined to see normative pretensions as essential to anything worth thinking of as 'philosophical'. Accordingly, he would prefer to see philosophy-as-epistemology give way to some more openly normative undertaking: politics or cultural criticism. But neither Quine nor Rorty allows room for normative epistemology.

Quine and Rorty take this line because they tacitly assume that philosophical theories, as normatively significant, must aim to be true *a priori*. In effect, they *equate* normatively significant epistemology with epistemology-as-first-philosophy. There is no reason to make this equation. As I have characterized it in this book, epistemology is not wedded to either autonomy or infallibility.

Among philosophers, it is true, there has been a recurrent tendency to claim certainty and finality for their theoretical systems. But even philosophers who have claimed to provide definitive solutions to philosophical problems have recognized that their positions need to be established, rather than just announced; and to advance arguments is to invite critical responses. The tradition of epistemological theorizing is a tradition of theoretical change: fallibilism in action.

As for the autonomy of epistemological reflection, it is never complete. Our epistemological views are never cut from whole cloth but are always influenced, openly or tacitly, by the current state of knowledge: in particular, by what we take to be our paradigm cognitive achievements. For example, the demonstrative ideal of knowledge is a casualty of the rise of modern science.

Giving up the idea of epistemology-as-first-philosophy leads also to a blurring of boundaries within philosophy. If epistemology is not first philosophy, there is no reason to draw bright lines between it and other philosophical sub-disciplines. Philosophy becomes rather more seamless. This result, the natural consequence of epistemology's abandoning the ideal of autonomy, is to be welcomed. As we have seen, epistemological issues cannot be usefully discussed in complete isolation from topics in the theory of meaning and the philosophy of mind.

Philosophers who advocate a naturalistic approach to epistemology sometimes intend only to reject the high apriorism mandated by the idea of epistemology as first philosophy. If this is naturalism—and it is certainly part of what Quine and even Rorty have in mind—I have no objection to it. My quarrel is not with this methodological naturalism but with the reductive naturalism that aspires to account for knowledge in wholly natural-scientific terms. Epistemology resists this kind of naturalization, not because there is anything supernatural about it, but because it is concerned with concepts that are irreducibly normative. Epistemology concerns the standards we should adopt, not just whatever procedure we happen to follow. In exploring the ideas of knowledge, justification, truth, and so on, we cannot lose touch with our actual practices, on pain of ceasing to be recognizably discussing the concepts in question. But the line between description and prescription is never a sharp one.

The epistemological views developed in this book sketch a distinctive picture of the constraints that do and (according to me) should inform our multifarious inquiries. In this sense, they are normatively significant. But as we have seen, we should not look to our general theory of knowledge for detailed advice about how to conduct particular investigations. Philosophy offers a broad understanding of our epistemic practices: it is not in the business of micro-management. If micro-management were all that Quine and Rorty objected to in the idea of normatively significant epistemological theorizing, again I would have no quarrel with them. But it is not all.

In suggesting that philosophical epistemology should give way to empirical science, Quine assumes, somewhat casually, that epistemology's successor will retain its predecessor's focus on the individual knowing subject. Why should this be? If epistemology is to give way to some empirical undertaking, why psychology rather than the history of science or the sociology of knowledge? The individualistic tendencies in ancient epistemology reflect ancient philosophy's moral-practical orientation. Those in modern epistemology are an artefact of Cartesian scepticism. Since Quine is not concerned with either ethical or sceptical issues, his individualism lacks a clear motive.

In later writings, Quine comes to agree that epistemology and scepticism are not easily disentangled.[6] His way of saving the idea that epistemology should be naturalized is to argue that scepticism arises out of a scientific or at least an empirical discovery: the realization that the world is not always as it seems. Scepticism is an overreaction to the discovery that we are liable to error. A better account of our cognitive powers, developed from within our evolving scientific picture of the world, will allow a more balanced assessment of our epistemic predicament. This could be considered a rudimentary diagnosis of scepticism's appeal. There is even something right about it. But it does not go nearly far enough. The mere fact of error does not lead to interesting forms of scepticism, or indeed any form, save in conjunction with ideas about the standards we must meet to count as having knowledge. What these ideas ought to be is not a straightforward scientific question. Nor is it immediately obvious what the sceptic's ideas are, still less whether we should go along with them. To answer these questions, we need a much deeper diagnosis than Quine offers. Furthermore, in so far as Quine has positive epistemological ideas, they involve some measure of externalism: we are to assess our reliability from the third-person point of view characteristic of scientific inquiry. But we cannot simply confront the sceptic with an externalist reply. We must earn the right to make use of externalist insights by embedding them in a deeper diagnosis of the sceptic's epistemological presuppositions. Such a diagnosis is what I have tried to provide.

Therapy and theory

It is easy to suppose that taking a diagnostic approach to sceptical problems indicates an urge to put an end to epistemological theorizing. But to think along these lines is to ignore my distinction between therapeutic and theoretical diagnosis.

Therapeutic diagnosis treats philosophical problems—epistemological problems included—as pseudo-problems generated by misuses or misunderstandings of language. By contrast, theoretical diagnosis treats them as genuine, but only given a definite background of theoretical, generally epistemological, commitments. While far from sharp, this distinction has it uses. Its importance becomes apparent when we reflect that a philosopher committed to the death of epistemology will want neither to solve epistemology's problems in a theoretical way nor to acquiesce in their insolubility (as Quine shows some tendency to do). His aim will be to effect an exit from any form of philosophical theorizing. This is a plausible goal only for someone committed to a very pure form of therapeutic diagnosis. Therapeutic diagnosis, in its purest form, aims at exposing epistemological problems as illusory, thus making them disappear without theoretical residue.

To effect such a disappearance has never been my goal. By identifying and criticizing the assumptions hidden in traditional sceptical arguments, theoretical diagnosis inevitably suggests an alternative picture of knowledge, which we cannot guarantee to be problem-free. This is why I follow my presentation of contextualism with discussions of relativism, objectivity, and progress. The aim is to show that the contextualist picture can deal with objections it seems to invite. I do not pretend to have offered the last word on any of the questions I have explored. This is not a claim any fallibilist ought to make. The idea of effecting an exit from all philosophical commitments is an attempt to place oneself beyond criticism. There is no reason to suppose that this can be done.

According to my diagnosis, both scepticism and theories that attempt to provide direct responses to it are committed to the Prior Grounding Requirement. I doubt that the Prior Grounding conception of knowledge and justification results simply from a disinterested (mis)reading of ordinary epistemic practices. It is far more likely that the Prior Grounding conception has deeper theoretical roots.

An obvious suggestion is that the Prior Grounding conception results from the lingering influence of the demonstrative ideal, itself derived from taking geometry as the paradigm of genuine knowledge. I have no doubt that this is part of the story. But it is not the whole story. The ultimate source, I suggest, is the moral-practical orientation of much (if not all) ancient philosophy. The philosophical ideal is a life according to knowledge, as opposed to tradition. This ideal of rational autonomy demands that knowledge be something that one can secure and know that one has secured for oneself. Of course, this ideal could never have been plausible, in the absence of examples of knowledge seeming to live up to it. But axiomatic geometry was on hand.

Ancient sceptics value the Agrippan trilemma because it undermines this ideal. But they know that we have to live, which means holding some common-sense opinions in a common-sense way. The Pyrrhonians recommend—if that is the word—that we regulate our everyday opinions by doing what we all do anyway: accept the guidance provided by our biological drives, our passions, the customs in which we have been brought up, and our professional education. But the Academics develop a fallibilist conception of sceptical assent. They think of sceptical assent as an alternative to knowledge. I think that they offer a glimpse of what we can see today as a better way to understand knowledge itself: contextualism.

The Prior Grounding Requirement, linked as it is to a demonstrative, infallibilist conception of knowledge, is both out of step with knowledge as we find it and, in any case, more trouble than it is worth. This pragmatic move will seem unreasonable to sceptics and traditionalists, who will demand to know which picture of knowledge is the true one. Following up this objection uncovers an even deeper traditional commitment: a commitment to epistemological realism, the idea that epistemic criteria are built into the nature of knowledge or justification, rather than being standards that we set (and can revise).

Epistemological realism is misguided theoretically and pragmatically. It offers no real understanding of everyday epistemic practices and is a source of problems we would be better off without. If we avoid it, we sidestep the charge that, if we cannot say which picture of justification fits the epistemic facts, the sceptic wins. Alternatively—and this comes in the end to pretty much the same thing—we are justified in taking a pragmatic approach to the whole issue. The question to ask is not, flat-footedly, which conception of justification gets the nature of justification right, but what we gain by thinking of justification in one way rather than another.

Contextualism gives us a picture of knowledge and justification that stays close to the phenomenology of everyday epistemic practices, that articulates a fallibilist conception of rationality, that is friendly to the socially distributed and historically situated character of knowledge, and that offers a principled escape from traditional sceptical conundrums. This is why we should adopt it.

I have referred to contextualism as offering a 'picture' of knowledge. Is a picture a theory? It depends on what we expect from a theory. Certainly, there is a way in which contextualism is less theoretically ambitious than traditional approaches to epistemology. To turn away from epistemological realism is to give up on the ideas of generic sources of knowledge and of a fixed order of reasons. Giving up on these ideas, the contextualist finds little theoretically interesting to say about what can be immediately known, what sorts of things must be known by inference, what can be taken as default entitlements, and so on. His answer is always: it depends. . . on the current state of knowledge, on the sort of inquiry we are engaged in, on the costs of going wrong versus those of missing a chance to go right, on the real-world error-possibilities. For the contextualist, there are limits to the extent to which knowledge and justification are objects of theory. The differences between contextualism and its traditionalist rivals are not just differences *within* the theory of knowledge: they are differences *about* the theory of knowledge.

Hearing this, someone may say that the contextualist picture isn't a theory. For my part, I think that philosophical theory is often in the business of sketching broad conceptions, so I see no reason to be overly puritanical about the word 'theory'. But I will not quibble. Wittgenstein once remarked that a philosophical problem has the form 'I don't know my way about'. If the ideas developed in this book help us find our way about the epistemological terrain, they are theory enough.

Notes

1. See 'Epistemology Naturalised', in Quine (1969). Rorty (1979) is probably the most widely discussed obituary. The most recent—and also deserving of close attention—is McDowell (1994).
2. The equation of the death of epistemology with the death of philosophy is explicitly argued for by Rorty (1979), and is equally apparent in McDowell (1994).
3. Like Hobbes before him, Locke finds Descartes's interest in extravagant forms of scepticism risible: '[I]f . . . any one will be so sceptical, as to distrust his Senses, and to affirm that all we see and hear, feel and taste, think and do, during our whole Being, is but the series and deluding appearances of a long Dream, whereof there is no reality; and therefore will question the Existence of all Things, or our Knowledge of any thing: I must desire him to consider, that if all be a Dream, then he doth but Dream, that he makes the Question; and so it is not much matter, that a waking man should answer him'. Locke (1975), 634.
4. An important recent discussion of these issues can be found in Wright (1992). See also Wright's paper 'Truth: A Traditional Debate Reviewed', in Blackburn and Simmons (1999). Stroud (2000) is a scrupulous, critical examination of arguments to the effect that colours do not belong to 'objective reality'.
5. Hacking (1999), ch. 4.
6. Quine (1975), *passim*. For more detailed criticism of Quine's argument, see Stroud (1984a), ch. 6 and Williams (1996a), 254–65.

Works Cited

Austin, J. L. (1961), *Philosophical Papers* (Oxford: Oxford University Press).
—— (1962), *Sense and Sensibilia* (Oxford: Oxford University Press).
Ayer, A. J. (1954), *Philosophical Essays* (London: Macmillan).
—— (1956), *The Problem of Knowledge* (Harmondsworth: Pelican).
—— (1959) (ed.), *Logical Positivism* (New York: Free Press).
Barnes, Jonathan (1984) (ed.), *The Complete Works of Aristotle*, vol. 1 (Princeton, NJ: Princeton University Press).
Bender, John W. (1988) (ed.), *The Current State of the Coherence Theory* (Dordrecht: Kluwer).
Berlin, Isaiah (1979), *Concepts and Categories* (Harmondsworth: Penguin).
Blackburn, Simon and Simmons, Keith (2000) (eds.), *Truth* (Oxford: Oxford University Press).
Blanshard, Brand (1939), *The Nature of Thought*, vol 2 (London: Allen and Unwin).
Bloor, David (1976), *Knowledge and Social Imagery* (London: Routledge).
Boghossian, Paul (1996), 'Analyticity Reconsidered', *Nous* 30, pp. 360–91.
BonJour, Laurence (1985), *The Structure of Empirical Knowledge* (Cambridge, Mass.: Harvard University Press).
—— (1998), *In Defence of Pure Reason* (Cambridge: Cambridge University Press).
Bouwsma, O. K. (1969), *Philosophical Essays* (Lincoln, NE: University of Nebraska Press).
Bradley, F. H. (1914), *Essays on Truth and Reality* (Oxford: Oxford University Press).
Brandom, Robert (1994), *Making It Explicit* (Cambridge, Mass.: Harvard University Press).
—— (1995), 'Knowledge and the Social Articulation of the Space of Reasons', *Philosophy and Phenomenological Research*, 55, pp. 895–908. Repr. in Sosa and Kim (2000), 424–32.
—— (1998), 'Insights and Blindspots of Reliabilism', *The Monist*, 81, pp. 371–92.
Buchler, Justus (1955) (ed.), *Philosophical Writings of Pierce* (New York: Dover).
Burnyeat, Myles (1982), 'Idealism and Greek Philosophy: What Descartes Saw and Berkeley Missed', *Philosophical Review*, 91, pp. 3–40.
Carnap, Rudolf (1961), *The Logical Foundations of Probability* (Chicago: University of Chicago Press).
Cavell, Stanley (1979), *The Claim of Reason* (Oxford: Oxford University Press).
Chisholm, Roderick (1982), *The Foundations of Knowing* (Minneapolis: University of Minnesota Press).
Churchland, Paul (1981), 'Eliminative Materialism and the Propositional Attitudes', *Journal of Philosophy*, 78, pp. 67–90.
Clarke, Thompson (1972), 'The Legacy of Skepticism', *Journal of Philosophy*, 69, pp. 754–69.
Clay, Marjorie and Lehre, Keith (1989) (eds.), *Knowledge and Skepticism* (Boulder, Col.: Westview).
Cohen, Stewart (1988), 'How To Be a Fallibilist', *Philosophical Perspectives*, 2, pp. 91–123.

Conee, Earl and Feldman, Richard (1998), 'The Generality Problem for Reliabilism',
   Philosophical Studies, 89, pp. 1–29. Repr. in Sosa and Kim (2000), 372–86.
Cottingham, J., Stoothoff, R., and Murdoch, D. (1984) (eds.), *The Philosophical Works of
   Descartes*, vol. 2 (Cambridge: Cambridge University Press).
Davidson, Donald (1984), *Inquiries into Truth and Interpretation* (Oxford: Oxford
   University Press).
DeRose, Keith (1995), 'Solving the Skeptical Problem', *Philosophical Review*, 104, pp. 1–52.
Dewey, John (1984), *The Quest for Certainty, Later Works*, vol. 4 (Carbondale, Ill.: Southern
   Illinois University Press).
Dretske, Fred (1970), 'Epistemic Operators', *Journal of Philosophy*, 67, pp. 1007–23.
—— (1972), 'Contrastive Statements', *Philosophical Review*, 81, pp. 441–37.
—— (1981), 'The Pragmatic Dimension of Knowledge', *Philosophical Studies*, 40,
   pp. 363–78.
Elgin, Catherine (1996), *Considered Judgment* (Princeton, NJ: Princeton University Press).
Engel, Mylan (1992), 'Personal and Doxastic Justification in Epistemology', *Philosophical
   Studies*, 67, pp. 133–50.
Feyerabend, Paul (1981), *Realism, Rationalism and Scientific Method: Philosophical Papers
   1* (Cambridge: Cambridge University Press).
Fogelin, Robert (1994), *Pyrrhonian Reflection on Knowledge and Justification* (Oxford:
   Oxford University Press).
Garfinkel, Alan (1981), *Forms of Explanation* (New Haven, Conn.: Yale University
   Press).
Gettier, Edmund (1963), 'Is Justified True Belief Knowledge?', *Analysis*, 26, pp. 144–6.
Goldman, Alvin (1967), 'A Causal Theory of Knowing', *Journal of Philosophy*, 64,
   pp. 355–72.
—— (1976), 'Discrimination and Perceptual Knowledge', *Journal of Philosophy*, 73,
   pp. 771–91.
Goodman, Nelson (1955), *Fact, Fiction and Forecast* (Cambridge, Mass.: Harvard University
   Press).
Grice, H. P. and Strawson, P. F. (2000), 'In Defence of a Dogma', *Philosophical Review*, 65,
   pp. 141–58.
Guttenplan, Samuel (1975) (ed.), *Mind and Language* (Oxford: Oxford University Press).
Hacking, Ian (1981) (ed.), *Scientific Revolutions* (Oxford: Oxford University Press).
—— (1999), *The Social Construction of What?* (Cambridge, Mass.: Harvard University
   Press).
Hadot, Pierre (1995), *Qu'est-ce que la philosophie antique?* (Paris: Gallimard).
Harman, Gilbert (1969), 'Quine on Meaning and Existence', *Review of Metaphysics*, 21,
   pp. 124–51.
—— (1973), *Thought* (Princeton, NJ: Princeton University Press).
—— (1977), *The Nature of Morality* (Oxford: Oxford University Press).
—— (1986), *Change in View* (Cambridge, Mass.: MIT Press).
Hempel, Carl G. (1965), *Aspects of Scientific Explanation* (New York: Free Press).
Horwich, Paul (1998*a*), *Meaning* (Oxford: Oxford University Press).
—— (1998*b*), *Truth*, revised edn. (Oxford: Oxford University Press); first published
   (Oxford: Blackwell, 1990).
Hume, David (1975), *Enquiries Concerning Human Understanding and the Principles of
   Morals*, ed. L. A. Selby-Bigge, rev. P. H. Nidditch (Oxford: Oxford University Press).
—— (1978), *A Treatise of Human Nature*, ed. L. A. Selby-Bigge, rev. P. H. Nidditch (Oxford:
   Oxford University Press).

Kant, Immanuel (1964), *Critique of Pure Reason*, trans. Norman Kemp Smith (London: Macmillan).

Kaplan, Mark (1985), 'It's Not What You Know That Counts', *Journal of Philosophy*, 82, pp. 350–63.

Keynes, J. M. (1921), *A Treatise on Probability* (London: Macmillan).

Kitcher, Philip (1992), 'The Naturalists Return', *Philosophical Review*, 101, pp. 53–114.

Kornblith, Hilary (1980), 'Beyond Foundationalism and the Coherence Theory', *Journal of Philosophy*, 97, pp. 597–612.

—— (1983), 'Justified Belief and Epistemically Responsible Action', *Philosophical Review*, 92, pp. 33–48.

Kripke, Saul (1980), *Naming and Necessity* (Oxford: Blackwell).

Kuhn, Thomas (1962), *The Structure of Scientific Revolutions* (Chicago: University of Chicago Press).

Lakatos, Imre and Musgrave, Alan (1970), *Criticism and the Growth of Knowledge* (Cambridge: Cambridge University Press).

Lehrer, Keith and Paxson, Thomas D. Jr. (1969), 'Knowledge: Undefeated Justified True Belief', *Journal of Philosophy*, 66, pp. 225–37.

LePore, Ernest (1986), *Truth and Interpretation: Perspectives on the Philosophy of Donald Davidson* (Oxford: Blackwell).

Lewis, David (1999), *Papers in Metaphysics and Epistemology* (Cambridge: Cambridge University Press).

Locke, John (1975), *Essay Concerning Human Understanding*, ed. P. Nidditch (Oxford: Oxford University Press).

McDowell, John (1994), *Mind and World* (Cambridge, Mass.: Harvard University Press).

—— (1995), 'Knowledge and the Internal', *Philosophy and Phenomenological Research*, 55, pp. 877–93. Repr. in McDowell (1998), 395–413 and in Sosa and Kim (2000), 413–23.

—— (1998), *Meaning, Knowledge and Reality* (Cambridge, Mass.: Harvard University Press).

McGinn, Marie (1989), *Sense and Certainty* (Oxford: Blackwell).

Malachowski, Adam (1990), *Reading Rorty* (Oxford: Blackwell).

Moody-Adams, Michelle (1997), *Fieldwork in Familiar Places* (Cambridge, Mass.: Harvard University Press).

Nozick, Robert (1981), *Philosophical Explanations* (Oxford: Oxford University Press).

Peacocke, Christopher (1993), 'How Are A Priori Truths Possible', *European Journal of Philosophy*, 1, pp. 175–99.

Pollock, John (1967), 'Criteria and our Knowledge of the Material World', *Philosophical Review*, 76, pp. 28–62.

—— (1974), *Knowledge and Justification* (Princeton, NJ: Princeton University Press).

Popper, Karl (1963), *Conjectures and Refutations* (London: Routledge).

—— (1972), *Objective Knowledge* (Oxford: Oxford University Press).

Price, H. H. (1932), *Perception* (Oxford: Oxford University Press).

Putnam, Hilary (1975), *Mind, Language and Reality: Philosophical Papers 2* (Cambridge: Cambridge University Press).

—— (1978), *Meaning and the Moral Sciences* (London: Routledge).

—— (1981), *Reason, Truth and History* (Cambridge: Cambridge University Press).

Quine, W. V. O. (1960), *Word and Object* (Cambridge, Mass.: MIT Press).

—— (1961), *From a Logical Point of View*, revised edn. (New York: Harper).

—— (1969), *Ontological Relativity and Other Essays* (New York: Columbia University Press).

—— (1975), 'The Nature of Natural Knowledge', in Samuel Guttenplan (ed.), *Mind and Language* (Oxford: Oxford University Press).

—— (1990), *Pursuit of Truth* (Cambridge, Mass.: Harvard University Press).

Ramsey, F. P. (1990), *Philosophical Papers* (Cambridge: Cambridge University Press).

Rorty, Richard (1979), *Philosophy and the Mirror of Nature* (Princeton, NJ: Princeton University Press).

Russell, Bertrand (1961), *A History of Western Philosophy* (London: Allen and Unwin).

—— (1969), *The Problems of Philosophy* (Oxford: Oxford University Press); first published 1912.

Sellars, Wilfrid (1963), *Science, Perception and Reality* (London: Routledge).

—— (1997), *Empiricism and the Philosophy of Mind*, with an Introduction by Richard Rorty and Study Guide by Robert Brandom (Cambridge, Mass.: Harvard University Press). First published in Herbert Feigl and Michael Scriven (eds.), *Minnesota Studies in the Philosophy of Science*, vol. 1 (Minneapolis: University of Minnesota Press, 1956). Repr. in Sellars (1963).

Sextus Empiricus (1933), *Outlines of Pyrrhonism*, vol. 1 of *Sextus Empiricus*, ed. R. G. Bury, Loeb Classical Library (London: Heinemann).

Shope, Robert (1983), *The Analysis of Knowing* (Princeton, NJ: Princeton University Press).

Skyrms, Brian (1975), *Choice and Chance*, 2nd edn. (Encino, Cal.: Dickenson).

Soames, Scott (1999), *Understanding Truth* (Oxford: Oxford University Press).

Sosa, Ernest (1991), *Knowledge in Perspective* (Cambridge: Cambridge University Press).

—— and Kim, Jaegwon (2000), *Epistemology: An Anthology* (Oxford: Blackwell).

Strawson, P. F. (1952), *Introduction to Logical Theory* (London: Methuen).

Stroud, Barry (1984a), *The Significance of Philosophical Scepticism* (Oxford: Oxford University Press).

—— (1984b), 'Skepticism and the Possibility of Knowledge', *Journal of Philosophy*, 79, pp. 545–51.

—— (1996), 'Epistemological Reflection on Knowledge of the External World', *Philosophy and Phenomenological Research*, 56, pp. 345–58.

—— (2000), *The Quest for Reality* (Oxford: Oxford University Press).

Thayer, H. S. (1982), *Pragmatism: The Classic Writings* (Indianapolis: Hackett).

Unger, Peter (1971), 'A Defence of Skepticism', *Philosophical Review*, 80: 2, pp. 198–211.

Vogel, Jonathan (1990), 'Cartesian Scepticism and Inference to the Best Explanation', *Journal of Philosophy*, 87, pp. 658–66.

Williams, Bernard (1978), *Descartes: The Project of Pure Enquiry* (Harmondsworth: Pelican).

Williams, Michael (1988), 'Scepticism without Theory', *Review of Metaphysics*, 61, pp. 547–88.

—— (1996a), *Unnatural Doubts: Epistemological Realism and the Basis of Scepticism*, corrected paperback edn. (Princeton, NJ: Princeton University Press); first published (Oxford: Blackwell, 1992).

—— (1996b), 'Understanding Human Knowledge Philosophically', *Philosophy and Phenomenological Research*, 56, pp. 359–78.

—— (1998), 'Descartes and the Metaphysics of Doubt', in John Cottingham (ed.), *Oxford Readings in Philosophy: Descartes* (Oxford: Oxford University Press); first published in A. O. Rorty (ed.), *Essays on Descartes' 'Meditations'* (Berkeley: University of California Press 1986).

—— (1999a), *Groundless Belief: An Essay on the Possibility of Epistemology*, 2nd edn. (Princeton, NJ: Princeton University Press); first published (Oxford: Blackwell, 1977).

Williams, Michael (1999*b*), 'Fogelin's Neo-Pyrrhonism', *International Journal of Philosophical Studies*, vol. 7 (2), 141–58.

—— (2001), 'Contextualism, Externalism and Epistemic Standards', *Philosophical Studies* (forthcoming).

Wittgenstein, Ludwig (1958), *Philosophical Investigations*, 3rd edn., trans. G. E. M. Anscombe (Oxford: Blackwell).

—— (1969), *On Certainty* (Oxford: Blackwell).

Wright, Crispin (1992), *Truth and Objectivity* (Cambridge, Mass.: Harvard University Press).

Index